This book is to return

KU-660-188

WITHDRAWN

Writing in action

Writing in Action provides a step-by-step, practical guide to the process of writing. Although the emphasis is on creative writing, fiction, poetry and drama, it also covers autobiographical writing and the writing of reports and essays. Because this is a book about process, rather than product, *Writing in Action* also looks at the practice of adaptation and editing.

Writing in Action:

- shows new writers how to get started
- encourages experimentation and creativity
- stimulates critical awareness through the inclusion of illustrative texts
- encourages writing as a skill, as well as an art form

This book is crammed with practical suggestions and self-evaluation exercises, as well as invaluable tips on style, sentence structure, punctuation and vocabulary. It is an ideal course text for students and an invaluable guide to self-study.

Paul Mills has taught and developed courses in Creative Writing at Manchester and Leeds Universities and at the University College of Ripon and York where he now teaches in the English Department. His third book of poems, *Half Moon Bay*, was published by Carcanet in 1993. His recent play, *Never*, was performed at West Yorkshire Playhouse in 1995.

EG01276

Writing in action

Paul Mills

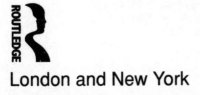

London and New York

EG01276   808.02 NL

EALING TERTIARY COLLEGE
LEARNING RESOURCE CENTRE · EALING GREEN

First published 1996
by Routledge
11 New Fetter Lane, London EC4P 4EE

Simultaneously published in the USA and Canada
by Routledge
29 West 35th Street, New York, NY 10001

© 1996 Paul Mills

Typeset in Times by
Ponting–Green Publishing Services, Chesham, Bucks
Printed and bound in Great Britain by
Clays Ltd, St Ives PLC

All rights reserved. No part of this book may be reprinted
or reproduced or utilised in any form or by any electronic,
mechanical, or other means, now known or hereafter
invented, including photocopying and recording, or in any
information storage or retrieval system, without permission
in writing from the publishers.

British Library Cataloguing in Publication Data
A catalogue record for this book is available from the
British Library

Library of Congress Cataloguing in Publication Data
A catalogue record for this book has been requested

'In the Waiting Room' from THE COMPLETE POEMS
1927–1979 by Elizabeth Bishop. Copyright © 1979, 1983 by
Alice Helen Methfessel. Reprinted by permission of Farrar,
Straus & Giroux, Inc. The lines from 'Rape' are reprinted
from THE FACT OF A DOORFRAME: Poems Selected and
New, 1950–1984, by Adrienne Rich, by permission of the
author and W. W. Norton & Company, Inc. Copyright © 1984
by Adrienne Rich. Copyright © 1975, 1978 by W. W. Norton
& Company, Inc. Copyright © 1981 by Adrienne Rich.

ISBN 0–415–11988–X (hbk)
ISBN 0–415–11989–8 (pbk)

For my mother

Contents

Acknowledgements

For several years I have taught a course in creative writing for first and second year students at the University College of Ripon and York St John, and the contents of this book have developed as a result. I owe a debt to many of the students of the course from years back, and to friends and colleagues who have offered advice on particular chapters and issues. Keith Watson, Chris Butler and Chris Jackson were especially helpful in reading through and commenting on the chapter on language. Leila Roberts and Beth Cowton offered valuable comments on the writing exercises. I am especially grateful to David Mac-Andrew and Joe Vicary for reading through the completed typescript and making the needed suggestions for final corrections, to Michael Glencross, Anita Parr, Hazel Purvis, Sarah Lawson-Welsh and Sheila Carr for their practical help and encouragement, and to Anne Price for arranging a period of study leave for me. There have been several occasions when discussions with friends stimulated my ideas, and in particular I wish to thank Elizabeth Sandie whose interest and support have influenced this book at every stage. Also I would like to express my gratitude to Julia Hall of Routledge for commissioning the book and for being such a communicative editor. My acknowledgement of help in developing my ideas extends further back, but in particular I thank Norman MacCaig and Peter Keating who taught me how to write.

The author and publishers would like to thank the following who have kindly given permission for the use of copyright material: Faber and Faber Ltd, for excerpts from 'Ocean 1212-W' in Sylvia Plath's *Johnny Panic and the Bible of Dreams*; Bloodaxe Books Ltd, for excerpts from Miroslav Holub's 'The Fly', reprinted by permission of Bloodaxe Books Ltd from *Poems Before & After* by Miroslav Holub (Bloodaxe Books, 1990); Random House, for excerpts from Norman MacCaig's 'February – Not Everywhere' and 'Other Self, Same Self'; *Stand* magazine, for reproduction of Anne Spillard's 'No Legal Existence', which first appeared in *Stand* magazine, vol. 21, no. 3, 1980, as one of two stories combined under the title *Night and Day*. The publisher has made every effort to trace copyright holders and would be glad to hear from any who have not been traced.

Introduction

In this book I have set out to explore poetry, fiction, drama and autobiography in ways that lead to writing. The principle I hold is that reading precedes writing, stimulates writing, and that confident writers are also confident readers. I would encourage anyone beginning to write by saying that they can learn most from the poems, plays and stories they enjoy. I hope this book will extend that enjoyment, as well as making it purposeful.

One of the pleasures and aims of reading is to learn something more about how to write. I see writers as researchers of their craft, experimenters who learn most from practice, but who also know and understand what other writers have done and how they operate. I have tried to get close to the experience of writing, to understand creative language as painters understand colour and forms in space. Part of this understanding will be intuitive, but an intuition that comes from familiarity.

Along with introductions to the different genres, this book gives a good deal of emphasis to practical writing exercises. Some of these are demanding, and deliberately so, since their aim is to stimulate experiment. Not all of the exercises fit neatly under chapter headings, and I have included some in a separate section (see 'Introductory writing exercises' Chapter 1). These and the others can be used selectively and added to. There will be many not included which individual writers and groups have found useful, and those I give may generate further ideas. But no book of this kind can fulfil the role of the teacher who is able to work closely with the student as her or his own writing develops, sympathise with its unique sets of demands, suggest what to read as a stimulus, and help to further the trial-and-error process which all writers are engaged in. Even if the methods I suggest provoke disagreement, I hope that the process will itself benefit. Writers need to talk to each other about writing, as most people do who practise any of the arts. It is through such discussions that fresh ideas and new techniques come to light. So I assume that all readers of this book will feel the beginnings of a sense of involvement – enough to want to argue, discuss, experiment.

This book is written for those who are beginning to experiment and discover the rewards of writing, who may well be involved in a course on creative writing either at sixth form or undergraduate level, who are working with writing groups or on their own. As well as chapters on writing as an art form, there are two chapters (Chapter 1, 'Structure and style', and Chapter 6, 'Writing to persuade') that might seem a little out of place in a book dealing mainly with creative writing. Chapter 1 outlines some basic principles of effective sentence construction. It explains the use of certain linguistic terms, but in a way that illustrates (as do the central chapters) the decisions that writers can and do make in the process of putting words together for a reader. I am thinking here of my readers as practitioners. Punctuation and sentence construction are not always taught with an exclusively practical outcome in view, and this chapter aims to help writers increase their confidence with the medium they are using.

I have this point in mind as well with Chapter 6. All writing, in a sense, aims to persuade. It is, I believe, an intention worth encouraging. It enables the writer to take possession of ideas and present them confidently. This chapter begins with a section on writing academic essays. Having worked for a time in the USA, I was struck by the obvious fact that in Britain and elsewhere we somehow assume that writing essays in schools, colleges and universities is a skill students apparently grow up knowing how to practise on their own; a mystique surrounds the exercise. The teaching of creative writing does acknowledge that writing is a skill, that a degree of technical learning is involved, that certain conventions operate which readers will recognise – even if instinctively. Thus by extending the range of this book, I am following a line of questions which people ask when they begin to explore writing as art: How do I write a short story? How do I start? The same questions apply to writing an essay, as well as to an opinion or survey article. The line I take follows the needs of my readers, and includes all forms of writing which may concern them at one time or another.

The real implication of this point is that creative writing has now become an institutional activity, and that those who sign up for its courses could also be writing essays in some other part of their programme. Art, music and drama composition, as well as the established training of actors – all these have long been institutionalised without the word suggesting some kind of trap. But do writers need institutions to learn in? For a long time, writing has privileged itself above other forms of art by mystifying its procedures, and our coyness about the word 'technique' seems partly a reluctance to tear off a veil and stare boldly into unconscious processes. Institutions can teach 'technique' effectively, and solitary writers can learn for themselves just as well. 'Technique' is not everything, but then no single qualifying experience is, was, or ever will be 'everything' – including the reading of this book, or any book on the subject.

To have creative writing in institutions means that it is beginning to be taken seriously – for the complex variety of reasons by which people do come to take things seriously and value them. But whether English Studies departments should be the only ones to adopt this attitude (and not all of them do) is another matter. Writing is multidisciplinary, not just because all disciplines require it to be practised in some form but because, for creative writing, students may come from disciplines outside English Studies.

When I was a student at Edinburgh in the late 1960s the writing classes I attended, run by Norman MacCaig, attracted students from all over the university. We were being taught (shown, invited to explore) the practices of an art – how others do it, how we could develop it for ourselves – and the combination worked. This was happening in an institution, and was of course funded and supported by it. But there is an argument for having creative writing attached to English departments in universities and schools, and valued by them more, and that is that such courses have a special way of developing the experience of reading. There are decisions that writers have to make – with the language itself, as well as with the structures of whole works, and to experience those decisions for oneself enables that knowledge to be internalised; it becomes much more than just tracts of dissociated information.

To establish this point, I would say that our system of social values encourages the belief, rightly or wrongly, that it is possible to challenge received opinion through the use of powerful images and convincing arguments. In such a system, writing can become a form of non-violent demonstration. Effective writers will become more discerning readers, and it is therefore in everyone's interest if learning to write promotes more critical reception and resists the influence of specious but plausible reasoning. One way of getting to know a genre or topic well is to follow up the option of writing within it. Those who know at first hand the problems of struggling with a piece of narrative will also read narrative in the knowledge of its techniques and how these work in practice. Getting published need not be the only reward for those who write; the practice of writing sharpens the practice of reading; confident readers are harder to deceive and therefore a vital challenge to those writers who do publish and are thought of as 'good' in the public view.

In shaping this book I have quoted, sometimes at length, from poems, stories, articles and plays. Each chapter is structured to move from illustrative reading and commentary towards writing. I chose some of the excerpts for their contrast and variety. But I would still have liked to include a great many more, and rely on the fact that much more could, and no doubt will, be provided by readers and teachers independently. By referring often to well-known writers I aim to serve a prior reading and recognition factor in my audience, but then, so much variety and richness exists that no one book can hope to confirm the choices others make when deciding which examples to use as guides. Even when commenting on sentence construction and punctuation in Chapter 1, I found it worthwhile to quote from novels, stories, poems and articles, but here too there were so many more examples I could have chosen. At best, those I have selected (and this point applies to each chapter) will stimulate a demand for more reading than I could possibly supply.

One other point to make here is that I sometimes refer to the readers of this book as 'readers' when actually I mean 'writers'. Should I assume that everyone who reads it is either a writer, or a writer 'not yet' – a potential writer? Certain readers will perhaps be people with no writing intentions. Although for the most part my aim is to connect with those who do or who want to write, those who mainly read and teach reading will not, I hope, find that this book is trying to minimalise what they do. Writers need readers and teachers, and each needs the other in a process which involves them collectively. Because we are now speaking about the future, the power and measure of what gets written is a matter of shared action.

One barrier against this idea is the strange assumption that 'creative writing' is a separate activity from other forms of learning, that teaching and reading are not part of it, that, for example, reading Shakespeare or metaphysical poetry has no connection with what we do when we write poetry ourselves; this idea feeds on the feeling that writing and reading literature are inimical and separate: one is major, serious and curricular, the other minor, flippant and self-indulgent. In the past, teachers have enforced this distinction partly I suspect to defend themselves against the creativity of their students.

Another common argument is that reading and studying literature destroys any ability to write oneself, as if a diet of Auden, Ginsberg, Graves, Plath or Eliot somehow dries up the imagination and prevents it from functioning. But were these writers when they started deliberately deprived of access to earlier literature, to literature of their own period, or anything written outside of so-called 'literature'? Did they read no history or anthropology, no science, no current popular journalism? Were they not interested in ideas, or in practised techniques and structures, as if such a diet might damage their own appetite and desire for artistic meaning? Why do we need to smother, protect and mystify creativity, seal it off from living ideas, from other writing or forms of art, or from any talk of learning about technique? Clearly this notion was nonsense for writers in the past; is it nonsense now? I would say yes; such a state of anxiety is unfounded, and is itself one source of the damage we do to students beginning to write if we try and separate the study of literature (or any other discipline) from writing as a practice. The romantic mythology which surrounds creativity is a major source of the damage. Writers need to learn how they can learn, how to make their own decisions confidently, how to enjoy reading and ideas.

In speaking of an ideal, therefore, I would argue that creative writing need not be simply a minor and end-stopped branch-line of English Studies. The barriers which identify separate disciplines might soon begin to make room for writing which is less English-based. It seems difficult to imagine a situation where students of the life sciences, the pure sciences, the broader humanities, are encouraged to write about lenses, genes, atoms, prehistory and spacetime, not just in terms of information significance but as cultural symbols too. And yet this is what writers continually do and always did. An English Studies training was never the sole prerequisite for writing, nor do writers produce their work only for students carefully trained in the concepts of English Literature. But this futuristic glimpse assumes that the sciences (for example) have begun to think about meaning in a symbolic (not just a literal) form, that science too is a way of inventing stories about reality, is a signifying narrative itself, and will eventually become a humanities subject.

The problem then is to insist that creative writing is a serious and valued activity, while removing from it the confining supports which traditional disciplines rely on for their status. But this problem is faced by many new interdisciplinary projects, and the problems are being solved. The creative writer can choose to work with a wider range of interests than the confining ones of the old subject definitions. The walls are already thinning. We are beginning to hear what is going on in the professionally sealed laboratories with their no entry signs. Writing in the next century might need to assume another kind of reader: one who belongs to a less restrictive educational culture.

Writing this book has made me think far more than ever before about language, and especially about the creative function of language: What is it for? What is it that feeds the imagination? What is it that imagination supplies? The word itself has gone through a history and acquired certain additions: the social imagination, the romantic, the scientific, the popular. My only answer is the broadest one: that imagination is a way of revitalising our interest in the world, and in each other, and that those who possess it are inquisitive and curious about everything. Within its reach there is everything to explore; nothing is forbidden. But we need to understand the ways and means, the technical business of how to construct bridges between writers and readers, writers, actors and audiences.

I often read a piece of work by one of my students which comes across as forceful, moving or amusing, and controlled – it is speaking to me as somebody would in a conversation, and yet it is showing that degree of control marked by a new attitude towards style. I know they have discovered something, that they have become confident. Very often the degree of control has taken me by surprise. But what makes style? Is its performance predictable? Two students recently acted the end of an Ibsen play for a class with no more than on-the-spot preparation. As chance would have it one of the two was wearing a leather jacket and mini-skirt and had pale blonde, spiky hair: she was playing the part of the mother, Mrs Alving in *Ghosts*. The performance left myself and the class speechless. She looked so profoundly unlike any Mrs Alving that there has ever been or could conceivably be. Was it a glimpse of this play in the twenty-first century? Was it her way of being completely that mother, while wearing punk clothes? What had we seen? Why was the incongruity so powerful? The interaction with her and her son had somehow managed to give us the whole play, yet it had been virtually unrehearsed. Something astonishing had happened.

My point is that with writing classes and spontaneous performance events, extraordinary things can occur. Someone with little obvious potential to begin with can make quite sudden and surprising progress, and it isn't easy to be clear why that has happened. All I can say is that something has been attempted, not shirked. The imagination does need rules and training; it needs to be given every possible chance, and it needs definite freedom outside the rules. But even given the most sensitive guidance, there is no science to it; nor does this book aim to provide one.

Chapter 1

Structure and style

SENTENCE AWARENESS

To write effectively in English, as in any language, requires an understanding of its structure. The basic structure of written English is the sentence. The sentence crosses all differences of genre and is found in all registers, from the most formal to the least. So what are sentences, and how are they made? The sentence is a fundamental invention of the mind. One of its uses is to show a completed action in the past, an ongoing action in the present, or a predicted action in the future. It says: something happened ('The pound fell yesterday to an all-time low'), is happening ('We are being invaded by scorpions'), or will happen ('Petra will fight them every inch of the way'). It can also say something must happen ('Australia must win the Ashes'), or is desired to happen ('Charlotte is longing for it all to end'). In another of its uses it describes a state, again in the past, present or future, as in these three sentences:

1 The centre of the town resembled a building site.
2 The situation remains difficult.
3 Tomorrow will be rainy.

The failure to understand sentences can lead to unwanted obscurity, and sentence construction therefore carries gains and losses for style.

The term *grammar* is frequently used to describe our knowledge of the separate parts of a sentence. Sentences contain clauses, clauses contain phrases, phrases contain words, and words themselves can be broken down into even smaller units. But *sentence awareness* is not the same thing as learning the rules of grammar. A sentence can be grammatical but functionally inadequate. Grammaticality is therefore a necessary but insufficient measure for judging how language creates meaning. The basic assumption of this chapter is that sentences were invented not only to indicate features of the world generally but to control emphasis and to organise information, and that we can therefore speak of good and bad, effective and ineffective sentences.

What I have said can be put in another way; writers make decisions. In structuring a sentence, it is important that we understand what we are doing, and why, and how sentences are formed. We need to be sure about the vital building materials of sentences, which of these parts can be moved about or discarded, and what the consequences of such rearranging will be. In simple sentences we may have comparatively little room for decision, but as our sentences become more complex, the situation requires that we do decide; the options will inevitably increase.

Even in very short and straightforward sentences we have some choice, as in the example below:

1 The young heiress hit the ball.

A writer may not wish to draw this kind of attention to the girl's status and may decide instead to write simply:

2 The girl hit the ball.

But whichever is chosen, and both are just as grammatical and effective as sentences, we can't choose to rearrange the words to produce:

3 The ball hit the girl.

without altering the meaning of what we are saying. And if we wrote:

4 (a) The girl the ball which broke the window. *Or*
   (b) That girl hitting a ball.

we would have produced a group of words which do far more than simply change the meaning: the words in example 4 do not make sentences at all. Why? Sentence construction has rules, and these rules limit our decisions fundamentally. The words in example 4 break a fundamental rule about sentences, and that is that all sentences must have a *main verb*.

Main verbs

In the most basic sentences of all, one or two words are enough to form a sentence. If begun with a capital letter and ended with a full stop, the word *Stop* is a sentence. *Speak. Listen. Help. Forget it. Hurry. Give up. Shut up. Come here. Go away.* All these are sentences. But place the following words between full stops and capitals, and they do not make sentences: *Paper. Telephone. Girl. Peterborough. Custard.* None of these is a sentence because the primary rule is that every sentence must contain a *main verb*; it must command, project or complete an *action*, express a *desire*, or describe a *state*. (The word *Telephone* is ambiguous in this context however, since if someone came into a room where I was sitting and shouted it, it could be understood as a command. But the spoken word would imply an unspoken verb: *Answer it*, or, *It's for you.* And the same would be true of *Custard* if it implied: *Do you want any?* or *Peterborough* if it meant: *There's a phone call from there. Answer it.*)

But the word groups in example 4 are not sentences: the first shows no action at all, the second leaves the action unmarked in *time*. The 'hitting' could be happening in the past, present or future. We anticipate there is something more to be said. Both groups in example 4 can be extended to form sentences by introducing a main verb and its time sense:

5 (a) The girl *hit* the ball which broke the window. *Or*
   (b) That girl hitting a ball *walked* straight into my party last night.

The first rule of sentence writing is deciding that your sentence has a main verb. This verb means that someone is telling us something either in a written or spoken form. *Chambers Concise Dictionary* tells us something if it is written on the cover of a book. But the sentence 'This is *Chambers Concise Dictionary*' means that someone is writing, or writing as they would speak to us *directly in time*. The phrase *Chambers Concise Dictionary*, however, has no speaker and no past, present or future. When hearing about an action, for example, your reader must be in no doubt about what has happened, is happening, will happen or what somebody wants to happen. Of course, we also have negative forms of the verb: 'did not happen, will not', etc., as well as 'may not, would not', but there too we can hear the speaker's claim to tell us something definite or projected, or hear the expression of a wish. His or her knowledge of a state or an action in time is still clarified, and this is what sentences are for. Behind sentences describing states or actions there is a *speaker* who is saying to us: 'This *is* something', or, 'I (see it, have seen it, want it to, believe it will, command it to, suppose it might, see it did not) happen.'

Main verbs and subordinates

If a sentence has two or more verbs, as in example 5(a), 'hit' and 'broke', some will be *main verbs* and others will be subordinate.

The *main verb* in this case is 'hit'. The second verb 'broke' is subordinate, and the word group containing it is called a *subordinate clause*: 'which broke the window'.

In example 5(a) 'The girl hit the ball' is the *main clause*, and contains the *main verb*.

Clauses join up to form bigger groups, and these we call sentences. But if these get too long, and contain too many subordinate clauses, such sentences can become ineffective.

A sentence can contain any number of verbs, and usually only one will be the main verb, and if that verb is not placed in a clear and obvious position the sentence will again become ineffective.

Sometimes two or even more main clauses can join up, but even then each main verb will need to be clear and obvious. In the following *joined* clauses, the main verbs are marked out:

> 6 The cat *sat* on the mat and the yellow puppy *walked* away with a howl.

Two basic things which we all use when interpreting sentences are (1) our knowledge of the grammar of our language (as native speakers we internalise this knowledge as we learn our language), and (2) our short-term memory. If more clauses beginning 'and . . .' were added on to example 6, the sentence would be grammatical, *but* our short-term memory could not cope with the amount of information it contained. While still grammatical, the sentence could even extend into infinity.

Subject and object

The *subject* of example 1 is 'the young heiress', and this clause is a sentence with an *object*: 'the ball'. Not all *subject + verb* clauses have objects. The following do:

- She turned on the radio.
- He was arranging the picnic.

These do not:

- The salmon struggled in the net.
- The thunder broke.

The verb 'struggled' can never have an object. Other examples of verbs without objects are: 'arrives, blooms, differs, prevails, decays'. We can't *arrive* something, or *bloom* something. In these verbs the action completes itself without an object, and we call these verbs *intransitive*. The verb 'broke' can have an object; in fact, it usually does, though not in the sentence above. In 'The ball broke the window' it becomes *transitive*, with 'the window' as object.

The subject is always the answer to a question about the verb. If you place *Who*? or *What*? directly in front of the verb, you will form a question, and the answer to that question will be the subject:

> The young heiress hit the ball.
> WHO hit the ball? *The young heiress (subject)*.

In longer sentences, subordinate clauses and other material can cluster around the subject and the object:

> 7 The young heiress (*subject*) who was descended from the
> Marquis of Doncaster
> hit (*main verb*)
> the ball (*object*), which bounced into the shrubbery.

But we can increase the contents of each of these three clusters. The sentence will still be grammatical, but if we fill some or all of the clusters with too much information, the sentence will start to collapse.

8 The young heiress, who was second cousin to the late
   Marquess of Doncaster whose ancestral line stretched
   back to the Swedish, Greek and Austrian dynasties
   which were frequently connected by marriage in the
   second half of the seventeenth century
   hit
   the ball which was donated to her family by Queen
   Christina of Sweden and lost during a return match in
   the environs of Hampton Court and afterwards due to
   neglect caused by bouts of plague, influenza and panic
   in the family was often left out in the rain or at
   times the snow, and remained undiscovered for three
   hundred years until one day the gardener ran over it
   with a wheelbarrow.

This sentence is still completely grammatical, and it still could in theory go on for ever. The *main verb* has no chance at all of being recognised for what it is: the main drive of the sentence. Surrounded with all that detail, it disappears. In the third cluster, for example, all kinds of new subordinate clauses are breaking out and adding themselves on to the main clause.

Here is another example of a sentence; again infinitely extendable but still grammatical. It still carries a *subject + verb* structure:

         large, ferocious, orange
9 The^
              which was recovering from an
              unsuccessful cyst operation
         cat ^
                  gradually, awkwardly, painfully
         sat^

                            which had been fitted
                            with underfloor heating
                            especially for the
                            purpose, but all to no
                            avail.
              on the mat^

Writers and readers instinctively react against sentences of this length, and with good reason. Our short-term memory just cannot absorb all that information at one hearing. To organise it for ease of communication we would have to break it down into shorter sentences, each with its own main verb. One main verb cannot perform that superabundance of work. And main verbs must dominate. It is when we are faced with large amounts of information that we have to make decisions about how to control it, what to put in each cluster, how many sentences to use, how to choose the best verbs and position them carefully. If you look at the passage quoted by George Orwell below (p.25) you can see what happens when verbs such as 'have', 'is' and 'are' are forced to do all the work. At this point rules of grammar will not help. Instead we need principles of coherence.

You might argue that no one in their right mind would ever write anything resembling examples 8 or 9. The writer would know instinctively not to do it. But they might write something like this and not recognise there was a problem:

10 The living conditions of families with young children vary more greatly than in any other type of household.

To a lesser extent, the problem here is the same as in examples 8 and 9 – the tiny verb 'vary' is having to cope with a heavy weight of *subject* as well as an equally large element after the verb. Two joined main clauses (along with two main verbs) may be needed to share the excess load:

11 Living conditions vary in all types of household, but variation is greatest among families with young children.

In his valuable essay on language and style, 'Politics and the English Language', George Orwell states a preference for the use of strong, active, simple verbs over vague, weak, complicated ones. His example of the former are verbs such as 'break, stop, spoil, mend, kill'. But all too often in modern prose such verbs are replaced by vague sounding verbs such as 'prove, serve, form, play, render, have the effect of, give rise to, exhibit a tendency to, serve the purpose of'.[1] Orwell's point is that verbs such as those in the second list typically produce sentences whose meanings are incoherent.

Objects, complements, adverbials

Not all verbs are followed by an object. So what do we call those elements which are *not the object*? Verbs such as 'is' and 'seems' don't have objects, and instead are followed by a *complement*. Here is an example of a verb with a complement:

Sylvia (*subject*) is (*main verb*) a teacher (*complement*).

Adverbials are a rather different matter, but we have to recognise them because they too have a functional role. Unlike a complement, an adverbial does not always *follow* a verb; it can be placed anywhere, but wherever it is it must always relate strongly to the process the verb describes, and the reader will need to sense that strong connection.

Adverbials can be a single word or a group of words. Just as the subject answers the question – Who? What? – so the adverbial typically answers a question, and in this case, too, the question is about the *verb, about the time, place, manner of, and reason behind, the verb's process or statement*. So adverbials are important in sentences because of their close relationship to a process going on in time. Also, if an interesting style depends to an extent on being specific about time/place/attitude, adverbials will be very useful indeed. The adverbials below are printed in italics:

Yesterday I saw Michael *in Sainsbury's*.

Quietly this morning beside the subsided herds of water, I walk.

Many readers will recognise that the last example sounds literary, intriguing and unusual, and it is in fact taken from a poem (see also Chapter 3, p.84). Here, 'quietly' and 'this morning' are typical adverbials. The long phrase beginning 'beside . . .' also is an adverbial, in spite of its length and oddness. What is not typical is the number of adverbials together in one sentence. If any more were added to the third example, the sentence would become incoherent.

In using these adverbials, the writer here has risked including what probably amounts to the maximum number possible in one sentence, but has arranged them so that each one comments on the process 'I walk'. In terms of style, the characteristic way of arranging adverbials is to follow the sequence – manner, time, place – and the writer has kept to this sequence exactly.

Sentence structure: a test

These three adverbial sentences don't cause their readers too much difficulty, but, as with sentences having objects and complements, problems do occur when the sentence you are writing gets too complicated. Now that we know how to distinguish all the basic elements in a sentence, let us try out our sentence awareness by seeing what happens when we read sentences that combine these elements and do become more complicated. Some sentences combine them more effectively than others, but can we tell the difference and say why?

Look at the following two sentences. Both are grammatical, but which of them in your view is the more coherent?

12 Most teachers are white Anglo-Saxon, which links with the Swann Report saying that some ethnic minorities are neglected, in my view this is wrong.

13 Five years after the Swann Report called for action to increase the number of ethnic minority teachers, the profession remains overwhelmingly white, Anglo-Saxon.

Many readers will notice first of all that example 12 contains a basic punctuation error. The comma after 'neglected' should be a full stop or a semi colon (see Punctuation below, p.17), and 'in my view' the start of a new sentence. But I have put in this error because joining sentences with commas is a very common mistake, and I wanted to reproduce the kind of style we often find in the work of beginning writers.

That apart, both sentences make use of the same material, and aim to express the same view of it. We can show the elements of examples 12 and 13 as follows:

Most teachers (*subject*) are (*main verb*) white Anglo-Saxon (*complement*), which links with the Swann Report saying that some ethnic minorities are neglected (*sub clauses*), in my view this is wrong (*new sentence*).

Five years after the Swann Report called for action to increase the number of ethnic minority teachers (*subordinate clause*), the profession (*subject*) remains (*main verb*) overwhelmingly white, Anglo-Saxon (*complement*).

In example 12 the *subject + verb* structure occurs at the beginning, and leaves the background information to trail behind it in a series of disorganised phrases, clauses, and even a new sentence joined to the first one by a comma. The subordinate clause beginning with 'which' is trying to attach itself to something, but what? In example 13 the background information is given at the beginning, and the *subject + verb* structure placed at the end for emphasis. The arrangement of the elements is a narrative – first: what happened in the past; second: the outcome in the present.

Example 12 produces a naive style, while example 13 is the work of an experienced writer. We can compare these sentences by using a simple metaphor of control: the first resembles a dog-handler pulled about by a group of dogs on separate leashes which all become entangled; the second is so tightly reined that the dogs drive forward and pull the sled.

Look at example 12 again. The word 'this' could refer to the fact that ethnic minorities are neglected, to the fact that most teachers are white, or even to the Swann Report itself. And by 'ethnic minorities' does the writer mean teachers, or perhaps pupils? And what does 'links with' suggest? What kind of linkage is it? This flimsy verb will not tell us. So much meaning rests on that link, and yet its precise meaning stays unspecific. Instead of relying on weak and uninteresting verbs such as 'are', 'is' and 'saying', example 13 chooses 'called for action' and 'remains' – much stronger. The final part added on in example 12 is really another sentence in itself, joined to the first by a comma, as we have seen, and to join sentences with commas exemplifies one other disorganised feature of style.

Both examples 12 and 13 express a *personal* view, but the second viewpoint rests its case on the *evidence*, and how that evidence is structured. It does not therefore have to revert to the slightly apologetic 'in my view this is wrong'. In example 13 we already know what is wrong, and why, and how the situation could be corrected.

Sentence structure: some principles for writers

From this analysis we can begin to construct a few principles for sentence organisation. As the information you are managing becomes more complex, the decisions you make will carry greater consequences.

- Choose verbs carefully. Make them as specific and forceful as you can. A main verb drives a sentence along and holds it together, but other verbs can help. Place verbs carefully, i.e. not all near the beginning but well dispersed. To place the main verb near the end generates emphasis.
- Know which verb is your main verb, and which words constitute the subject of your sentence. If your sentence extends into a complement, try not to make the complement over-long, full of trailing phrases, phrases beginning with 'which', 'ing' words, and 'ands'.
- See if you can position some information *in front of* the *subject + main verb* structure. When beginning to write, people often start off with the subject and then fill in the rest as it occurs to them. But it can help to begin with the minor information and lead up to the *subject + main verb*: the major information.
- Experiment. Decide on the order of phrases. Be aware that sentences consist of parts, and that these parts need to be strongly connected. The reader needs to see clearly how they relate. For this reason, short, well-structured sentences will often read more effectively than long, complicated ones.

To make these rules hard and fast would be a mistake, however. A useful way of arriving at an effective style might equally involve finding a piece of writing that appeals to you. You can then begin to appreciate how it works. Here is a piece written by the artist Paul Nash after one of his visits to the trenches in 1917. In that year he returned to the front as an official war artist. This is what he saw and felt:

> Sunset and sunrise are blasphemous, they are mockeries to man, only the black rain out of the bruised and swollen clouds all through the bitter black of night is fit atmosphere in such a land. The rain drives on, the stinking mud becomes more evilly yellow, the shell holes fill up with green-white water, the roads and tracks are covered in inches of slime, the black dying trees ooze and sweat and the shells never cease. They alone plunge overhead, tearing away the rotting tree-stumps, breaking the plank roads, striking down horses and mules, annihilating, maiming, maddening, they plunge into the graves which is this land; one huge grave, and cast up on it the poor dead. It is unspeakable, godless, hopeless. I am no longer an

artist interested and curious. I am a messenger who will bring back word from the men who are fighting to those who want the war to go on for ever.[2]

Reading this passage I can see some of my own rules broken instantly. Commas join sentences, 'ing' words proliferate, but quite clearly Nash has no need to end his piece with 'in my view this is wrong'. Instead he makes the evidence argue persuasively. Rather than being a mistake, his way of joining up sentence to sentence with commas adds to the urgency of the writing. His phrases form into lists, and by this means we can see how they relate even when the sentences are filled with information. We have no trouble wondering how the pieces of sentences fit. The passage is strewn with powerful and accurate verbs: 'ooze . . . sweat . . . never cease . . . plunge . . . cast up'. He places us where we can see. He inspires savage indignation, the only possible response.

In thinking about points of effective style, we might therefore add one more rule. If we compare this passage with example 13, we can see that they have something in common even though their subject matter could not be more different. Both writers feel strongly, and know what they think. They don't dither. They make every word, every phrase, add something, and they must do this because they care passionately about what it is they are trying to say. They also know all the evidence for that urgency, have thought about it deeply, and need to bring it before us. Nash himself was not a professional writer. He had simply found a subject matter that could not be left to the chance inaccuracies of half-hearted observation and muddled thinking – the enemies of good style.

Eccentric structures: stylisation

The following poem by Berthold Brecht does not at first appear to be a sentence:

Pleasures
The first look out of the window in the morning
The old book found again
Enthusiastic faces
Snow, the change of the seasons
The newspaper
The dog
Dialectics
Taking showers, swimming
Old music
Comfortable shoes
Taking things in
New music
Writing, planting

Travelling
Singing
Being friendly.[3]

The reason it doesn't is because it isn't. In order to communicate, some word groups do not need to be arranged in sentence form. But they still require a structure the reader can learn. This group makes use of its shape on the page, and also has the appeal of a stylised list: what has 'dialectics' to do with singing or comfortable shoes? Quite a lot possibly. Just because this list is so peculiar, the reader senses both a speaker and actions, and knows that the speaker relates to those actions strongly. The actions listed are eccentric enough to appeal to a sense of individual choice.

A sentence may say something odd and inventive:

Jonathan is a walking criminal tendency.

Here, a specific concrete word 'Jonathan' stands beside an abstract concept 'walking criminal tendency' so that we ask: Can a person act like an abstract concept? Can an abstract concept act like a person? The judgement could be affectionate; we can hear a voice with attitude speaking through. The reader becomes involved in asking questions – enjoyable questions, not produced by bewilderment or confusion – and this involvement marks one feature of effective style. To say instead 'Jonathan has criminal tendencies' loses that effect. It forces its readers to question the basis for the statement: we are not intrigued but puzzled, even suspicious; the speaker could be wrong.

One other point about stylisation. All language exists within a social context, and experienced writers often appeal to readers by cutting across this terrain from an odd angle. If, for example, all the gravestones in a churchyard were traditionally carved with the words: 'And his beloved and faithful wife', while one stone said: 'And his beloved wife' readers would have to draw only one conclusion, but they might say that the inscription had style. It is worth remembering what readers are likely to experience through the media (a common if ephemeral stimulus, but also a rich source of public language) and to locate your ideas within a range of cultural experiences which almost all of us know about. To refer, as one radio comedian did recently, to a well-known older member of the royal family as manager of the Bottle Bank of England unites two areas of cultural knowledge which are normally worlds apart; this comic deviancy is satirical, but not unaffectionate, and by stylising its perceptions it attracts our interest. In a similar example, the journalist Andrew Rawnsley, writing about high salaries in the privatised Water Authorities, referred to sewage being changed into champagne.[4]

PUNCTUATION

If you look at the writing in this chapter and the next ('Autobiographical writing') you will see that I have been making use of a wide range of punctuation features. There are dashes, colons, semicolons, speech marks, question marks, brackets, as well as capitals, commas and full stops. Inconsistencies between different rule books on punctuation need not deter you from trying out as many of these features as you can, so long as you are consistent in your own limits. As with sentences, certain features are compulsory, while others permit a greater degree of choice. And as with sentences, rules operate more strictly where the simpler forms are involved.

The following rules are meant to act as a guide to decision-making. They also show the places where a basic rule must operate in conventional punctuation. If your aim is to punctuate eccentrically (as Brecht does above) you will still benefit from knowing a conventional system.

Every act of language implies a speaker, and used successfully, punctuation increases the sense of a voice. Unless one is Irish, even something as simple as a full stop at the end of a sentence will mean a drop in the voice, however slight. Brackets suggest the tone of an aside. Sentences joined by commas evoke urgency. Colons prepare the voice for a possible list, while dashes make way for short spontaneous intrusions. The life in a good deal of writing depends more than we think on its punctuation.

The following comments aim to explain as many uses of punctuation as possible. Not all will be relevant to your needs at any one time, but if in doubt you can look back at the relevant parts of this list; it is intended to cover the range of features in current practice.

In later examples I have illustrated punctuation forms by using quotations from recent or contemporary writers. Here you will see punctuation used inventively. See if you can copy some of their inventiveness in your own writing. Once you have access to the rules and knowledge of them it becomes possible, and desirable, to try out new effects.

Capital letters, full stops (C.)

Rule: Capital letters signify proper names, as for instance in 'Jonathan' or 'Chicago'.

Rule: A capital letter marks the beginning of a sentence. It implies that the end of the sentence will follow and will be marked by a full stop, exclamation mark or question mark Some people like to end sentences with several exclamation marks!!! But while this form might be suitable in a personal letter, it looks naive elsewhere and implies embarrassment. The usual form is as follows:

> 'The whole tendency of modern prose is away from concreteness.' (*George Orwell*)

These two rules are conventional, but a writer can decide to increase the status of a non-sentence word or word group by placing it between capital and full stop. This feature is sometimes found in stage and advertising dialogue:

Q. Chocolates?
A. No, Maltesers.

A writer can increase the status of a word by starting it with a capital, i.e. by giving it the status of a proper name. The word *City*, for example (with a capital), normally means either the banking and commercial district of London or a football team.

Word groups occurring between capitals and full stops are normally assumed to be sentences. If a word group is placed between a capital and a full stop, *and is not a sentence*, then that punctuation will be eccentric. It may be a mistake; the word group may actually be part of a preceding sentence, so check.

If your sentence ends with a quotation using speech marks (see below), always place the full stop *after* the speech marks. This is the true end-of-sentence point.

Apostrophe S ('s and s')

Rule: Never use either of these forms with an *s – plural*. Use only to indicate belonging, as here: *Satan's motives = the motives of Satan*.

Rule: The apostrophe should follow the last letter of the last word after the *of*.

The room of the women becomes *the women's room*.
The skill of the bricklayer becomes *the bricklayer's skill*.
The attitude of the parents becomes *the parents' attitude*.
The exclamation marks of the headmistress becomes *the headmistress's exclamation marks*.

Rule: Apostrophe S can be used to indicate a shortened form, for example:

He has arrived becomes *He's arrived*.
Who is that? becomes *Who's that?*
It is Father Christmas becomes *It's Father Christmas*.

To correct a common mistake, please note:

it's = it is
its = belonging to it

Colon (:)

Rule: A colon introduces a list. By introducing a list, or citing an example, a colon makes clear to your reader how information is organised, as follows:

The old woman's needle had three uses: killing frogs, lancing boils, and third, picking her teeth.

It can also precede a single-item list, as in this sentence:

Pinter's dialogues unite speech with violence: the violence of revenge.

Rule: A colon introduces speech, or a quotation. It can precede the use of speech marks when a short quotation is needed, as below:

I needed a slogan: 'strike lucky with England's Glory matches', but decided instead on: 'England's Glory: thicker, stronger matches'.

A colon can also precede a long quotation, as after 'below', or 'as follows'.

Semicolon (;)

Rule: A semicolon joins together two linked sentences:

'Freedom is never voluntarily given by the oppressor; it must be demanded by the oppressed.' (*Martin Luther King*)

All there is to writing is having ideas; to learn to write is to learn to have ideas.

Rule: Semicolons may mark divisions between longer items in lists.

Clichés: never just horror but abject horror; not just embarrassment, but acute embarrassment; not only beautiful but breathtakingly; not just an inferno but blazing; the sunlight always blinding; never just a simple crash but resounding; the imagination always, of course, fertile. Abject, acute, breathtaking, speechless – resounding exaggeration I call it, in every case.

For inventive uses of sentences, colons and semicolons, see the examples below by Angela Carter, Woody Allen and John Fowles.

Comma (,)

Rule: Commas can mark divisions between word groups, and a pause in the voice. But rather than being a rule every time the use of commas has become a matter of personal style.

If the rhythm of a sentence does not make the divisions within it clear, a comma will help.

Commas are not always required even when the voice does pause. To sprinkle sentences with commas can look patronising, as if readers can't be expected to make up their own mind where to pause. I still felt I needed one after 'patronising' above. Quite appropriately the following sentence has no commas:

I had come to this lunch because the editor had sent me a note saying he had read some of my scribblings and would like to discuss the possibility of my writing something for *Playboy.*

Rule: Commas divide few-word items in lists. See the example by J. G. Ballard below.

Use commas for emphasis, to make clear the divisions between word groups. In lists the word 'and' is not normally followed by a comma.

Rule: Commas can be used to introduce speech words.

He said, 'Let me introduce you to my friends.' *Or*
'Let me introduce you to my friends,' he said.

The use of a comma can alter the meaning of a sentence:

My friend, Clara, is a bus driver.

Remove the commas and the sentence means that the speaker has several friends, not just the named one. The sentence with commas could also mean that the speaker is addressing 'Clara' about another friend who is a bus driver. A similar instance might be:

The reason, madam, is that I have just joined the RAF.

Commas can be used like semicolons to link sentences together, but only when doing so is appropriate. This usage generates narrative urgency and is not suitable for registers such as academic prose or formal report writing. It increases the pace of reading. The passage by Paul Nash (see p.15) is a good example. Another might be:

Florence began to talk, she told me everything, her sister had been arrested, her father was deported and unable to communicate, she had only her friends. 'And me, you have me,' I whispered. She gripped my hand.

Inverted commas, speech marks ('. . .')

Rule: Single inverted commas are placed around the titles of book chapters, individual articles and poems and short quotations.

Inverted commas also indicate borrowed phrases and words. It often implies that the words borrowed are someone else's judgement, opinion or usage, or that the words have become a cliché. It can imply a tone of embarrassment, disapproval or sarcasm:

The 'meal' consisted of three tomatoes, a packet of digestives and a banana.

Remove the inverted commas and the tone reverts to straight information. Ask yourself whether you do want to show disapproval, disagreement or embarrassment. You may not. If not, remove the punctuation. If you are embarrassed by a phrase you have written, it may be better not to use that phrase or word at all but to find others. Inverted commas do not excuse clichés or slang, so if you feel you want to excuse them, ask yourself why you wanted them in the first place. If, for instance, you describe certain characters in a story as having 'done a bunk' this usage might be quite acceptable, or it might not be. It might be aiming to give an impression of the words the characters themselves would be likely to use, or it might suggest that you, the writer, are stuck and can't think of a better choice of expression.

If, as another example, you placed the words *greenhouse effect* in inverted commas, it could imply that you wished your readers to regard the whole phenomenon with suspicion: the 'greenhouse effect' *so-called*. In reality you would be disowning it, so be careful. Do not place inverted commas round words unless you are very clear about your intentions.

Brackets and dashes

Brackets suggest an alternative way of referring to something, e.g. *Beethoven's next symphony (his Fifth)*. They can also add minor information quickly. Without pursuing a point in full, they can remind your reader of a previous point made:

> There are three folk-tales (though some would claim there were four) in which Sir Gawain appears.

> Remember you can always cross out anything you have written. (It is after all only a rough draft.)

Brackets are useful for indicating your tone of voice, as in an aside or *sotto voce* comment.

As with brackets, dashes are used for adding something, but *without* reducing its status as information.

> By writing a postcard from one character to another – what did she say, how did she say it, why did she send it to him? – you will learn something about them you couldn't have guessed.

If the questions in *dashes* were instead placed in brackets, the contained ideas would be made to seem less important than the main sentence. In the above sentence therefore, dashes are the better choice.

Emphasis (underline, italics, three dots)

Underlining emphasises a single word or phrase. The same effect is often produced in print, as in this book, through the use of italics. These forms can enable your readers to identify certain important words and word groups. It is also a way of making your writing more voiced.

Three dots (ellipsis) are frequently used to shorten a long quotation by missing out the inessential parts of it. But this punctuation can also increase voice quality. Unlike the simple quotation-shortener form, it entails a deliberate pause, activates interest and suggests that what follows will be significant.

In Milton's view we should be critical only of Satan's motives, not God's. . . . Why is this?

The passage by John Fowles below is a good example of the use of three dots for suspense.

Punctuation effects: some examples

Look carefully at the following examples of punctuation. The most unusual example (in the passage from Toni Morrison's novel *Beloved*) contains virtually no punctuation at all. This passage describes the experience of a black girl in a crowded ship travelling from Africa to America during the slave trade. The gaps suggest long time periods, horrifying but unchanged circumstances: the gaps will only be followed by the same things.

Using a range of punctuation effects, Angela Carter also evokes an extreme: a defenceless existence struggling for life in the primitive northern forest and its legendary horror. She isolates words in lists, and divides up items with semicolons and commas but not full stops. The effect suggests continuity and background. Long sentences produce this continuity, while words split up by punctuation sound savage, short and dramatic: a background impression but also immediate impact. In the passage about the Conservative MP, John Fowles shifts through an enormous amount of material by using a variety of punctuation forms (colons, semicolons, dashes, brackets, three dots). These keep us reading where a plodding sentence-by-sentence style would fail. By mixing humour with self-centred abruptness, Woody Allen uses punctuation to mock the self-regard of pompous diary-like writing. Orwell quotes a passage which differs from the others, and in it we see a failure to communicate. The writer he quotes speaks of 'on the one hand . . . on the other' and even uses italics. In spite of this the structure of this passage collapses under the weight of abstract ideas. Orwell quotes this example to serve as a warning, and rightly so. Assaulted by the sheer number of complex concepts, the reader's mind is soon transformed into a jelly-like mass at the prospect of sorting them out; no alternative punctuation could possibly restructure this passage for us or rescue it from confusion.

We can therefore see that punctuation can help, but only if the content of what is said permits it to. If it cannot, the content itself may require drastic revision. Punctuation can organise sentences, phrases, word groups and single words into lists, instances, comments, significant structures; it is a principal means of controlling emphasis. To make use of a wide range of punctuation can in most cases stimulate the writer's voice, and therefore the experience of reading. The selection below illustrates something of the range of these effects when used inventively. The writers who use them know the rules but are clearly deciding between the available forms. Through this inventiveness, writing immediately becomes more accessible and interesting, and the reason is that in every case (the exception being the passage quoted by Orwell) we hear a voice speaking; we hear meaning organised for a reader.

Angela Carter

It is a northern country; they have cold weather, they have cold hearts.

Cold; tempest; wild beasts in the forest. It is a hard life. Their houses are built of logs, dark and smoky within. There will be a crude icon of the virgin behind a guttering candle, the leg of a pig hung up to cure, a string of drying mushrooms. A bed, a stool, a table. Harsh, brief, poor lives.[5]

One beast and only one howls in the woods by night.

The wolf is carnivore incarnate and he's as cunning as he is ferocious; once he's had a taste of flesh then nothing else will do.

At night, the eyes of the wolves shine like candle flames, yellowish, reddish, but that is because the pupils of their eyes fatten on darkness and catch the light from your lantern to flash it back at you – red for danger; if a wolf's eyes reflect only moonlight, then they gleam a cold and unnatural green, a mineral, a piercing colour. If the benighted traveller spies those luminous, terrible sequins stitched suddenly on the black thickets, then he knows he must run, if fear has not struck him stock-still.

But those eyes are all you will be able to glimpse of the forest assassins as they cluster invisibly round your smell of meat as you go through the wood unwisely late. They will be like shadows, they will be like wraiths, grey members of a congregation of nightmare; hark! his long, wavering howl . . . an aria of fear made audible.[6]

John Fowles

When John Marcus Fielding disappeared, he therefore contravened all social and statistical probability. Fifty-seven years old, rich, happily married, with a son and two daughters; on the board of several City companies (and very much not merely to adorn the letter-headings); owner of one of the finest Elizabethan manor-houses in East Anglia, with an active interest in the running of his adjoining 1,800-acre farm; a joint – if somewhat honorary – master of fox-hounds, a keen shot . . . he was a man who, if there were an -arium of living human stereotypes, would have done well as a model of his kind: the successful City man who is also a country land-owner and (in all but name) village squire. It would have been very understandable if he had felt that one or the other side of his life had become too time-consuming . . . but the most profoundly anomalous aspect of his case was that he was also a Conservative Member of Parliament.[7]

Woody Allen

Thought: Why does man kill? He kills for food. And not only food: frequently there must be a beverage.

Today I saw a red-and-yellow sunset and thought, How insignificant I am! Of course, I thought that yesterday, too, and it rained. I was overcome with self-loathing and contemplated suicide again – this time by inhaling next to an insurance salesman.

Should I marry W.? Not if she won't tell me the other letters in her name.[8]

J. G. Ballard

All the same, Jim would have liked to eat the ship. He imagined himself nibbling the masts, sucking the cream from the Edwardian funnels, sinking his teeth into the marzipan bows and devouring the entire forward section of the hull. After that he would gobble down the Palace Hotel, the Shell Building, the whole of Shanghai . . .[9]

George Orwell

In his essay 'Politics and the English Language' Orwell quotes this passage by an unnamed writer:

On the one side we have the free personality: by definition it is not neurotic, for it has neither conflict nor dream. Its desires, such as they are, are transparent, for they are just what institutional approval keeps in the forefront of consciousness; another institutional pattern would alter their number and intensity; there is little in them that is natural, irreducible, or dangerous. But on the other side, the social bond itself is nothing but the mutual reflection of these self-secure integrities. Recall the definition of love. Is not this the very picture of the small academic? Where is there a place in this hall of mirrors for either personality or fraternity?[10]

Toni Morrison

All of it is now   it is always now   there will never be a time when I am not crouching and watching others who are crouching too   I am always crouching   the man on my face is dead   his face is not mine   his mouth smells sweet but his eyes are locked   some who eat nasty themselves   I do not eat   the men without skin bring us their morning water to drink we have none   at night I cannot see the dead man on my face   daylight comes through the cracks and I can see his locked eyes   I am not big small rats do not wait for us to sleep   someone is thrashing but there is no room to do it in   if we had more to drink we could make tears   we cannot make sweat or morning water so the men without skin bring us theirs   one time they bring us sweet rocks to suck   we are all trying to leave our bodies behind   the man on my face has done it   it is hard to make yourself die forever   you sleep short and then return   in the beginning we could vomit now we do not   now we cannot   his teeth are pretty white points someone is trembling   I can feel it over there   he is fighting hard to leave his body which is a small bird trembling   there is no room to tremble so he is not able to die   my own dead man is pulled away from my face   I miss his pretty white points[11]

ASPECTS OF STYLE

Paragraphs

In the punctuation section of this chapter I suggested that in order to emphasise the voice rhythm of a sentence and to structure it effectively for a reader, a wide range of punctuation marks are available and can be used, sometimes experimentally. I omitted any discussion of paragraphs, however. Paragraphing allows a greater degree of freedom than the other forms. While their uses are limited to the division of word groups within sentences, paragraphs operate outside the sentence cluster by uniting finished sentences into blocks.

The word *paragraph* derives from a now obsolete symbol (*IP*) known as a paraph mark. Our current practice is to signal the beginning of a paragraph by indenting the first word of the next line, or by placing a whole line space between paragraphs. But until the invention of paper in the fifteenth century, all writing was scripted on to vellum, a parchment prepared from calf hide. The rarity of vellum discouraged such wastefulness of space as we now have, and to indicate divisions in a page of script, paraph symbols were placed in the margin to mark changes of sense. Clearly such changes are inevitable and desirable, and need to be marked in some way.

The basic paragraph structure (the one above provides an obvious example) begins with detailed information, specific reference, and moves towards summary. Paragraphs therefore enable writers to pause, consider and reflect before going on to their next available point. Long staircases are only possible in very large houses, while those of a less ambitious sort need staircases that stop, pause and continue round the next corner, and this feature also fits the requirements of most readers.

The basic paragraph outline therefore serves both writers and readers. Because writing needs to supply a series of direction changes, this happens usually after about 150 words or fewer (but not more), and if the block goes on considerably longer than that, readers (and writers) are likely to get uncomfortable and begin to anticipate a change which isn't happening. The same unease must have existed long before the invention of paper; readers of parchment would start to hope for a ¶ sign in the margin. Change is necessary and therefore fundamental, but it also needs to be marked. The writer may be aware of a change of sense, but if he or she fails to mark it the reader will see a block of continuous script and begin to feel seriously discouraged.

To change the sense, and mark it: this is the rule, and the only rule about paragraphs, and this rule allows for a number of decisions. If we look back at the examples given above, we can see that paragraphs don't need to occupy anywhere near the 150-word-sized space, nor do they need to proceed in every case from specific reference to summary. That outline indicates the conventional set of procedures, and is likely to be found in formal articles, academic essays and in most examples of continuous prose argument. But if we explore outside those types of discourse, we are likely to see inventive uses of paragraphs. Look, for example, at the Angela Carter passages. The first sentence of both her stories is a paragraph in itself. A quality of decision is in force here and permitted; the writer is making a confident choice of effect.

All the quoted examples above are in paragraphs. Ballard ends his short one-sentence paragraph with three dots: a summary implying that the action could go on. Woody Allen's diary reserves a paragraph for each statement, however bizarre. Only Fowles has stayed within the convention – the final piece of detail completes the portrait – while Morrison's paragraphs in this part of her novel move hopelessly but gradually towards an exit for the speaker from her suffering.

Redrafting

The drive behind effective style is decision: knowing where you have freedom and where you do not, where you have choice and where you must stick to the rules.

As we found in examples 12 and 13 above, both writers chose to express the same idea but differed in their decisions about sentence structure and about which words to select.

Let us assume that the writer of example 12 accepted our advice and rewrote the sentence to read more like example 13. In doing so, the writer would have achieved a more effective means of expression than their first attempt produced. Certain kinds of advice, in certain instances, will help writers to make effective decisions. But in other instances the advice might sound like this: 'What you have written is perfectly sound and communicates very successfully, but *as an experiment* why not try rewriting it in a new way. You will learn something, and can always, if you decide to, go back to your first alternative.'

All the same, Jim would have liked to eat the ship. He imagined himself eating the masts, eating the cream from the Edwardian funnels, eating the marzipan bows and the entire forward section of the hull. After that he would eat the Palace Hotel, the Shell Building, the whole of Shanghai. . .

If J. G. Ballard had brought this paragraph to his writing tutor for comment, he might well have received the second type of advice, which would be: 'Yes, you have an exciting idea here, but try rewriting the passage by substituting a range of expressions for "eating" – then decide which alternative you prefer.'

In this example, we can see how choices about *vocabulary* affect impact. The question is: why is the published version preferable? There may be a good many reasons.

Another set of choices involves *tenses of verbs*. Suppose Angela Carter had written her first draft of 'The Werewolf' in the *past tense*, thus:

One beast and only one howled in the woods by night.

The wolf was carnivore incarnate and he was as cunning as he was ferocious; once he'd had a taste of flesh then nothing else would do.

At night, the eyes of the wolves shone like candle flames, yellowish, reddish, but that was because the pupils of their eyes fattened on darkness and caught the light from your lantern to flash it back at you.

Using present tense verbs is a major option, and redrafting can explore these options. Compare Angela Carter's version (p. 24) with the passage above. Can you describe the change of attitude which the alteration from past to present has produced?

As a final example, the sentence below, written by a student, contains an interesting idea but is limited in its vocabulary.

I feel there is a lot of insecurity amongst authority figures which leads to them not doing much in fear of losing their relative superiority.

How would you advise her to redraft it?

Clichés

One mark of a developing writer is the urgency to give themself advice and then to decide whether to act on it.

Some of you will notice my choice of the word *themself* here. Why did I use it? Was it desirable? Why didn't I simply put 'the writer . . . himself'? Are there other alternatives? I could have chosen to say, 'the writer . . . herself'? Maybe I should have. This problem is becoming increasingly familiar. To use unquestioningly the masculine form has now become a kind of cliché unacceptable because it suggests sexism and conformity. It produces that cliché feeling readers recognise; the writer hasn't *thought enough* about what he or she is actually saying. But to use the neutral form as I have chosen, or to use 'herself' – the feminine – could be clichés too now, unfortunately.

Clichés prevent us from thinking about what exactly we are trying to say and about how to find accurate ways of saying it. They are borrowed substitutes for our own choice of expression. By using clichés we imply we are capable only of responding to the obvious and of using the obvious and unexamined expression for an idea. We write 'home is where the heart is' and so avoid exploring what our home really does mean to us.

By saying 'themself', I imply that the term 'writer' can refer to both males and females – an obvious point – but I also imply that I am aware of the use of sexist language, that I have confidently examined the problem and made my decision in the light of it. This attitude has in itself the mark of becoming a new cliché, however. If I wanted to sound entirely original and even start a trend, maybe I should have said: 'the writer . . . *it*self' – complete neuter and hence possibly the least offensive of all, though not a good choice for other reasons.

Fortunately, we can in most cases purge our work of clichés without becoming entangled in this problem. Here are some examples of clichés from Alan Bennett's monologue 'Soldiering On' in the series he wrote for television entitled *Talking Heads*. The speaker is Muriel, a woman in her late fifties. A few days after her husband's death, some unexpected guests arrive for the funeral:

> It's a funny time, three o'clock, too late for lunch but a bit early for tea. Besides, there were one or two brave souls who'd trekked it all the way from Wolverhampton; I couldn't risk giving them tea or we'd have had a mutiny on our hands. . . . One's first instinct was to make a beeline for the freezer and rout out the inevitable quiche, but I thought, 'Muriel, old girl, that's the coward's way out'. . . however, Mabel warmed up the proceedings with one of her famous soups, conjured up out of thin air, so we lived to fight another day. . . . Still it was a bit sticky at the start as these occasions generally are. There were people one didn't know from Adam (all the Massey-Ferguson people for instance, completely unknown quantities to me), and then lots of people I knew I should know but didn't. But whenever I saw anyone looking lost I thought of Ralph and grabbed hold of someone I did know and breezed up saying, 'This is Jocelyn. She's at the Royal College of Art. I don't know your name but the odds are you're in agricultural machinery,' and left them to it. It was a case of light the blue touch paper and stand clear.[12]

The clichés here belong to the woman character, not the writer. The title 'Soldiering On' is a cliché itself (it's what you must do in well-regulated moneyed families when 'things get on top of you'). If you can identify the clichés in this excerpt, you will see how they are used for comic effect; clichés are used by people when they avoid thinking directly about what is happening to them. The clichés here create a sense of a character, and infiltrate her style with class-bound attitudes. The woman speaks as people of her social group would expect her to, and Bennett's writing has caught that 'soldiering on' attitude exactly: jollification (in spite of the tragic circumstances) and specious, rather silly, exaggeration.

The rule is that clichés should be avoided, otherwise we shall begin to sound like Muriel. If we want to write Muriel-like monologues however, clichés will be very useful indeed. If we want to write as ourselves, clichés will make us sound like somebody else: someone addicted to socially conditioned speech habits, and unreflective about the language they use.

Here is a list of available (and avoidable) clichés. Because it disowns exaggeration, preferring instead exactness and honest statement, good style usually resists them:

tears stung my eyes
in the pit of my stomach
in floods of tears
speechless
indescribable
sickening
stunned silence
(blind/stricken) with terror
I could feel my heart pounding
the price to pay
selfless abandon
blind acceptance
trembling anticipation
hasty retreat
golden opportunity
stark contrast
stern warning
nagging doubt
constant reminder
echo
link
conflict with
totally (anything)
blatant (anything)
abject (anything)

I include the last three items because they often occur in the style of beginning writers. Although they can be used effectively, they may suggest a needlessly exaggerated tone. This list could be continued. There may be occasions when certain items really do fit exactly what is required. But all too often these constructions indicate tiredness of thought, naivety, evasiveness. It is a small but necessary step to dismantle the phrase and rediscover its meaning through other words. All clichés should be treated in this way: reject them and find new means of expression. One way of doing this is simply to get rid of the exaggerating adjunct (muted, stark, infinite, boundless, totally, abject, etc.) and to see if the word that remains does the work you want. If it does not, you will need another word or word group to contact your intended meaning. The exception, of course, is when you are scripting word groups by other speakers, as in monologues and dialogues. On those occasions clichés make powerful *indicators* of naivety and evasion.

Referents

Finally, let us assume that the writer of sentence (12) refused to accept our advice and instead asked us for more explanation of why that sentence is problematic. Here it is again:

12 Most teachers are white Anglo-Saxon, which links with the Swann Report saying that some ethnic minorities are neglected, in my view this is wrong.

We could easily reply by asking the writer what the word 'this' refers to. As we discovered, 'this' might refer to 'most teachers are white', or to 'the Swann Report saying that some ethnic minorities are neglected'. We might think we know the writer's intention, but grammatically the word 'this' could refer to either phrase.

The word 'this' is sometimes a danger in sentences, especially if the reader is left with doubts about what 'this' means. 'This' and 'it' and 'which' usually refer back to something said previously – possibly even a large number of 'somethings' – and we need to be sure which one. To begin a sentence with 'this' or 'it' will send readers back to the previous sentence, and if that previous sentence was unclear, the meaning of the new one will also be lost. The following sentences make use of referents (as marked).

We didn't believe *her story which* was typical. (ineffective)

She said *she* had sprained her wrist *which* was normal. (ineffective)

She said *she* had sprained her wrist; we didn't believe *it*.
(effective, although the second 'she' could still be referring to someone else)

We didn't believe her story about her wrist; *it* looked normal, and anyway she told lies all the time. (effective)

The point here is to cut down on the number of referents, and to make *each sentence say the thing in full* rather than just leaving the meaning to chance. When explaining a situation, writers need to spell things out directly more often than not. Don't assume your readers will know the information beforehand, or will somehow be able to work it out for themselves. Too much reliance on referents takes short cuts through meaning and produces obscurity, as in sentence (12) and the first two sentences in the above extract. If you make each sentence say something *definite and different from* your previous one, your readers will pay more attention. As far as possible, each sentence should form a new, clear, independent statement.

Readers and writers

As writers, our job is to guide our readers and not take them on unannounced mystery tours. But the territories we enter may not always be clear to us to begin with. Writers make use of common knowledge and shared experience even while exploring new ideas. Concrete words such as 'house', 'garden' and 'river' are therefore far less hazardous than abstract words such as 'life', 'dream', 'reality' and 'socialism'. Words with powerful and specific associations are always more useful than loose and general abstractions.

Similes and metaphors can be effective because they combine new impressions with shared and knowable ones. If we say 'life is like a river' we are relying on the fact that readers already know something or enough about rivers to make sense of the comparison. The comparison isn't very interesting, however; it needs stimulating details. Does it help if we then make the comparison more detailed? If we say that 'life is like the River Tagus' we would have to assume our readers didn't know enough about the River Tagus to understand what we meant, and we would therefore have to explain its location and what sort of river it is (a scorched dried up canyon or a torrent, or both at different seasons of the year); in other words, to share our special knowledge with them first. This would make a much more significant comparison, but risks being obscure unless we explain.

As a less hazardous example, if we say that the inside working of a digital computer resembles Los Angeles at night, we are assuming readers will have more knowledge of cities than they do of computers, will therefore make some sense of the connection, and will gain from the image's visual impact. Each of these assumptions is probably correct, and the likeness just about specific enough to attract interest. If you look at Sylvia Plath's metaphors for the sea (Chapter 2, p.61), you can tell how she is working on the problem of mixing her own insight with the reader's prior knowledge and experience. She has to guess at those and make assumptions, and doing so is part of the writing process. The difficulty with some metaphors however is that readers have either heard the comparison before and don't therefore find it very interesting or, faced with too much newness, feel confused. Another problem is that metaphors rate high on interest value but low on information value. A comparison between Los Angeles and a computer would not be of much help if found in a user's manual.

The example of metaphor highlights an issue central to writing and reading.

A degree of common knowledge must be established before new meanings can be produced, and writing, like any sign system, moves back and forth between the shared and the new. If it succeeds it will be because the writer is aware of the distinction and able to operate confidently in between. Too much timid reliance on shared knowledge produces a lack of interest (as clichés do); boredom quickly follows. Disregard for the reader's prior experience creates obscurity, with the same result: boredom and impatience. So the business of moving back and forth – back to the reader and forward into the new – describes the kind of action writers perform. How well they do it depends on their sense of their readers but also on their feeling for the new thing to be said. It also depends on how they write sentences. Imagine you are your reader; what impact is your sentence producing? Does it turn the reader's mind to pulp – like the passage quoted by Orwell – or bring about sharpness, shape, understanding?

As writers, we can decide to acknowledge the reader and allow that imaginary presence to shape how we write, and this decision will affect our style at the sentence level as well as in the overall structure of a piece. Whether we are writing a poem or a user's guide, our choices will be influenced; our readers will not share the same sets of expectations. So effective writing begins with an acknowledgement of its readers.

At the same time, effective writing stimulates fresh interest, reveals unforeseen insight: writers could begin to experiment, for example, with punctuation, the use of dialect forms, or with the expression of fresh and unformed ideas. All that matters is that as writers we know what is appropriate, have confidence in our choices, know when readers need help, and know when we are giving them something new. It matters too that the writer's own interest be fully involved. Whatever the topic or theme of a piece of writing, that excitement is the drive of a confident style.

INTRODUCTORY WRITING EXERCISES

These exercises are to help you develop the focus and style of your writing. Some of them can be developed into stories and poems, or referred back to when you are writing in one of these forms. The suggested length for each exercise is about 800 words, but this of course is provisional. There are advantages to getting things said in a compact form fully and quickly; on the other hand you might decide to continue beyond this length.

Observation

1 Take a notebook and visit a place where you can observe a scene carefully and in detail: a place where crowds gather, or where there are plenty of things to see and hear. Write in the present tense.

   Your reader will know that the place, people and events you describe are present and happening. Nothing is invented. There could be one particular item catching your attention, or several: people, objects, colours, sounds, smells, and you will be giving yourself the chance to notice far more than you would normally. You may want to capture a broad impression to begin with, but try to move as quickly as possible into close-up. If you see a face that interests you, let it fill the whole frame. Notice how people stand, walk, behave with their bodies and hands. Are they eating, drinking, speaking (some overheard dialogue will help your reader to glimpse the typical atmosphere)? There may be a kind of behaviour associated with this place, and if so, try to catch what is typical, but do this also in detail. Or there may be no people present. Your interest may be focused on the place itself. Your writing might be complete at one sitting, or you could write notes and develop these later.

2 Describe your district, city, town or village by using a series of close-up shots. Avoid unspecific reaction words: nice, great, wonderful, friendly, exciting, boring, ugly, ideal. Instead of naming them directly, try to *convey* these reactions by the way you write about the place, people, sights, sounds. You may well have feelings about, and an attitude to the place, and these could be positive or negative or a mixture. But again, try to make the reader experience these reactions; show rather than tell; go for sensation and visual impression: what is it really like to be there, on certain days, at certain times?

Sensation

1 Many people who have lost their sight or hearing are able to allow their other senses to compensate for the missing one. Far from lacking vividness, the other sense impressions can be acute. Try to imagine the world without your sight and hearing, and focus your writing on a short period of time; record your impressions. Write with as much exactness and attention to detail as you can, so that your reader will share the experience.

2 Imagine you have overdeveloped hearing, touch, taste or smell. Concentrate on one of these senses, and explore how they change your experience of the world. Instead of writing about experience generally, focus your reactions on to a particular place or event. But don't merely invent or exaggerate things just for effect. Try to live inside this sensation for a short period, and see what impressions you collect. Write them down as exactly as possible so that your reader will experience them as you do.

3 Write about particular kinds of weather or climate (snow, rain, wind, hail, sleet, thunder, sun, mildness, coolness, the moment when you sense a season changing). Inside each of these obvious words there will be a whole range of sensation reactions and qualities to record. Write in the present tense, so that you can record exact changes and contrasts: cloud-formations, weather effects in familiar surroundings as well as their impact on yourself

and your feelings. How do these different types of weather make you feel? Again, try to convey the feelings rather than simply name them. You might try this in prose or poem form.

4 Allow one colour, object or person to fill the whole of your attention. Keep your focus narrow and clear, and make your reader feel the presence of this person or object as physically as possible: they are not like any other anywhere, they are unique, but you can still describe them using metaphors (in fact every available means) to reveal that uniqueness of posture, build, skin texture, size and bulk – that presence. If you are writing about a colour, try to give it as much substance and vividness as you can by revealing all the varying shades within the colour-name, as if you are experiencing these for the first time, or have been suffering from yellow or green deprivation.

It might help you to give it an actual substance: a fruit, its presence in a painting, a fabric – the red of plastic is not the same as that of a rose – the yellow of a wash-leather is different from the yellow of fire.

Culture images

You have the choice of one object which represents a significant cultural marker. Every civilisation is a mixture of cultures and counter-cultures, some dominant, some marginal. You may feel you belong to a smaller culture within the dominant one. You may object to the images through which your culture, or the dominant one, represents itself, or you may approve of them. Ethnic images in dress and furniture, typical objects in a DIY superstore or large garden centre, new kinds of domestic technology – all these could be useful. Objects can represent an image of a particular social class, its tastes and its way of life. Fashion comes into this system of representations. Types of dress, hair-style, ornament – all these consciously or subliminally convey social meanings and group identifications. Images are strongly represented in advertising: the typical car advertisement of the moment, the use of environmental images in advertising. Choose an object or image that has strong interest value for you: one you disapprove of, approve of, or simply think worth investigating. Explore some reasons why it is, or should be, seen as a culture image.

Photographs and paintings

Browsing through magazines and newspapers in any one week can produce a whole range of photographs, paintings and computer graphic effects. If you cut these out they can have more power than when surrounded by print and story coverage. You can either write about their impact in connection with the caption or story, or see what impressions they generate on their own. Perhaps not surprisingly, there is an obvious difference between advertise-ment photographs and 'real' photography, and, as a rule, the latter can offer more powerful stimuli for writing. We at least know that somebody is not just trying to sell us something but to make us *see* something with its own value. What are the thoughts of the figures and faces in a photograph/painting, or of the photographer/artist? How do the subjects in the picture relate to their setting, to each other? Does the use of perspective affect your response?

Free writing

Here you are free to write what you want and how you want, but the idea is to focus your thoughts on one particular topic. It could be anything: a film you have just seen, a book you have just finished reading, a decision you are trying to make, a place you have visited, your partner, your children, your parents. The idea is to collect your thoughts, but in a way that will enable you to understand your thinking and point of view when you return to read your writing a week, a month, or even some years later. It is best to write quickly, and let your ideas tell you what to write. This form of writing can be very fruitful. It overcomes the sense of being blocked, which all writers experience from time to time. It may help to think of yourself only as your reader, but by working with details and specific thoughts you will produce a record of your ideas, attitudes and impressions as and when you wrote them down.

Once you have developed this method, you may find that it comes in useful when writing in the other forms. Let your ideas flow; if you are writing down some thoughts for a short story, for example, you then look back over your work to select your best ideas.

NOTES ON WRITING

Writing for a reader

Every written text, whether it aims to be published or not, involves a relationship between the writer and reader. In free writing you are your own reader, but as that reader you will still need to receive a clear picture of the ideas, impressions and feelings you were experiencing at the time.

The presence of the reader might seem at first a very unwelcome and even inhibiting factor, a kind of tyranny you would much rather do without. But once you have accepted it as a fact, the writing experience becomes not more difficult and inhibited, but easier and less fraught. And the reason for this is that readers are not only eager to be kept involved, they also respond to the strength of the *writer's* involvement with what she or he is trying to say. If you, the writer, are involved, your reader will follow. If you are bored, your reader will quickly follow by losing interest. Your reader instinctively senses the strength of commitment you feel towards the subjects you write about.

So what are the signs of commitment which readers recognise and enjoy? You can perhaps agree on this from your own reading. By commitment I don't necessarily mean some serious moral theme, nor do I mean some political dogma or party bias. At this stage, all I imply is a sense of excitement. It is possible to write an interesting and committed book about fly-fishing or building model aeroplanes; people do so for readers who share the same set of obsessions as the writer, and feel the benefit of reading a book written by an expert on the subject. But that kind of writing clearly relates to the general reader on only a few occasions.

The point however still holds. Your appeal to your reader depends on the extent to which your are prepared to become an expert on your topic, to know it, even if your topic is a scene in a piece of fiction or autobiography, or a character in a story, or a moment of time in a poem you are writing. The word 'expert' could be off-putting, but all I mean is being prepared to take an extra step, a closer look, to ask an unusual question, to observe, feel and think about something with forceful and detailed attention, to go into detail and not be quite satisfied with the usual or stereotypical way of presenting a scene, character or event. The keyword here is *focus*, and sharp focus implies above all an extra degree of engagement, a degree of excitement which, if the writer feels it, the reader will too. And fortunately, most writers, like their readers, want to take that extra step themselves, and need that detailed feel for the texture and roughness of an experience. Writers and readers actually want the same thing.

Keep writing

You may have an idea for a story or a poem or a piece of autobiographical writing; you may have less than a clear idea, more a hunch or an instinctive interest in a piece of dialogue, a character or a place, whether real or imaginary. It may be that some experience or sensation has left an image with you even though you have forgotten the details and circumstances. Though time has passed you remember something: the look of a group of trees, or a face locked in anger or hesitation, or a room in a certain house you no longer visit, or a place in a dream or some imaginary country. You decide you want to explore this image further; you start to write, but what you have written looks flat and uninteresting compared with the original. It's important at this stage that you do not give up after the first try, but allow yourself to keep writing.

Very few experienced writers succeed at the first go, or even with the third or fourth attempt. Instead, they enter the struggle; they permit themselves to experiment, and if you follow this path you will at the very least learn something about how language works, about how words form themselves into phrases, how meanings come to be wrestled with. The chapters below will not always remind you of this rule, but since it is fundamental to every act of writing it is worth keeping it always fresh in your mind. If at the first try you are going to be satisfied with nothing short of perfection, you will not be giving yourself the chances you need: the chance to learn as much as you can about words, the chance to experiment. It is preferable therefore to start with rough ideas, sketches, attempts, and to build up the pressure gradually.

Language as art

Every word in the dictionary is available for the creative writer to use: scientific phrases as well as street slang, medical terms as well as the language of advertising. Certain types of language are of special interest to writers and will have specific impacts on readers. Here are some of them.

The rhythms of speech

Language written to imitate the spoken word: dialect, dialogue, voice quality, accent, slang. This type may involve a deliberate break with the sentence structures of modern Standard English, replacing it with phrases or single words. More formally, it can also involve the elaborate use of punctuation for emphasis as in speech: the use of brackets and dashes to indicate asides: language conversing, demonstrating, arguing, refuting.

Language drawing attention to itself

Language as sound, echo, texture and substance: its visible shape on the page, rhythm qualities, internal or end rhyme, stress patterns, metaphors, similes, puns, borrowed words or phrases from other writers, features which traditionally mark out literariness. Community-owned language, slogans, buzzwords, for example, are often borrowed for literary use by writers. Peter Shaffer, Harold Pinter, Alan Bennett and Victoria Wood, among contemporary writers, are experts in the use of cliché, drawing attention to the staleness of public language by making what is familiar sound unfamiliar, mocking or comic.

Language as search

Language that is continually revisiting the real which lies beyond language, out of its usual reach; language that is, to use T. S. Eliot's phrase, 'a raid on the inarticulate, with shabby equipment' – which faces the unknown, unavailable or pre-verbal levels of experience. The writer here is trying to reveal what cannot easily become articulated. The obvious words and forms will not suffice, so more inventive and searching constructions of words are required to bring to light what is obscure or forgotten. We can see this function of language operating in John Berger's thoughts about his mother in Chapter 2 (see p.43).

Here, Berger is trying to read the signs of his mother's strange inaccessible personality, and teaching us how to read them as he does so. Language as search could be called language extending itself.

Frameworks

Behind this book lies a basically held view about the creative process. On the one hand we are working within the accepted conventions and frameworks, and when it comes to a single piece of writing one way to begin is to have a sense of what its overall structure might be like. But the actual process of composition is only partly determined by that framework. If pushed against, the fractures in the frame begin to show, and out of that pressure of working within a frame, something new and quite unprescribed can happen. The writing begins to develop almost independently of the writer and independently of what he or she thought it would be about or would be like. The colours we set out with begin to mix. We need something – a framework, a sense of structure – but the excitement comes when this structure begins to evolve by itself, to find its own shape.

Editing

No piece of writing is really finished until it has been lived with and read through several times. Here are some questions to ask yourself while editing and revising one or more of the exercises above.

1 *Sentence awareness.* See if you can strengthen your sentence structure. Make sure your main verbs and main clauses are visible and not weakened by trailing subordinate clauses. Each sentence must be formed so that your reader will hear, grasp, understand. Try experimenting with new punctuation: colons for lists, semicolons for closely linked sentences.
2 *Economy.* Does each sentence add something to the previous one? Does each one reveal something new about your topic? Is each sentence making clear a definite written statement?
3 *Register.* This term describes the appropriateness of a piece of language to the social context in which it is received. Slang, for example, indicates an informal context. In the above writing exercises you should assume you are writing for a general reader and your register should be not too formal and not too informal. It should also be consistent.
4 *Structure and rhythm.* When reading through your work, see if it leads from one point to the next clearly and rhythmically. If you are writing about sensations, your style could become influenced by your feelings and be based more on impressions than on clearly presented ideas. But even if this

is so, imagine yourself as the reader: Are the feelings sharp and powerful enough to get through? Does your writing have pace, rhythm, interest? Will your reader feel lost, and if so can you correct this problem?

5 *A reader.* If you possibly can, find someone who will read your work sympathetically, but who will say clearly when they don't follow, lose the thread, or get bored. This occurs in all writing and should be a matter of simply making some corrections.

Time out

We need each other's encouragement, and to share our experiences of writing, but also as writers we need to work independently. We may also need to do certain things which, paradoxically, do not involve words. So the last point you might consider is this: if you have a piece of writing in mind, or in some half-finished state – which is actually the case for almost all writers much of the time – stop, go for a walk, draw a picture, enjoy something different, go window-shopping, or even fly-fishing, but observe, take notice, bring to your surroundings and other people an extra special level of attention, see them as unfamiliar and worth all your attention, store up what you see, hear or think, and let it lie in that part of your mind which has no obvious practical function, which isn't continually worrying about what you have to do today or next week. Writing needs that stocked reservoir of real but aimless sensations. When the time comes and you need them, they'll find you.

Chapter 2

Autobiographical writing

The flamboyant dancer and eccentric, Isadora Duncan, when asked to write her autobiography, almost lost her nerve at the suggestion. 'I confess that when it was first proposed to me I had a terror of writing this book. Not that my life had not been more interesting than any novel and more adventurous than any cinema and, if really well written, would not be an epoch-making recital, but there's the rub – the writing of it!'[1] She admits that even given her interesting life (she obviously held few doubts about the heights of its significance), something else is required, by which she meant the skill of transferring that sense of significance and excitement to her readers.

Your life may well be stocked with exceptional happenings, exotic voyages, famous or infamous friends, but if you spend the bulk of your time, as most of us do, within the realms of the ordinary, is anyone going to be interested in what you write? Asking this question is understandable but far from drawing a negative response the answer is, yes, they will. And they will because if you write in a way which will make people want to read and go on reading, it doesn't matter how interesting or dull you judged your experience. You will yourself discover where the interest lies, which is the point of autobiographical writing; you will have engaged your reader and yourself. The idea of this chapter is to help you write something which people will read not because your name is the epoch-making Isadora Duncan, but because you have written it in a way which provokes attention. What finally counts is the writing of it.

If you succeed in discovering the right words, the exciting angle, you might then face the next set of questions which stumped Isadora:'How can we write the truth about ourselves? Do we even know it?' But you have at least one advantage. No one is asking you for your whole life story from birth up to yesterday. Autobiographical writing is not the same thing as writing a complete autobiography. This chapter is asking you to specialise and select – not to give the whole of the truth even if that were possible – but to aim your attention at one particular memory or set of incidents, and as we shall see there are many ways of doing this.

FINDING A FOCUS

Even if you do decide to tell your life story so far, you will not be able to achieve it without focus, by which I mean close-up (rather than only wide angle) shots. Ideally you need both, but without close detail and a sense of perspective your readers will feel less convinced that it is worth their while to look through the particular lens you have set up. I stress the idea of a camera deliberately. A wide angle shot looks like this:

> I was born in 1968 and at the age of four attended a small primary school on the outskirts of Norwich, the largest town in East Anglia. My father is an architect and for two years was employed on rebuilding work to the cathedral. My sister worked in a bakery in the main street. My best friend lived outside the town at a pig farm near Taverham. When I was nine, my mother attended a WEA class on industrial archaeology.

Close-up shots prevent the slide from one piece of information to another by selecting a point of interest and holding it, thus:

> I am standing in the middle of a sweep of green. I stare at a point near the spire where a ladder perches and a tiny figure is climbing from rung to rung.'Come on!' a voice calls, 'you'll be late, hurry up,' but I go on looking. The figure I can see, high up in the wind, is my father.

Something as simple as a voice calling – a small enough detail in itself – can add tension and generate involvement, but only if the focus has been adjusted down to that scale. Impact depends as much on minor effects as on broad strokes of background information, and this will be true whether or not the information is interesting, exotic, or concerns outrageous events and well-known people. Even where the events *are* outrageous, the small details count, as we shall see.

The skill in all autobiographical writing is finding a way of setting up the camera so that you can control the resulting shot, the one with appeal and maximum interest value. You do not have to worry too much about inventing the details since these are there already in your memory. You need to develop an accurate retrieval system, but the fact is that, as soon as you begin to aim your attention in one specific direction, you find you begin to remember more than you thought. You might begin with an actual photograph of a place or person of particular interest to you. At the back of your mind, what you thought of as nothing but a faint trickle or irrelevant source is in fact the whole reservoir; the more you attempt, the more you can recover.

Your choice of how to focus your writing might not be quite so easy as I have made out. You might, for example, need to provide a certain amount of background information. What I suggest is that you think carefully about how much, how little, and how to avoid sliding from one piece of information to another without knowing when or how to stop. Avoiding such a slide means finding a point of focus.

Why autobiography?

Autobiographical writing draws directly on the writer's personal experience, but apart from the point of reviving what you know, its value lies in training the act of attention, in thinking about your reader – how to get them interested and involved – and in making your own decisions: the kind you will need to make when handling future writing projects.

Autobiographical writing is a useful place to start. The forms it takes are different and your first step will be to assess the various types of approach. You could decide, for example, to make your piece of writing into a story, to build it around a portrait of someone you know, to record a change in your thinking about some experience which has affected you, or evoke a scene in a poetic way. The examples given below illustrate these different modes and there will be others which you could draw on for ideas. The ones I have selected preview in miniature the subjects of further chapters in this book: fiction, poetry, writing about ideas, thinking about audience, and thinking about writing in terms of film and other media. Elements of fiction, drama and persuasion are all present in autobiographical writing. Writing of all kinds combines image-making and comment; much is also drawn from the writer's experience, and here we can see some different ways of contacting that experience.

CHOOSING A FORM

Before you reach the point of balancing close-up and background detail, your first decision will be to choose the kind of autobiographical writing which has the most appeal to you, and as you will see from the examples below, this genre can take a number of forms. The first step is to read carefully some examples, and discover ways in which these examples differ.

Attempting to understand these differences will help you decide what your approach might be. A discussion about them will also help you decide; my own comments, therefore, do not aim to cover every point worth raising.

This first example is a portrait, and printed in full.

'Mother' by John Berger
From the age of five or six I was worried about the death of my parents. The inevitability of death was one of the first things I learnt about the world on my own. Nobody else spoke of it, yet the signs were so clear.

Every time I went to bed – and in this I am sure I was like millions of other children – the fear that one or both of my parents might die in the night touched the nape of my neck with its finger. Such a fear has, I believe, little to do with a particular psychological climate and a great deal to do with nightfall. Yet since it was impossible to say 'You won't die in the night, will you?' (when Grandmother died, I was told she had gone to have a rest, or – this was from my uncle who was more outspoken – that she had passed over), since I couldn't ask the real question and I sought a reassurance, I invented – like millions before me – the euphemism See you in the morning! To which either my father or mother who had come to turn out the light in my bedroom would reply, See you in the morning, John.

After their footsteps had died away, I would try for as long as possible not to lift my head from the pillow so that the last words spoken remained, trapped like a fish in a rock pool at low tide, between my pillow and my ear. The implicit promise of the words was also a protection against the dark. The words promised that I would not (yet) be alone.

Now I'm no longer usually frightened by the dark and my father died ten years ago and my mother a month ago at the age of ninety three. It would be a natural moment to write an autobiography. My version of my life can no longer hurt either of them. And the book, when finished, would be there, a little like a parent. Autobiography begins with a sense of being alone. It is an orphan form. Yet I have no wish to do so. All that interests me about my past life are the common moments. The moments – which if I relate them well enough – will join countless others lived by people I do not personally know.

Six weeks ago my mother asked me to come and see her; it would be the last time, she said. A few days later, on the morning of my birthday, she believed she was dying. Open the curtains, she said to my brother, so I can see the trees. In fact, she died the following week.

On my birthdays as a child, it was my father rather than she who gave me memorable presents. She was too thrifty. Her moments of generosity were at the table, offering what she had bought and prepared and cooked and served to whoever came into the house. Otherwise she was thrifty. Nor did she ever explain. She was secretive, she kept things to herself. Not for her own pleasure, but because the world would not forgive spontaneity, the world was mean. I must make that clearer. She didn't believe life was mean – it was generous – but she had learnt from her own childhood that survival was hard. She was the opposite of quixotic – for she was not born a knight and her father was a warehouse foreman in Lambeth. She pursed her lips together, knitted her brows, as she calculated and thought things out and carried on with an unspoken determination. She never asked favours of anyone. Nothing shocked her. From whatever she saw, she just drew the necessary conclusions so as to survive and to be dependent on nobody. If I were Aesop, I would say that in her prudence and persistence my mother resembled the agouti. (I once wrote about an agouti in the London zoo but I did not then realise why the animal so touched me.) In my adult life, the only occasions on which we shouted at each other were when she estimated I was being quixotic.

When I was in my thirties, she told me for the first time that ever since I was born she had hoped I would be a writer. The writers she admired when young were Bernard Shaw, J. M. Barrie, Compton MacKenzie,

Warwick Deeping, E. M. Dell. The only painter she really admired was Turner – perhaps because of her childhood on the banks of the Thames.

Most of my books she didn't read. Either because they dealt with subjects which were alien to her or because – under the protective influence of my father – she believed they might upset her. Why suffer surprise from something which, left unopened, gives you pleasure? My being a writer was unqualified for her by what I wrote. To be a writer was to be able to see to the horizon where, anyway, nothing is ever very distinct, and all questions are open. Literature had little to do with the writer's vocation as she saw it. It was only a by-product. A writer was a person familiar with the secrets. Perhaps in the end she didn't read my books so that they should remain more secret.

If her hopes of my becoming a writer – and she said they began on the night after I was delivered – were eventually realised, it was not because there were many books in our house (there were few) but because there was so much that was unsaid, so much that I had to discover the existence of on my own at an early age: death, poverty, pain (in others), sexuality. . . .

These things were there to be discovered within the house or from its windows – until I left for good, more or less prepared for the outside world, at the age of eight. My mother never spoke of these things. She didn't hide the fact that she was aware of them. For her, however, they were wrapped secrets, to be lived with but never to be mentioned or opened. Superficially, this was a question of gentility, but profoundly, of a respect, a secret loyalty to the enigmatic. My rough and ready preparation for the world did not include a single explanation – it simply consisted of the principle that events carried more weight than the self.

Thus, she taught me very little – at least in the usual sense of the term; she a teacher about life, I a learner. By imitating her gestures I learnt how to roast meat in the oven, how to clean celery, how to cook rice, how to choose vegetables in a market. As a young woman she had been a vegetarian. Then she gave it up because she did not want to influence us children. Why were you a vegetarian? I once asked her, eating my Sunday roast, much later when I was first working as a journalist. Because I'm against killing. She would say no more. Either I understood or I didn't. There was nothing more to be said.

In time – and I understand this only now writing these pages – I chose to visit abattoirs in different cities of the world and to become something of an expert concerning the subject. The unspoken, the unfaceable beckoned me. I followed. Into the abattoirs and, differently, into many other places and situations.

The last, the largest and most personally prepared wrapped secret was her own death. Of course I was not the only witness. Of those close to her, I was maybe the most removed, the most remote. But she knew, I think, with confidence that I would not pursue the matter. She knew that if anybody can be at home with what is kept a secret, it was me, because I was her son who she hoped would become a writer.

The clinical history of her illness is a different story about which she herself was totally uncurious. Sufficient to say that with the help of drugs she was not in pain, and that, thanks to my brother and sister-in-law who arranged everything for her, she was not subjected to all the mechanical ingenuity of aids for the artificial prolongation of life.

Of how many deaths – though never till now my own mother's – have I written? Truly we writers are the secretaries of death.

She lay in her bed, propped up by pillows, her head fallen forward, as if asleep.

I shut my eyes, she said, I like to shut my eyes and think. I don't sleep though. If I slept now, I wouldn't sleep at night.

What do you think about?

She screwed up her eyes which were gimlet sharp and looked at me, twinkling, as if I'd never, not even as a small child, asked such a stupid question.

Are you working hard? What are you writing?

A play, I answered.

The last time I went to the theatre I didn't understand a thing, she said. It's not my hearing that's bad though.

Perhaps the play was obscure, I suggested.

She opened her eyes again. The body has closed shop, she announced. Nothing, nothing at all from here down. She placed a hand on her neck. It's a good thing, make no mistake about it, John, it makes the waiting easier.

On her bedside table was a tin of hand cream. I started to massage her left hand.

Do you remember a photograph I once took of your hands? Working hands, you said.

No, I don't.

Would you like some more photos on your table? Katya, her grand-daughter, asked her.

She smiled at Katya and shook her head, her voice very slightly broken by a laugh. It would be so difficult, *so* difficult, wouldn't it, to choose.

She turned towards me. What exactly are you doing?

I'm massaging your hand. It's meant to be pleasurable.

To tell you the truth dear it doesn't make much difference. Which plane are you taking back?

I mumbled, took her other hand.

You are all worried, she said, especially when there are several of you. I'm not. Maureen asked me the other day whether I wanted to be cremated or buried. Doesn't make one iota of difference to me. How could it? She shut her eyes to think.

For the first time in her life and mine, she could openly place the wrapped enigma between us. She didn't watch me watching it, for we had the habits of a lifetime. Openly, she knew that in that moment her faith in a secret was bound to be stronger than any faith of mine in facts. With her eyes still shut, she fingered the Arab necklace I'd attached round her neck with a charm against the evil eye. I'd given her the necklace a few hours before. Perhaps for the first time I had offered her a secret and now her hand kept looking for it.

She opened her eyes. What time is it?

Quarter to four.

It's not very interesting talking to me, you know. I don't have any ideas any more. I've had a good life. Why don't you take a walk?

Katya stayed with her.

When you are very old, she told Katya confidentially, there's one thing that's very, very difficult – it's very difficult to persuade other people that you're happy.

She let her head go back on the pillow. As I came back in, she smiled.

In her right hand she held a crumpled paper handkerchief. With it she dabbed from time to time the corner of her mouth when she felt there was the slightest excess of spittle there. The gesture was reminiscent of one with which, many years before, she used to wipe her mouth after drinking Earl Grey tea and eating watercress sandwiches. Meanwhile, with her left hand she fingered the necklace, cushioned on her forgotten bosom.

Love, my mother had the habit of saying, is the only thing that counts in this world. Real love, she would add, to avoid any factitious misunderstanding. But apart from that simple adjective, she never added anything more.[2]

Although I described this piece as portrait-writing, it contains almost no physical description. How then does Berger succeed in bringing his mother's presence alive to us on the page?

A number of remembered incidents: the child saying goodnight to his parents, his fear of the dark as their footsteps recede, his mother's knitted brows ('She never asked favours of anyone'), her habit of wiping the corner of her mouth after drinking Earl Grey tea, moments in the final days of her life, and some of the things she said to him at the time when she was dying; all are points of focus. But the main drive of the writing is its ideas: the connection between his writing and her secrecy, between autobiography and loneliness, and the final importance of love. Coming from someone known for her reticence on the most important matters, this idea – that love is what counts in the end – carries weight, and is added into the memory of her last days as a suitable epitaph for her by her son.

The first idea in this passage comes near the beginning.

'Autobiography' Berger writes, 'begins with a sense of being alone. Yet. . . .

All that interests me about my past life are the common moments. The moments – which if I relate them well enough – will join countless others lived by people I do not personally know.' His aim is not an epic recital but the catching of what is ordinary and commonplace, and yet no less mysterious for that. Berger here is acknowledging one of his fears. He is almost afraid to write autobiographically because such writing implies a kind of loneliness, and loneliness is, to him as to most of us, something we secretly dread. Autobiography is too private, too personal. No one will understand or feel any connection with what we say. How can we make contact with our readers? Memory, where the focus is on each one of us privately, can make us feel alone, uncomfortably so, like children in the dark when the footsteps recede. We are alone, so what do we have to say for ourselves, about ourselves, to others?

Berger confronts this fear, and we know that he intends to deal with it carefully. If he relates them well enough, those private moments will join with other moments lived by his readers, and this for him is one of the aims of autobiographical writing: it is to find a way of writing, remembering and speaking which will break down the barriers that separate writer from reader or listener, so that both can begin to inhabit a common space; so that, in effect, the footsteps will return.

The whole truth?

We therefore need to think as carefully as Berger about what is meant by *relating things well*. Does it mean telling the whole truth or story? Some readers might regard Berger's portrait of his mother as somewhat idealised. Is there a difference between their relationship as it was and the way he presents it? Does the picture suggest a reconciliation? And doesn't that suggest a previous discord? Has he converted something which was a problem to him (her lack of explanation of important matters, her lack of interest in the content of his books) into a virtue he can now celebrate? Is this autobiography telling the truth, or only an acceptable part of the truth?

These are just some of the questions which readers ask about autobiographical writing. It is these questions which make it such a fascinating form to attempt. As the writer you are in control, but can you ever give a complete picture of your experience? Are you able to hint rather than tell? You are controlling the hints you give your readers. In autobiographical writing, the first thing you will need to do is persuade your readers that those experiences did happen and did consist of those remembered moments. But you may be trying to provoke curiosity by leaving things unsaid, as Berger himself leaves certain things unsaid.

Selecting details: writing from the centre

The first rule of relating things well is knowing how and when to be specific. Berger does not tell us very much about the time when his grandmother died, but he does specify what the touch of fear felt like each night when his light was switched off, and in even more detail his method of trapping the voice saying goodnight in the sudden dark. To write so specifically he must have revisited that experience and put himself into the child's exact feeling of anxiety. He is writing from the *centre* of that anxiety. The only difference is that he now has an adult's command of language and confidence in expressing these complex feelings as accurately as he can, and is able to discuss them in front of an adult audience. The main drive, as I have said, is discussion, but he flavours it with detailed recall, some narrative and a great deal of careful reflective thought.

Does the word 'reticent' describe his mother? It is a word I used for her earlier. Instead of using it Berger unpacks the feeling behind this word, a feeling he aims to revisit in all its complexity. A one-word description wouldn't be enough to serve the picture he aims to find. He aims to find a set of words derived from his ideas, his observations, and from her own sayings. The writing provides a substitute place, now she is dead, for her to be in existence ('The book would be there, a little like a parent') . It offers a good example of language as search (see p.38).

One reason he does not specify about death is that he probably does not have any exact memories of its signs, more a pervading impression that it was everywhere. Yet he does have a sense, a physical sense, of the dark, of those receding footsteps, and of that first moment of isolation. As a writer he knows that these are the moments he must re-enter and re-create. Why? It is the same when he strokes his dying mother's left hand, or recalls her habit of wiping her mouth after drinking Earl Grey tea and eating watercress sandwiches. Why specify what kinds of sandwiches or what brand of tea, or which of her hands he massaged? Why revisit the memory in such detail? Why place those details just before the end, next to the last paragraph? Again he has found the details which mark for him the centre of his experience of his mother – her gestures, the slight movement of a hand, her sayings about love. To go back to my comments at the beginning of this chapter, those gestures and sayings which Berger remembers are quite ordinary and commonplace, but no less mysterious or meaningful. Her hand movements and the things she said are both of equal importance, and are so because both belong at the centre. He makes us feel that we, his readers, may also have memories equally slight, but equally central, equally significant.

At the centre there are no big explanations about his life. Why not tell us something about himself – about the quite remarkable fact that he left home for good at eight years old? This whole passage fails to provide what we might call straight information: born when, attended which school, etc. The fact that the family lived in Lambeth is added as an afterthought, as is the fact that the writer now lives abroad. We know at once so much and so little. Why leave out these supposedly important facts and in their place tell us about the way his mother wiped her mouth with a handkerchief? He has chosen the details of greatest importance *to him*. But these are the details that do so much to invite our participation as readers. The impact of exact reference and close-up acts as a charm to remove the barriers between reader and writer, and opens a path for us to find in the writer's space the common spaces of understanding and meaning, but it also leaves a great deal still unexplained. Is the lack of wider explanation a loss or a gain? The impact of these details and these secrets is to intrigue us, to provoke imagination. Berger is controlling what he says to us, along with what he does not, in the same way as his mother did with him when he was a child.

Themes and ideas

Finally, we have the ideas in the passage: writing and secrecy, loneliness and love, isolation giving way to connection. Through his ideas the writer makes further contact with his readers. He chooses to describe those moments of experience which, he believes, are of interest to us all, moments belonging not just to himself but 'lived by people I do not personally know'. Is this why he doesn't make too much obvious reference to his own personal circumstances or private history: the facts which make him separate and different? Ideas are the net by which he brings those moments to the surface, while exactness of detail, close-up, focus and immediacy are the features which give them life, which convince us of their reality.

Berger uses ideas and exactness to fuse together the personal and the general. He uses these tools to bridge a gulf and escape his autobiographical isolation. He can be sure that his readers will feel accommodated and not left out. He has found those moments and ideas which readers relate to, and most important he has made them specific, exact and personal.

Shock tactics

But that is not the only way to attract your reader. Another method might be shock, outrage, the use of a grotesque image which sharply *disrupts* our sense of a shared world.

Below are the opening paragraphs from Marianne Faithfull's auto-biography. Her method is to deal with a common subject, the mother and child relationship, but not in the way we anticipate.

'My Earliest Memory' by Marianne Faithfull

My earliest memory is a dream about my mother covered in armour, a coronet of snakes entwined around her head. I am three years old. I'm in my bed, in the little room with blue curtains. In the dream it is daytime, and sunlight is streaming through the curtains. Everything is blue, the blue of Ahmed's hashish and jewellery shop in Tangier. Blue curtains blowing in the wind. And beyond them a garden. The green green green of an English lawn. I hear a voice calling me; 'Come, Marianne, come.' I feel helpless. I have no choice.

'Marianne! Marianne!' the voice calls again, so piercingly this time that I get out of bed. I float to the window the way Alice does, with her feet just off the ground. I open the curtains and fly down to the end of the garden, where my mother has planted an asparagus patch. I see a fantastic figure looming over me. It is my mother-as-goddess, wearing armlets, breastplates and greaves like the ancient warrior queen Boadicea. She is cooking, raking the coals with a pair of tongs. She lifts me in her arms and places me on the fire. The dream ends as I lie down and allow her to roast me on the grill.

This happens night after night; again and again she arranges me on those hot coals. The dream always stops at that point. There is no pain, not really a nightmare at all, but rather a ritual that I obscurely recognise. A very Middle-European apparition – a proper, collective-consciousness dream about the mother, the goddess. Some form of training perhaps. It certainly prepared me for later life![3]

We don't need to know anything about the writer to sense the impact of this opening passage. Anyone could have written it. We don't need to know about her involvement with the Stones, Mick Jagger or drugs, or what her hit records in the 1960s were, or even how appropriate a beginning this is for a very bizarre and fascinating story. The passage is bizarre and fascinating in itself. The first sentence holds and provokes interest. A profoundly significant stereotype: the caring mother whose voice calls out our name so we come running and are lifted into her arms, has been altered into its opposite. The mother here is a female warrior of terrifying strength and size. If mothers traditionally provide food for their children and call them when it's ready, here is a child placed on a grill and cooked. The tone of almost hallucinatory extravagance changes what might be threatening and ominous to something quite comic, but not entirely so. The fact that we are reading an autobiography must influence the questions this opening invites: Does the child accept her unusual treatment? Did her mother resemble this monstrous apparition in any way? If this is a test, will Marianne finally pass it and survive? What does it signify?

Note, too, the presence of exact reference:'the blue of Ahmed's hashish and jewellery shop in Tangier. . . . Alice . . . with her feet just off the ground . . . the end of the garden, where my mother has planted an asparagus patch.' Once again, the details carry the claim of authenticity, the feel of a world uniquely real to the writer; a lesser degree of exactness would simply mean less familiarity between writer and world. Without that sharp focus and personal knowledge writers are less convincing, and readers less convinced. Without that sense of a world real to the writer, the reader loses interest and stops reading.

Narrative

To respond to this next example of autobiographical writing, it probably does help if readers know something about the writer in question. Armand and Michaela Denis were a husband and wife team whose films of African wildlife first appeared on television in the 1950s. But whether we know this or not, the passage still uses certain obvious bridge-building techniques. Here, in the opening pages of her autobiography, the story tells how Michaela met her husband.

'Cupid in the Clouds' by Michaela Denis
At the heart of all adventure lies self-fulfilment.

I didn't know this when I was fashion-designing and moving among the smart set in New York. The lure of the big city held me and swept me more or less limp from one week to the next. I loved my work, but my life was really a tangle of ragged ends. Something vital was missing.

There were times when my whole being protested against the empty social round through the city's concrete canyons and under its bright lights. Then I would stay at home and lock my door against the world.

Love and marriage, they say, always lie at the bottom of a woman's thoughts. I can honestly say I had no such ideas – at least, not consciously. But my sophisticated friends did the conventional thing and dangled eligible young men before me. I couldn't have been less interested.

Outside my work I had two passions – travel books and animals. I had grown up with them and they had helped to form my character and outlook. The most wonderful hours of my youth had been spent dreaming over maps in travel books and pretending that our domestic pets were wild creatures in forests.

But there was nothing I could do about making these dreams real. We have to take life as we find it and to make our own opportunities within the scope allotted. But new prospects are apt to open up unexpectedly. Then suddenly the whole world is transformed.

It happened to me at a party in New York. I had accepted the invitation as a matter of course. It was just another party where I should see friends and indulge in small-talk, drink a couple of martinis, and return home without a ripple on the surface of my thoughts and feelings.

As soon as I entered the room, however, I became conscious of something different. A very tall man rose from his chair and took my hand as our hostess murmured our names. His was Armand Denis.

My heart leapt. This was Armand Denis, the famous explorer, whose travels in the wild areas of the world had brought him fame and the gratitude of all animal lovers, for he was not a hunter but a student and photographer of the untamed creatures of forest and jungle.

I was rather overcome and had little to say for myself. Armand Denis has a magnetic personality which draws people to him naturally. I made no attempt to resist. In less than a minute after meeting him I knew that I was in love; but I had not the slightest idea what he thought of me.

So it came about that not long afterwards I found myself in South America, sitting next to Armand Denis in a large sedan car, driving over the Andes. Before and below us stretched a scene of unparalleled magnificence. Ahead lay our destination – Potosi, the highest town in the world. The way to it was strewn with death-traps. This was the worst season of the year for car travel among the precipitous mountains. For days it had rained; now snow was falling. Over the terrifying complex of hairpin bends and crumbling paths stretched the immense grey, snow-laden sky, and below, between the great peaks, depths of unfathomable steel-blue.

Armand was silent and calm. I glanced at him and marvelled at his imperturbability. We had just passed through a nerve-shattering experience. The road over which we drove had been dynamited for repair and no warning notices had been put up. Suddenly before us yawned a horrifying drop into the blue chasm. I stiffened into a column of ice. Arman, with only inches to spare, urged the car forward without a tremor.

Now all the ice in me had melted to an emotional pulp. I was suffering from a violent reaction. But Armand sat there, maddeningly aloof, threading his way round sickening bends with a matter-of-fact mastery. Not a flicker of feeling had passed over his handsome face.[4]

This form of autobiographical writing aims to tell a story. First of all the writer claims no interest whatsoever in anything to do with love affairs – only to plunge into one with both feet. To say the least we might think this is a bit disingenuous of her and somewhat ridiculously exaggerated, but the writing has a kind of derivative confidence, a sense of the theatrical about it, and a strong sense of narrative: this happened, and this transforming event was the trigger for even more outlandish experiences. It is quite obviously a performance.

Michaela Denis's is fictionalised autobiography, not in the sense of the events being in any way untrue, but in the sense that certain effects belong to a kind of fiction. John Berger's approach attracts its readers by discussing with them a number of familiar themes: the way adults talk to children about deaths in the family, a child's reaction to unnecessary but real fears induced by darkness. Michaela Denis's approach, by contrast, is to tell a story, and a story with recognisable character types: an unattached and impressionable young woman is meeting the man of her dreams.

Its aim is to attract readers by involving them in a conventional romantic story plot dominated by a heroine's youthful viewpoint. One evening at a party her life is transformed by the unexpected presence of a stranger. He is famous, talented, shares intriguing connections with the 'untamed', and possesses a magnetic personality. She has no idea what he thinks of her but is willing to risk everything, and almost immediately finds herself high in the Andes in a blizzard on one of Armand's precarious expeditions. She discovers he is courageous, dependable and strong – everything she could wish for. Settings and characters are highlighted for their glamour. No time is wasted on minor commonplace detail or explanation. 'And so it came about that not long afterwards I found myself in South America' is all we hear about it. For readers worried about the propriety of this, as some might well have been in 1955, Armand and Michaela sleep in separate vehicles and two days later get married. Michaela Denis's sense of what her readers want to hear is highly developed and accurate, though she does take a risk with that sudden shift of scene.

Michaela Denis is able to know what her readers want because of her own widely published role as a traveller and broadcaster. Most of us have to work a bit harder to achieve this rapport and build the neccessary connection with our readers. But it can be done. If readers expect a certain searching honesty, for example, Michaela Denis is not going to appeal as strongly as Berger who claims our attention because he deals with us and with his experience more personally, and without the obvious protection of reputation. His aim to achieve a common ground concerns him. He builds this very problem into his work and hence can discuss it directly with the reader without losing his confidence or control; he makes being honest the basis of his appeal.

At the same time, a sense of story can be useful in autobiographical writing, not least because readers everywhere understand the link between suspense and expectation which stories enhance. In Michaela's piece, the jump from New York to the Andes is a sharp feature and worth considering in story-type autobiography whether or not you have any such glamorous settings to call on. Contemporary readers are no longer impressed by the same things as readers of Michaela Denis in the 1950s. You can tell a story, and be honest as well. You don't need to arrange a trip to the Andes beforehand, but you may need to dramatise yourself a little, turn yourself into a character, and make that character sharply recognisable: it may not be wholly true and wholly real; the truth of it will be in its strong relation to other characters as well as to any differences of place.

The next example is a piece of unpublished autobiographical narrative by someone beginning to write. It controls some of the above features by means of its speed-momentum. We don't need prior knowledge about this writer. All we need begins with the first sentence and ends with the last. This scene also involves dangerous driving, though the place is more like Margate than Potosi:

'Permanent Nights, Winter 81/82' by Eric Jackson
1.45 a.m.

Sometimes I'd be half-asleep and it was difficult to tell how much was real and how much was just hanging behind my eyes. The alarm tearing into my dreams: a cold clenched fist in my stomach. Everyone else would be sleeping, Dad snoring in the next room. I'd sleep with most of my clothes on, slump out of bed – fatigue and resentment a single emotion – and do as much as I could in darkness.

Black coffee to scour a clogged throat, wake me up as if there were some purpose to this. Kid myself. In the bathroom I'd put the light on. Sting my eyes like shampoo does when you're a child. In the mirror always the same vampire face, the matted hair, red eyes, pale skin. So tired, so incredibly tired and fighting against it.

I'd tip cups of water, cold, over my head. A shock like toothache to bring me alive. After the coffee go outside shivering to try and start the van. Freezing in scarf, gloves, hat, everything. Often I'd fill hot water bottles and wear them inside my coat across the small of my back. The heater in the van didn't work and there were gaps around all the windows. Once I'd started the engine I'd have to get out again and clear the ice from the wind-screen. There'd be snow in the driveway and the cat's footprints over the roof of the van.

The drive to work. A roller-coaster of left over dream images and sudden black bends. Trees and walls leaping out of nothingness directly into my path. The line between sleep and wakefulness as blurred as the hedgerows rushing past. Reaching the outskirts of town – a flood of orange lights, the odd police car; cats and lovers hurrying home down some side-street; the warehouse.

Sometimes there'd be thick, bitter tea in unwashed cups. A treat if it was the foreman's night off. There'd be nothing to say. I'd be looking at their dead white faces, tanned by neon and touched by moonlight more than sun, thinking:'Is that me? Do I look like that?' Like defeat and acceptance and long since abandoned bitterness.

The machine would rattle and hum and my fingers, the skin too colourless to bleed, would crack on the strapping as the parcels piled up. In the yard, wagons shunted and lumbered ('Left hand down') spewing carbon monoxide into the loading bay, gears grinding and grating on my nerves. As far back as I could remember; as far forward as I could see.

They'd give me forty five minutes to do the deliveries, because they thought it was impossible. I'd do it in thirty five. Stack the parcels properly in the back, that was the key, then alter the brain to sleep while reactions took over.

I'd leave the yard with tyres spinning gravel and the door still half-open. Leave the window down to hear the engine, the screaming rubber, to flood the van with night.

Never cruising. Always accelerating madly or breaking desperately, blocking out the times, a dozen a night, when I'd leave the tarmac and lose control. Just for a second but long enough careering down unlit country lanes on the wrong side of the road, the rush of fear was the one spark of life in this robot existence.

Still in darkness I'd tear past the milk floats back into town, ignoring red lights, one way systems, pavements. ('If it's flat you can drive over it'.) And the metal of the van would screech in protest, remembering its twisted frame and buckled wheels and shattered glass not so many nights ago on a road exactly like this.

All this to possess those last ten minutes and say, 'These are mine.' To park on the road along the beach and hear the engine ticking as it cooled, and outside hear the surf and the gulls. I could watch the sea and watch the sunrise, watch the birds with marble eyes scavenging the empty chip bags, cocoa cola tins, rubbish stacks. See the first light paint the sky and glint across steel grey waves and the aluminium doors of Gilly's Fun Palace, Big Prize Bingo, and the Original Gypsy Rose Lee's Palmistry Stall with its faded pictures of Des O'Connor, Les Dawson, and Frankie Vaughan.

I didn't need her magic.

I saw my future and my past: a hall of mirrors reflecting to infinity in all directions with me at the centre, staring through the filthy windows of a Ford transit, watching the sea and shivering inside.

What do we know about this writer's feelings? From the last image he clearly feels trapped. His sense of relief is transitory, but we are not told this explicitly; we feel it without the need for direct comment. He could, for instance, have begun his piece with a list of explanatory details: 'Two years ago I was working shifts driving a van in Redcar for a transport company. I hated the job but needed money for a trip to the Andes, etc . . .' Would more data have benefited? The only information of this type is the merest: '1.45 a.m.'

By being real to the writer as he writes, this experience becomes real to the reader. Much of it consists of things which exercise physical rather than mental reactions, but even those parts which do reflect on the experience go a step further: 'Do I look like that? Like defeat and acceptance, and long since abandoned bitterness.' The writer assumes that given this particular set of conditions, most of us would respond as he is doing. That moment of freedom and peace at the end is one we can each relate to. 'All this to possess those last ten minutes and say, "These are mine."' The statement is both anonymous and personal, and succeeds in saying something about work and its squalid demands. And given that is the issue, the finer and more detailed the exactness, the stronger the bridge between writer and reader. Instead of explaining: 'Then we drank some tea', he almost chokes us with it; we can taste it. We feel we have experienced what he knows. We feel this because of the strong dominant viewpoint, but also because the writing is like a magnetic field; every detail points in the same direction. It has rhythm. It speeds. It drives impressions home phrase after phrase. The rhythm changes for the final paragraphs: 'All this to possess . . .' The sentences tick over like the engine; they are longer and slower than the stabbing rhythms. They reflect on what has happened, but without losing touch with the new circumstances: the litter and the gulls and the sea itself. And this rhythm is just as important for their meaning as what the words actually say.

Background information

There are times when some explanation is needed, and then how much, how little, is a matter of judgement. In the following passages, the writers are keen to explain to us who they are and how they came to be in a certain setting. Here, we need that background information.

'A Mural Nine Miles Long' by Mandy
I set off to Greenham as a critic – not as a critic of the issue of nuclear war/ weapons – but as a critic of what I expected would happen: of the long and passionate speeches, full of clichés, and 'guilt-tripping' statements about what we should all be doing. Basically I was tired of emerging middle class leaders in the peace movement making careers out of telling us what we should be doing and how we should be doing it! As a working class woman I've felt alienated from the peace movement and, worse still, guilty that the problems of surviving as a single parent, meant I had little energy left to direct into any campaign – no matter how important I felt that campaign to be. Nuclear disarmament is the ultimate issue of the day and so I've always made a point of attending most of the local and national demonstrations. In terms of the media, numbers are important, and so I was content to be a 'head to be counted'! However, after a while, this can be a demoralising and tedious way of making a protest – you come away feeling tired, anonymous, and with a feeling that the demonstration would have gone on quite well without you. I don't think that I'm alone in this feeling either – lots of people I know, especially women, have expressed the same feelings and have made the decision not to attend any more demonstrations for a while. People can and do feel alienated within a movement against a common cause.

On December 12th at Greenham Common it was different. All my own criticisms, based on previous experiences, disappeared within reaching a hundred yards of the fence. I don't think it was the day, the event, or the common cause which was responsible for making every woman present feel a vital part of the day – it was the fence itself. It united women on a common experience: the fear of nuclear war, the fear of total annihilation of all life on earth. This 'experience' transcended all class divisions, all race and ethnic divisions and united women in a way I'd never known before. The fence was transformed into a powerful work of art – a mural, nine miles long of common communication, a picture of spontaneous and deep emotion which linked every woman be they mothers or daughters, married or single, black or white, rich or poor, old or young. As far as I am concerned, it was the most important work of art this century, probably ever, precisely because I can think of no other painting, sculpture or whatever, which has expressed so much for so many. In such a short time, thirty thousand women converted a frightening fence into a living museum of hope. The fence was not planned as a painting or a mural would be. It will never be hung in a gallery in years to come and it could not even be photographed as a whole. Its only claim to existence is in the memories of those who participated in its creation. . . .

Women were asked to bring to Greenham items to hang on the fence. The response went way beyond anyone's expectations. Some of the items genuinely made you feel cold and frightened – not because they were scary but simply because you realised the heart searching that went into making the decision to leave the item on the fence. A woman I know wanted to hang a photo of her dead mother on the fence; it was the the only photograph she had and I could feel her inner turmoil as she quietly hung it on the fence with the others. She said later that she felt proud of herself and that she believed her mother would have wanted it. There were many instances like this one of people holding private memorial services to lost loved ones. It felt like the best way to let go of these sorts of photographs and, as my friend told me later, her mother died knowing that she had left life to continue, and by placing the photo on the fence of Greenham Common, my friend was making a personal plea for life.

Another thing which also struck the hearts of many, particularly the mothers, was the amount of contributions given by children: stories, poems, paintings, toys and photographs of their animals or brothers and sisters. For some of the older children, their fears were real – they understood what nuclear war was all about and expressed as much in terms of paintings and poems.

Mothers left their children's first baby-gro's with photographs of the babies pinned neatly to them. By the end of the day, there were so many baby-gro's that it looked as if they were all linking sleeves around the fence. You could find everything from a child's bottle to a child's first pair of shoes.

I could go on and on talking about the things I remember hanging on that fence but I won't because every single item was important in its own way and so I feel it would be unfair to pick out a few of them.

What was also very special about the day was that you had time to read all the messages, poems and stories, and to look closely at the photographs. The silence was haunting for about four hours as women quietly wandered around the fence. Initially, there was a great deal of emotion and sadness at the sheer force and intensity that the decorated fence presented, but after the women had had the time to walk around and read some of the things the mood changed. The fence was filled with so much individual hope and collective belief in the future it gave a surge of new energy into everyone's blood-stream. Women then collected anything which could be weaved into huge symbols, wool into messages and webs which linked the fence with surrounding trees, sticks were used to make crosses until the whole fence was woven into a continuous ocean of energy and love of life.[5]

'Thinking the Unthinkable' by Donald Morris, lieutenant

Quite a lot of the men when we got to Greenham were in something of a spin, particularly the young officers. I don't think they'd ever come across anything like it before, the sight of a large group of women who were well organised, well able to look after themselves, and well able to express their opinions of us and to us with some strength of feeling. A lot of the men had never seen women behaving like that, and couldn't get out of their minds the idea there must be some men somewhere in the background who were directing and controlling them. If it hadn't been so unpleasant and serious it might almost have been funny. It was unpleasant because here we were, facing women who were mostly our own age, and we didn't know what they were going to do. It made us nervous and edgy. On one occasion they all came up very close to the fence and started shaking it: it really did look like as though it was going to come down. What exactly we'd have done if there had been a mass break-in I'm not at all certain. Obviously there are contingency plans, our commanding officer knows exactly what he'll do in every possible circumstance. But they weren't revealed to us beforehand, so we were in the position of not knowing what the next order would be. We just hoped it wouldn't be anything dreadful.

I know it was said in Parliament that if necessary the soldiers would be ordered to fire. I can't be specific about this, but I don't feel they would pour a volley of shots into a group of unarmed demonstrators, I really don't.

I think it's very unfortunate that the situation ever arose that the soldiers should have had to go there to help hold the security of the perimeter. I won't say it isn't the fault of the women, and if they hadn't brought it about it wouldn't have happened. I've heard that argument advanced, but I think it's a weak one, on a par with the things the police say, like 'if you've done nothing wrong, you've nothing to be afraid of if you're arrested.' It had happened that someone in the police had felt they might not be able to contain any larger number of demonstrators if they suddenly appeared, so they asked the army for help. I suspect the soldiers were there as a deterrent, and I don't think there was ever any intention of them attempting

to disperse the women outside the fence. As far as I'm aware there was
no physical contact made between soldiers and demonstrators: all the
arrests were made by the police.

All the same, it was a very serious situation. In Ireland on the streets,
because of the numbers both of civilians and soldiers, it would have been
in the same category as a major riot. I think credit must be given to the
women for the fact that they kept the demonstration peaceful. I suppose to
an army officer it would be thinking the unthinkable to allow oneself to
believe they might in fact have a point in what they were doing and saying,
that our country would be if not safer, then in no way less safe if the
Americans took their missiles away. I've heard it argued in the mess that
these things are here in this country at the invitation and with the agreement
of the British government. But from what little I've read about the subject,
I think it was never debated in Parliament. So I don't think it could be
claimed it's the will of the majority of the people. Having said that though,
it has to be said it might be.[6]

Without the surrounding circumstances, the writers' thoughts, and particularly the impact of changes in their thinking, would not be available to
us. These last two examples offer another mode of autobiographical writing,
where focus is on a specific change of attitude and on exploration of the new
set of impressions.

Both passages follow the same pattern: from alienation to sympathy – a
renewal of sympathy in the case of the woman demonstrator, and in the case
of the lieutenant a more surprising change and one not fully articulated or
convinced. On whose authority do soldiers carry out orders? Is it the
commanding officer's, or the government's, or parliament's, or the wish of
the majorities of electorates? The writer is left facing a question too complex
for him, or for most of us, to answer. For this writer in these circumstances,
thinking itself is unthinkable, yet he is making the attempt. At the centre of
his experience are his doubts. Both writers are trying to get at that centre and
to tell us what they find there. Those four hours while the women read the
stories, look at the photographs, and think about what these signify, becomes
a powerful image of the whole experience; the centre is there, and from it
emerges a new energy.

Poetic autobiography

In the next passage the poet Sylvia Plath revisits the scene of her early
childhood by the sea in North America. The territory here is well-known to
her, a physical place, but her sense of it is not just recalled but revived by
the act of remembering. More and more comes back to her as she writes, but
the focus stays firmly on the sea which appears like a living thing in a range
of shapes.

From 'Ocean 1212-W' by Sylvia Plath

My childhood landscape was not the land but the end of the land – the cold, salt, running hills of the Atlantic. I sometimes think my vision of the sea is the clearest thing I own. I pick it up, exile that I am, like the purple 'lucky stones' I used to collect with a white ring all the way round, or the shell of a blue mussel with its rainbowy angel's fingernail interior; and in one wash of memory the colours deepen and gleam, the early world draws breath.

Sylvia Plath writes with anticipation and excitement. She has given herself complete permission to re-enter that world of her ocean childhood. She brings it to life: all of it. What will she discover?

Breath, that is the first thing. Something is breathing. My own breath? The breath of my mother? No, something else, something larger, farther, more serious, more weary. So behind shut lids I float awhile; – I'm a small sea-captain, tasting the day's weather – battering rams at the seawall, a spray of grapeshot on my mother's brave geraniums, or the lulling shoosh shoosh of a full mirrory pool; the pool turns the quartz grits at its rim idly and kindly, a lady brooding at jewellery. There might be a hiss of rain on the pane, there might be a wind sighing and trying the creaks of the house like keys. I was not deceived by these. The motherly pulse of the sea made a mock of such counterfeits. Like a deep woman, it hid a good deal, it had many faces, many delicate, terrible veils. It spoke of miracles and distances; if it could court, it could also kill. When I was learning to creep, my mother set me down on the beach to see what I thought of it. I crawled straight for the coming wave and was just through the wall of green when she caught my heels.

The sea is strange and obscure to her, alive, beautiful, but dangerous. Her writing has touched that ambivalence of response, and without loss of childlike curiosity:

I often wonder what would have happened if I had managed to pierce that looking-glass. Would my infant gills have taken over, the salt in my blood? For a time I believed not in God or Santa Claus, but in mermaids. They seemed as logical and possible to me as the brittle twig of a seahorse in the Zoo aquarium or the skates lugged up on the lines of cursing Sunday fishermen – skates the shape of old pillow-slips with the full, coy lips of women.

And I recall my mother, a sea-girl herself, reading to me and my brother . . . from Matthew Arnold's 'Forsaken Merman':

Sand-strewn caverns, cool and deep,
Where the winds are all asleep;
Where the spent lights quiver and gleam;
Where the salt weed sways in the stream –

> Where the sea-beasts ranged all around
> Feed in the ooze of their pasture-ground;
> Where the sea-snakes coil and twine
> Dry their mail and bask in the brine;
> Where great whales come sailing by,
> Sail and sail with unshut eye,
> Round the world forever and aye.

I saw the gooseflesh on my skin. I did not know what made it. I was not cold. Had a ghost passed over? No, it was the poetry. A spark flew off Arnold and shook me, like a chill. I wanted to cry; I felt very odd. I had fallen into a new way of being happy.

But would the sights and sounds of the sea, of any sea, anywhere, auto-matically produce the reactions she felt as a child? Her answer is No. It had to be that place on the Atlantic coast of North America: the sea by her grandmother's house. Living in England, 'in exile', she would be taken to the sea regularly as a cure for her nostaglia, but the cure never quite worked:

> The geography is all wrong in the first place. Where is the grey thumb of the water-tower to the left and the sickle-shaped sand bar (really a stone bar) under it, and the Deer Island prison at the tip of the point to the far right? The road I knew curved into the waves with the ocean on one side, the bay on the other; and my grandmother's house, half-way out, faced east, full of red sun and sea lights.

> To this day I remember her phone number: Ocean 1212-W. I would repeat it to the operator, from my home on the quieter bayside, an incantation, a fine rhythm, half expecting the black earpiece to give me back, like a conch, the susurrous of the sea out there as well as my grandmother's Hello.

Only through writing could she revisit that atmosphere:

> The breath of the sea then, and then its lights. Was it some huge, radiant animal? Even with my eyes shut I could feel the glimmers off its bright mirrors spider over my lids. I lay in a water cradle and the sea gleams found the chinks in the dark green window blind, playing and dancing, or resting and trembling a little. At naptime I chinked my fingernail on the hollow brass bedstead for the music of it and once, in a fit of discovery and surprise, I found the join in the new rose paper and with the same curious nail bared a great bald space of wall. I got scolded for this, spanked too, and then my grandfather extracted me from the domestic furies for a long beachcombing stroll over mountains of rattling and cranking purple stones.[7]

In this last sentence, Sylvia Plath could easily have written: 'then he took me for a long walk on the beach'. But the word 'walk' becomes 'a long beachcombing stroll' – so much more accurate – and the beach becomes 'mountains of rattling and cranking purple stones'. This refusal of the obvious simple name for a thing, and revisiting instead the original sensations we see most frequently in poetry. Much of these passages reads like an artist's notebook; largely she is beachcombing for poems, trying out special images, connections, sounds, letting her mind drift where it wants to go.

One other thing to notice in these passages: sensations, textures, colours and sounds have immediate meaning-quality and feed the writer's poetic, imaginative vision. Texture, colour (a shell's 'rainbowy angel's fingernail interior') merge, are a single substance; meaning clings to every shape and space (even a telephone number) because of its proximity to the sea.

But it isn't the sea anywhere. The drive of the writing is not to give us back what we already know but to show us how meanings collect and store themselves and to show ways of raiding that store. Because of this, the place must be felt as wholly unique to the writer: it relates to no one but her; she to nowhere but exactly that positioning of the coast.

General comments

Refusing the obvious, taking an extra step towards the real, is a quality which unites all these examples. They happen in the face of a puzzle. Experience has at some exciting point become puzzling. The writer isn't sure what he or she is going to unearth. The reader, too, isn't sure what will happen. But each of these writers is confident that the medium of words can make discoveries, or can at least enter the struggle by taking that extra step. The discoveries may be ragged or incomplete. They may not tell us the whole truth but only a fragment of it, and by choosing an odd angle, and leaving out information we might expect, they are filling the space with objects, words and thoughts which become more interesting to their readers than any amount of data or explanatory flatness. What is more, those objects, images, words and thoughts are the centre that the writer has been looking for. The movement of a hand, the habit of saying that love is what counts: in the centre of John Berger's portrait of his mother, both these facts are equal.

Another quality that these passages have in common is consistency of attention. There is always a referent: this woman, this dream, that party, that drive through the night, this experience at Greenham and, in each case, those resultant ideas. Another common factor is speech. They converse. They stay close to the way the writer speaks, and they do this even while allowing themselves the space to think and speak more carefully and accurately than they would otherwise do. Another word for this quality is attitude. A final point: in each of these excerpts the writer/autobiographer is seen in the company of one or two other people or small groups. In most cases the other people are dominant: sources of potential tension, they aid the writer/ protagonist's self-definition.

In this project, you need to think about which of these different approaches to autobiography best suits your own voice, and which best suits the topic you want to explore.

You may decide that the literary style of Plath will be a better approach than any of the others. You may wish to make narrative the main drive. The experience you choose might involve a change of thinking about some issue, so that you will be recording that change. The pieces on Greenham both do this without attempting to be literary or use narrative. You may wish to revive your memory of a person as Berger does. You may wish to identify yourself mainly in terms of class, gender and marital status as Michaela Denis and the woman at Greenham both do, or you may not. And when it comes to thinking about your readers, you may wish to begin with an eccentric and startling image like that in Marianne Faithfull's autobiography, or begin by involving your reader in a discussion of ideas.

The points listed below recap on what has been said so far about autobiographical writing.

- Significance depends on writing qualities, not on quantities of experience.
- As your own interest deepens and revives, so will the interestedness of your reader.
- An important way of reviving this depends on selecting details and moments for close-up.
- The most significant moments, images and ideas (for both reader and writer) will be those closest to the centre.
- Background information may be useful, but it's your decision as to how much you include. Some may be absolutely necessary. Too much can produce slide.
- Autobiographical writing trains your attention on what is already there in your memory. It teaches the importance of focus.

WRITING IN THREE STAGES

Stage one

Try to form a first impression of which among the above forms appeals to you most for writing.

For convenience, I have separated the examples into Portrait, Narrative, Change of Thinking, and Poetic/Imaginative. On occasions, these modes overlap, so that each can be found to some extent in the others. But in spite of that, the differences should be clear.

Discussing these examples, and others you may have found, will help you to decide your approach.

If you have problems making a choice, write down each of the above forms as headings, and write some notes under each. Your notes will consist of memories, ideas, images and sensations, and some idea of where to set up your camera and how to focus the lens. When you press the trigger, will your camera record a wide angle shot of your whole life, or a large section of it, or a moment in close-up? Who will be in the picture: yourself, yourself and someone else or a group of people?

Look back at what you have written. You have already made a start, but one (or perhaps two) of the headings will have appealed to you already and concentrated your mind more. These are the ones to continue exploring in detail. Underline any phrases and words which begin to trigger your thinking.

This is still the pre-writing stage, so you don't need to worry about your reader or about producing any final or acceptable script at this point.

Try to extend your notes on the words and phrases you underlined.

Stage two

The aim of Stage one was to stimulate your thinking, but it is important that you don't let your thinking go on for too long in note form only. You will need to stop making notes after a few minutes and take a break. This is the time to ponder your subject while doing something else for a while. You are taking possession, committing yourself. The next time you write will be time to make your discoveries.

Without using your notes as a direct guide, start again and write in paragraphs. Restrict yourself to forty or fifty minutes uninterrupted.

Theme

Look back at your writing. See if it has a theme. You may have recorded a change of attitude to your subject, told a story, gathered ideas round a portrait, explored the poetic qualities of a setting, its sounds and colour sensations. You may have discovered another approach not included here. Other words for *theme* are *attitude, aim, drive, purpose.* If in your view your writing lacks this quality, can you see why and take some steps to find what its theme might be?

Stage three

Whether or not you want to rewrite your piece will depend on how you feel about it and possibly on the comments you have received. You may want to start the process again from the beginning, leave what you have written as it stands, or make selected changes to your script. Whatever advice you receive, make your decision.

Redrafting

If, in your decision, you need a complete rewrite or to make changes, you could do so by looking back at the first part of this chapter and considering the following:

- Have you included some points of detailed focus?
- Can you discover any unclear or oversimplified statements? Do you intend to leave these as they are, or take further steps of investigation?
- Does your writing have a theme or attitude? If you can achieve one it will mean that you, and your reader, are confident that your writing has found a forceful and definite aim.
- Do you judge your writing as lacking meaning–significance for a reader? Try reading it aloud. Imagine it as a radio script read by someone else. Does it attract and hold a listener's attention?
- In your first paragraph, which effects will catch your reader's attention? Is it focus, ideas, control of information?
- Are there important points of information which your reader must know in order to feel comfortable with your writing?

Finally it is the writer who makes the decisions. But I hope it will be clear from the suggestions I have made that personal writing, like all writing, still has obligations to readers. By aiming to try and meet these obligations, the writer is likely to make discoveries about the topic and value them more, and writers therefore need actual readers as well as imagined ones.

Chapter 3

Writing poems

READING AND LISTENING

William Carlos Williams described a poem as 'a machine made of words', and in the first part of this chapter I want to look closely at some of these machines of words to discover how they are put together, how they perform as they do and why they are able to attract our attention as readers. As writers we need to learn how poems can be made by looking at certain examples of finished poems and finding out what kind of pleasure they aim to provide and how our imagination is being engaged. One peculiarity about poems is that they can exist in two places: on the printed or handwritten page; and in the air, as sound.

We hear poetry aloud either live at a reading, on radio or television, as poetic drama on stage, or very occasionally as part of a film soundtrack. It can also be read aloud by readers in private. If a poem is read silently on a page, the reader can read at his or her own pace; he or she controls the reading and can repeat it or go back over passages within a poem. Most reading is of this backtracking sort, and many writers would probably hold that if this is the case then a vital link is missing: the link that connects poetry with the sound of a speaking voice. If the reading is controlled by an outside source – the actor or speaker reading to an audience – then the audience is subjected to that control, and must listen or lose out. To read a poem aloud from the page enables it to come across as uninterrupted sound, and this at least is preferable to silent reading. Even silent reading can be *voiced*, but only if the reader is able to make the conversion from print to voice quality and to enjoy the words for their patterns and structures of sound as well as for the shapes of lines on a page. Poetry offers both these forms of pleasure: the shaped figure of it, and its voice.

Several writers have drawn attention to the quality of voice in poetry. Seamus Heaney writes about his work as rooted in the speech of his own region. D. H. Lawrence wrote poems reproducing the speech of his childhood background in north-east Nottinghamshire. The poet and dramatist Tony Harrison has experimented with poems which include phonetic symbols in the written text of his work, and which therefore demand that readers distinguish between forms of pronunciation. Printed, they look awkward; they challenge the whole idea of *book* poetry which Harrison was taught at school. Asking him to read Keats aloud in class, his teacher at Leeds Grammar School ridiculed Harrison's (nicknamed T.W.) Yorkshire dialect:

> 'We say [ʌs] not [uz], T.W.!' That shut my trap.
> I doffed my flat a's (as in 'flat cap')
> my mouth all stuffed with glottals, great
> lumps to hawk up and spit out . . . *E-nun-ci-ate!*[1]

Harrison contrasts his own Leeds voice ('stuffed with glottals, great lumps') with that of the teacher's so-called refined accent. Harrison was fortunate, in one way, in having a teacher who did insist on the reading and hearing of poetry aloud, but unfortunate in that his teacher also believed that a proper delivery required 'proper speech' – *enunciation* – not dialect. It may be unfair to cite Harrison's teacher as an example of a common mistake, but in the minds of many people poetry has come to be associated with high culture, excessive formality, and with making its first appeal to the trained intellect. Otherwise, it is slushy, sentimental, pretentious, self-pitying. Either way, the words of Sam Weller in Dickens's novel spring to mind: 'Poetry's Unnat'ral'.

Of course it is quite possible to write poems which pander to these objections, and the objections themselves are valuable and useful if they help to prevent that from happening. There is however some cause for identifying poetic language as the very opposite of intellect and abstraction. Writers often prefer the notion of poetry as unrefined and primitive: the kind of language you learn before you learn how to reason and think in abstract concepts. The psychologist D. W. Harding wrote about conceptual thought as having an origin and infancy; it does not appear fully-grown from the start; the language of poetry deals with thoughts as they are 'in their dumb cradles' – that is, in their earlier stages of growth. The language as learned in childhood, language close to its dialect origin therefore, exhibits more substance and stronger emotional power. Poetic language has a basic *physicality*; its sound-quality and sharply focused attention on what is immediate in the physical surroundings guarantees an appeal first to sensation. Poetic language offers language itself as a sensation; it makes language itself into texture and musical sound-structure. Writing in dialect is one of the methods of drawing attention to the texture, and away from the abstractable meaning or message of a poem. Instead of the usual question: what does it *mean*? the preferred question should be: how does it *speak*?

We need to be sure of one basic point, however. Poetry is for everybody to hear, and for everybody to write. To enjoy reading Harrison or Heaney we do not have to do it with an accent. Fortunately, it is not necessary to have an Ulster background or use Harrison's awkward-looking phonetic symbols in order to write for the voice. Nor is 'voice' the only means of enjoyment.

As we shall discover, not all poems *are* written for the voice; some writers deliberately choose to shape their poems for the page; some choose to let their poems inhabit both these dimensions.

To insist on the voice is a partial but important and neglected truth. Shakespeare, like Harrison, is a poet who wrote for the stage. Here is a piece from *Macbeth*:

> – Now o'er the one half-world
> Nature seems dead, and wicked dreams abuse
> The curtain'd sleep: witchcraft celebrates
> Pale Hecate's offerings: and wither'd Murder,
> Alarum'd by his sentinel, the wolf,
> Whose howl's his watch, thus with his stealthy pace,
> With Tarquin's ravishing strides, towards his design
> Moves like a ghost. Thou sure and firm-set earth,
> Hear not my steps, which way they walk.[2]

At this moment I am typing Shakespeare's text into a word processor. Until printed it only exists on a screen, but clearly this space is not the same as the one within our minds as we hear it happening. To retrieve it from being just writing inside a book you will need to read the piece from *Macbeth* aloud and let it come into being inside your thoughts: it gathers pace, builds, rushes forward. The page is flat, screenlike and uneventful, but the space of thought twists and shapes writing to an active image; it acts like skin to touch; it has that kind of surface. Words merely printed or on a screen cannot realise the impact-effect of words read aloud and heard.

One of the skills involved in writing poems is to discover what will reoccupy that screen of imagination. How does Shakespeare do it? Clearly some words if extracted from the text will create big difficulties: Who was Hecate? Tarquin? What was meant by 'sentinel', 'alarum'd'? But imagination does not hear this passage in terms of such problems of isolated meaning. Instead, it watches with a sense of events swept forward by murder's approach. Whatever the word 'sentinel' means in a dictionary, it contributes to and is joined with a flow of voice which cannot be stopped. Equally we sense, because these words are spoken by Macbeth himself, that what they produce is also imagined by him, and helplessly; he too is swept along. Against his better judgement, he aims to convince himself that he can kill. Night is not just the shadow side of the earth, but a place where things, including Macbeth's words, arrange themselves for atrocity. The verb-phrase 'moves like a ghost' placed at the end makes all previous phrases its tributaries; the murder must happen. The commentary is delivered in a horrified whisper, the whisper becomes a torrent, and nothing can convince like the inevitable.

I once had an argument with a friend about football and poetry: which offered the more aesthetic experience? With scholarly enthusiasm he said football of course. But it strikes me that the first response on hearing this piece from *Macbeth* is to punch the air and shout, *Yes that's it!* – not to stop and wonder who Tarquin was. Response first, replay and tactics later.

In Milton's poem *Paradise Lost*, the angels find Satan whispering into Eve's ear:

> Him there they found
> Squat like a toad close to the ear of Eve,
> Assaying by his devilish art to reach
> The organs of her fancy, and with them forge
> Illusions, as he list, phantasms and dreams.[3]

Both of these passages from Shakespeare and Milton strongly imply that the power of language can indeed be fearful: something more than just words when judged for effect. These writers correctly acknowledge the power that lies in their hands, not just in the hands of their villainous counterparts. The ultimate aim of Milton's poem is to whisper things conceived as a force for good, but the power of the whisper is the same: a transforming power, it gets inside the feelings and inclinations; close to the ear, it forges illusions and dreams. At this level, language is not just a series of acquired message-producing codes but an event in the mind before the rational angels intervene. By means of unusually strong voice rhythms, it suspends judgement and the reasoning faculties in favour of what T. S. Eliot called the 'auditory imagination': truly a devilish art.

The belief that poetry can do this more than any other of the verbal arts accounts for the belief that it carries high risk responsibility. Something out of the ordinary is implicated: the poet is a special kind of person, a legitimate trespasser on the sacred, someone whose own ear has been whispered into by powerful, devilish or divine messengers. It is not my aim to argue either for or against this view. The relationship between poet and community does not have to involve a tiny select minority of eminent writers and a large amorphous majority of non-writers. In certain communities everyone writes, not only the specialist. But in all communities where poetry has a presence, the belief holds that within the mind a space exists for words to generate meanings which will transform. In other words, imagination is real; hearing Milton or Shakespeare can still awaken it; it can be awakened with or without their methods and constructions of the world, and new forms of awakening can be found.

An act of attention

Writing that seduces, persuades, argues, comforts, contradicts – writing resembling speech but speech with impact: poetry can display all these tones in its register. It aims to throw a charge between two points: one, the subject, topic, piece of the world, and the other the reader's responsive imagination:

the space in the mind that responds to sound and image. It persuades, comforts, argues, finds a voice, makes use of rhythm, rhyme and forms of sound-quality with that imagination primarily in view. It aims to root itself there so that, like Eve, we become unwarily entangled. This would seem at first to require either very susceptible readers or very heavy methods of literary technology, neither of which we can count on. But fortunately, one drive of poetry is surprise: a sense that things in the world about us are surprising and that words, even obvious and simple words, can be organised to enhance surprise. A word often used to describe this effect of surprise is *defamiliarisation*, a 'making strange' of the things we usually think of as familiar and not worth a second look. The focus of a poem is so sharp that it defamiliarises; it does make things worth looking at twice, as in the poem below by William Carlos Williams. As we shall see, the language is straightforward; clever and elaborate metaphor is not necessary.

Proletarian Portrait

A big young bareheaded woman
in an apron

Her hair slicked back standing
on the street

One stockinged foot toeing
the sidewalk

Her shoe in her hand. Looking
intently into it

She pulls out the paper insole
to find the nail

That has been hurting her[4]

The art of this poem (as in the passage from *Macbeth*) is its organisation. It could have moved straight from the subject of the sentence ('A big young bareheaded woman') to the rest of the main clause ('pulls out the paper insole/ to find the nail'), but the intervening phrases delay the verb and all the information it supplies. Why? The poem needs to place this information at the point where it will surprise us. The structure prolongs our attention in the same way and for the same length of time as the poet's attention is prolonged by what he is seeing. He becomes absorbed, just temporarily, in someone else's absorption. We witness a sudden act of concentration: the woman's, and the poet's, and even though the event described might happen any day anywhere, something we might not normally notice has been brought close to our attention and valued.

POETIC FORM

Regular form

A common question is how to define the way poetry differs from prose, especially when faced with a piece like the one above. Its language seems too ordinary to be in a poem, and the subject itself far too commonplace for the elevated treatment we expect. But really the word 'poem' implies a space: what you put into it can be just what you decide you will put into it. It might be just a piece of the world discovered – or *re*covered from the flood of obscurity and forgetfulness that engulfs almost everything that happens to us. But this point cannot be securely made until we have looked more closely at poetic form, and especially at regular form features such as metre, rhyme, stanza – the terms which to most readers imply a use of strict and formal conventions. Are they useful? If so, how should we understand them? What, and how much do we need to know about them in order to write?

To write poems we don't need to know too much about these features – that would be the comforting answer at least. But when we come to look at free verse, which might appear to have rid itself of these conventions completely, it will be clear that not even free verse is free in this respect; behind that too is a finger tapping a desk: there might be stanzas of more or less equal length; there might even occur the occasional rhyme, and certainly there will be rhythm. To read regular verse and think about its conventions of stress patterns is good training. Reading it aloud however is probably of more use than learning elaborate rules. But as well as reading aloud, the questions we might ask are: Why use regular form? What does it do? At this point, some definitions will help.

Whenever we write and speak in English we make use of *stress pattern.* Phrases and words are divided up into syllables; some are stressed (*S*), others unstressed (*U*), as in the following headline:

City centres fall prey to march of malls

This phrase has ten syllables and five stresses, with a pattern of *S U, S U U, S U, S U, S.* If situated alongside others with the same pattern, this phrase would begin to sound like poetry, and could indeed be a line out of a poem. If surrounded by lines of the same pattern it would begin to sound in the reader's mind and would make the reader *sound it out* with emphasis on the stressed/unstressed beat. This stressed/unstressed feature (*S U*) we call *trochaic metre.* Because it occurs on its own as a newspaper headline, the phrase stands far less chance of becoming verse-like, but placed next to others of the same type they will start to influence and chime with each other. In the following lines the sequence of beats is regular (*U S*), and we call this metre *iambic*; iambic metre is the most commonly found metre in English verse. The lines below by Robin Bell are a good example of regular iambic metre:

The bridge is wide. The Forth is deep.
Iambic trains are made for sleep.[5]

As with all metrical verse however, one line needs another. The first line needs the second to become regular.

We can distinguish two kinds of form in poetry. One is found on the surface of poetic language and we can recognise it by noting *stress pattern* regularity, as above. Another example of surface form is *rhyme pattern*, as in the following poem by W. H. Auden:

From 'Twelve Songs'
Stop all the clocks, cut off the telephone,
Prevent the dog from barking with a juicy bone,
Silence the pianos with muffled drum
Bring out the coffin, let the mourners come.

Let aeroplanes circle moaning overhead
Scribbling on the sky the message He Is Dead,
Put crepe bows round the white necks of the public doves,
Let the traffic policemen wear black cotton gloves.

He was my North, my South, my East, my West,
My working week and my Sunday rest,
My noon, my midnight, my talk, my song;
I thought that love would last for ever: I was wrong.

The stars are not wanted now: put out every one;
Pack up the moon and dismantle the sun;
Pour away the ocean and sweep up the wood.
For nothing now can ever come to any good.[6]

Rhyme pattern and regular metre can often produce the comic effect of light verse, but the mood of this poem is serious; the flippant and serious effects are both there but firmly under control. The rhymes in this poem are regular; each stanza has four lines of two rhyming couplets. A number of lines, a sufficient number, have a regular stress pattern, but the rhyme has the highest degree of consistency. The regular number of stresses per line is four, as follows:

Stóp all the clócks, cút off the télephone,

Sílence the piános with a múffled drúm

He was my Nórth, my Sóuth, my Éast, my Wést,

Páck up the móon and dismántle the sún;

Póur away the ócean and swéep up the wóod.

Certain lines have six stresses, but most keep the consistency intact, and rhyme marks the strongest signifier here of regularity. But if we look at this poem from a quite different angle we can also see that it has another kind of form which has nothing to do with surface regularity. Stopping the clocks and cutting off the telephone, or making the policemen wear black cotton gloves, are not the same thing as dismantling the sun and pouring away the ocean. The poem moves from the small to the vast, away from the local towards the panoramic. To reverse that sequencing would alter the poem and destroy its emotional power. The sequencing is gradual but relentless and we might describe this form as the poem's inner structure or architecture, and identify it as a change of perspective or even a transformation.

So we need to be clear about these two kinds of form: *surface* patterning and *inner* patterning or *structure*. Why, then, does Auden's poem have both? Given that the inner structure is so obviously the more powerful, why have regularity? The answer is that the stress patterns and rhyme scheme act as a framework, a loom-like system into which odd and surprising details (the 'public doves' is a good example) are threaded. The poem creates a tension between expectation and surprise, and produces its extraordinary effects within the constant security of the rhyme. It is both predictable and unpredictable at once. The point of using regular form is to increase the reader's pleasure by combining reassurance with surprise, and thus to produce a heightened level of attention. Regular form does not need rhyme of course; in *blank verse* the lack of rhyme is compensated for by a regular number of stresses. Shakespeare and Milton make use of iambic pentameter: ten syllables, five stresses per line, the dominant form in English verse of their period.

We might then ask, since rhyme is so useful, why it has gone out of fashion, and the answer is that it has not. Tony Harrison uses it, as 'Them and [Uz']' illustrates; it can be found in a range of poems by many poets writing now. But there has been a shift of interest to inner structure as a method of achieving cohesion, and many people starting to write poems are influenced by that shift and less likely to begin writing like Auden. One reason might be the notion of freeing the voice from problems of mere technique, and the parallel idea that a poem should be unique, expressive, not systematised, in times which value individualism and personal disclosure. But I am guessing, and cannot do more than that. It follows, however, that we need to look closely at free verse structures.

Free verse structures

I can illustrate one type of structure by referring to a poem by the Czech poet, Miroslav Holub. Holub adapts his sense of structure from William Carlos Williams's statement about poetry: 'no ideas but in things', and as we can see, Holub's poem consists of 'things' placed next to each other in a list:

The Fly
She sat on a willow-trunk
watching
part of the battle of Crécy,
the shouts,
the gasps,
the groans,
the tramping and the tumbling.

During the fourteenth charge
of the French cavalry
she mated
with a brown-eyed male fly
from Vadincourt.

She rubbed her legs together
as she sat on a disembowelled horse
meditating
on the immortality of flies.

With relief she alighted
on the blue tongue
of the Duke of Clervaux.

When silence settled
and only the whisper of decay
softly circled the bodies

and only
a few arms and legs
still twitched jerkily under the trees,

she began to lay her eggs
on the single eye
of Johann Uhr,
the Royal Armourer.

And it was thus
that she was eaten by a swift
fleeing
from the fires of Estrees.[7]

Reading for structure identifies this poem as a *list* of related incidents. These incidents also form a *narrative of encounters*: the reproductive processes of the fly as it moves from object to object, mates and deposits its eggs. In this sense Holub's poem is a narrative. While the human objects stay fixed, it seems the ubiquitous fly has all the advantages until, of course, the last stanza. Each incident is given in close-up detail: naming the Duke, the Royal Armourer, numbering the cavalry charges, and the poem is strong enough to accommodate these details while not distracting readers from its overall structure. We learn it as we read; we anticipate; but even so, we are not prepared for the end. The poem's message has something to say about the futility of human processes, and also about the futility of non-human life, but at no point does it state this message directly; we hear the message because of the way the details in close-up are structured. And because of the poem's tone or voice – mocking, comic, observant, dispassionate – we are not inclined to identify it as a war poem with typical war poem attitudes: horror, outrage and sympathy for victims. But a war poem is certainly what it is: a deviant treatment of war within that tradition.

In free verse (here there are no rhymes or consistent metre), inner structure can completely displace surface regularity, *and for a free verse poem to succeed, that structure needs to be strong and audible.*

We saw how in Auden's poem the structure involved a shift from the specific to the panoramic. By leaving us with a glimpse of the fires of Estrees, 'The Fly' to an extent achieves this too. But the following poem, by Ted Hughes, begins with the vast, moves into close-up, then finally back to the wide angled shot. The first stanza establishes a condition, the subsequent ones offer specific examples and the final stanza confirms the original perspective. There has been no change, nor could there be. In musical terms, a pibroch is a lament. The structure enforces a single mood and theme.

Pibroch
The sea cries with its meaningless voice
Treating alike its dead and its living,
Probably bored with the appearance of heaven
After so many millions of nights without sleep,
Without purpose, without self-deception.

Stone likewise. A pebble is imprisoned
Like nothing in the universe
Created for black sleep. Or growing
Conscious of the sun's red spot occasionally,
Then dreaming it is the foetus of God.

Over the stone rushes the wind
Able to mingle with nothing,
Like the hearing of the blind stone itself,
Or turns, as if the stone's mind came feeling
A fantasy of directions.

Drinking the sea and eating the rock
A tree struggles to make leaves –
An old woman fallen from space
Unprepared for these conditions,
She hangs on because her mind's gone completely.

Minute after minute, aeon after aeon,
Nothing lets up or develops.
And this is neither a bad variant nor a tryout.
This is where the staring angels go through.
This is where all the stars bow down.[8]

We could identify the structure of this poem in another way as a set of *failed encounters*. At least the fly in Holub's poem mated and reproduced. Here the stone, the wind and the tree appear to share the same setting, appear to meet and act. They rush, drink, eat, struggle, try to feel a direction, fantasise omnipotence – the poem adds one thing to another – but whatever else might be added, nothing would be able to make any difference and it seems a fact of existence that this is so. The only change, if there is one, comes at the end. This place is also an object of wonder and ignorance: known or abandoned, this setting is everything. Any encounter happening there is limited, perhaps even impossible.

Settings and encounters

The settings and encounters in a poem will influence its structure. If you choose a wilderness setting like 'Pibroch', the structure might show repetition with little change, or it might show climatic and seasonal differences. Hughes chooses the first here, by and large, and the lines are set down in layers with minimal progression. The evidence builds up, the poem becomes longer; comment and vision are restricted by where the action and evidence are situated. If, for instance, the setting is a police station or an archaeological site, a marriage ceremony or a bar, the encounters and subsequent structures will be influenced. To check this point, look at the titles listed in the contents page of any recent poetry anthology. A quick random selection produced the following: 'Welsh Landscape', 'On the Farm', 'Open Waters', 'Talk in the Dark', 'Manchester', 'At the Day Centre', Family Group', 'Below Loughrigg', 'Alcatraz'. From the title alone readers will anticipate an encounter, either between people within these settings, between people and objects, between the objects themselves (as in 'Pibroch'), or between the poet–speaker and the place. You have a choice about how to structure a poem, and also a choice about setting. Does your setting lead towards fixed or open encounters, towards progressions, escape-narratives, confrontations, or does nothing alter? If it is open, what will the outcome be?

Free verse: extended treatment

The following poem by the American poet Elizabeth Bishop also describes an encounter. What happens when things meet is still the question. The setting for this encounter is not the strange world of battlefield or empty wilderness but the speaker's personal experience of a waiting room: somewhere closer to hand. The setting is open. The speaker – 'I' – is trying to make sense of the encounter, trying to feel (to borrow Ted Hughes's phrase) 'a fantasy of directions'. But unlike 'Pibroch', here the poet is thoroughly within the poem and its autobiographical setting. Here the poet needs time to reach her conclusions; the mood of considered careful exploration, therefore, leads towards a more open or extended treatment.

In the Waiting Room
In Worcester, Massachusetts,
I went with Aunt Consuelo
to keep her dentist's appointment
and sat and waited for her
in the dentist's waiting room.
It was winter. It got dark
early. The waiting room
was full of grown-up people,
arctics and overcoats,
lamps and magazines.
My aunt was inside
what seemed like a long time
and while I waited I read
the *National Geographic*
(I could read) and carefully
studied the photographs:
the inside of a volcano,
black, and full of ashes;
then it was spilling over
in rivulets of fire.
Osa and Martin Johnson
dressed in riding breeches,
laced boots and pith helmets.
A dead man slung on a pole
– 'Long Pig,' the caption said.
Babies with pointed heads
wound round and round with string;
black, naked women with necks
wound round and round with wire
like the necks of light-bulbs.

Their breasts were horrifying.
I read it right straight through.
I was too shy to stop.
And then looked at the cover;
the yellow margins, the date.

Suddenly, from inside,
came an *oh!* of pain
– Aunt Consuelo's voice –
not very loud or long.
I wasn't at all surprised;
even then I knew she was
a foolish, timid woman.
I might have been embarrassed,
but wasn't. What took me
completely by surprise
was that it was *me*:
my voice, in my mouth.
Without thinking at all
I was my foolish aunt,
I – we – were falling, falling,
our eyes glued to the cover
of the *National Geographic*:
February, 1918.

I said to myself: three days
and you'll be seven years old.
I was saying it to stop
the sensation of falling off
the round, turning world
into cold, blue-black space.
But I felt you are an *I*,
You are an *Elizabeth*,
you are one of *them*.
Why should you be one, too?
I scarcely dared to look,
to see what it was I was.
I gave a sidelong glance
– I couldn't look any higher –
at shadowy gray knees,
trousers and skirts and boots
and different pairs of hands
lying under the lamps.
I knew that nothing stranger

had ever happened, that nothing
stranger could ever happen.
Why should I be my aunt,
or me, or anyone?
What similarities –
books, hands, the family voice
I felt in my throat, or even
the *National Geographic*
and those awful hanging breasts –
held us all together
or made us all just one?
How – I didn't know any
word for it – how 'unlikely' . . .
How had I come to be here,
like them, and overhear
a cry of pain that could have
got loud and worse but hadn't?

The waiting room was bright
and too hot. It was sliding
beneath a big black wave,
another, and another.

Then I was back in it.
The war was on. Outside,
in Worcester, Massachusetts,
were night and slush and cold,
and it was still the fifth
of February, 1918.[9]

In this poem Elizabeth Bishop chooses free verse to illuminate an experience
which could easily be summarised as a cliché: 'in spite of age, family or racial
differences, we are all one and equal, and there is such a thing as shared
human identity'. But because it traces the awkward and clumsy dawning of
this perception so unsentimentally (notice the harsh judgement on Aunt
Consuelo), and is always at pains to relate it to actual circumstances, it ceases
to be a cliché and becomes real.

It faces the otherness of races represented in the *National Geographic*
('their breasts were horrifying'), the distant cry of pain from the other room,
the knees, clothes and bodies close at hand, the child's sense of her own
'other' identity – her name – and mixes them in a way which places herself
right in their midst: *they* are together; she is one among *them*. Instead of
belonging only to herself, she is part of everyone else. In this poem the
poet is made strange to herself. The poet's troubling anxiety about herself

produces images of falling and being engulfed. But it would not be possible for Bishop to reach this perception without the extended treatment, the searching trial-and-error exploratory form, the sense of everything sharply focused and never other than bafflingly present and actual. Rather than trying to encapsulate a feeling in one or two concisely structured meaning-saturated lines (a quality we often expect from poetry) the chosen form explores the experience gradually, moment by moment.

How free is free verse?

But again, we might ask, if wholly free of rhyme, metre, evenly lengthed stanzas and other forms of surface regularity, how does this piece of writing differ from prose? Could we not call such extended treatment prose – why is it poetry? The answer is really quite technical. As with the other examples of free verse given above, vestiges of regularity are still there. Look at the words at the end of every line in Bishop's poem – the place where rhyme ought to be (1) – and compare these with the words at the beginning of each line (2):

1 Massachusetts/Consuelo/appointment/her/room/dark/room
2 In/I/too/and/in/it/early

However you describe the difference, it is clear that (1) contains a predominance of nouns, is strong on information-significance, and that these are the words which, because they occur at the end, would have been strongly emphasised through rhyme. Clearly, when compared with (2) they carry *emphasis*, and do so even more when placed at the end. The verse structure therefore serves emphasis, in the same way and for the same reasons as rhyme marks out words at the ends of lines.

In free verse, significant words are normally placed at the ends of lines, while pronouns, adverbs, qualifiers – I/in/and/too – are found at the beginning. This quite simple rule is one practised by almost all writers of free verse.

Also if we count the number of stresses per line, the pattern is relatively consistent:

In Wórcester, Mássachúsetts,

I wént with Áunt Consúelo

to kéep her déntist's appóintment

All the lines look almost the same length, but there is more to it than that. Most of the lines have three stresses, some two: it varies, yet enough have three to make a sufficient consistency overall. Lines with two stresses are particular: 'Their breasts were horrifying', 'the *National Geographic*', 'another, and another'. A wavelike formation runs through those lines with only two stresses. Printed and therefore read as prose, these qualities would be lost. Rather than being consistent with formal verse the poem retains vestiges of regularity: we can hear the drum taps without becoming too conscious of orchestration; instead we hear her voice as it ponders, reflects, remembers, becomes confused, struggles to reach its conclusions.

In the first paragraph of this chapter I pointed out the importance of voiced as opposed to silent reading. We need to be able to convert print into voice. Unless we can do this, all reference to, for example, Bishop's voice will be meaningless, so how do we make that conversion?

First, the poet herself is making it possible by not including words that sound antiquated. We can forgive Shakespeare and Milton for using outdated and conventional poetic phrases such as 'O'er' and 'as he list' but not someone writing in our own time, unless they are doing it for ridicule effects or irony.

Anyone using these outdated words immediately sets up barriers for the voice. Bishop chooses her words from current usage. But look at the second stanza of 'In the Waiting Room'. The line beginning 'but wasn't' makes an odd impression. This and the lines that follow are arranged to produce a sense of afterthought: ideas are given in order as they occur, not arranged tidily and compactly. The word 'me' is twice positioned at the end, yet the second 'me' needs to be sounded emphatically. Even without the italics it would be emphasised by the close parallel between these words and *speech*. The ear hears these two 'me's' as different, and the same difference happens again with the 'my's' – 'my voice, in my mouth', and the repetition of 'I' just below it. The question is not just *what* did she think, but *how*. The printed lines are clues; they aim to tell us as much as they can about how those thoughts rushed into her mind at that moment. We can therefore value those thoughts and feel their influence; they operate like events in the poet's mind.

Free verse: compact treatment

February – Not Everywhere
Such days, when trees run downwind,
their arms stretched before them.

Such days, when the sun's in a drawer
and the drawer locked.

When the meadow is dead, is a carpet,
thin and shabby, with no pattern.

and at bus stops people retract into collars
their faces like fists.

– And when, in a firelit room, mother looks
at her four seasons, at her little boy,

in the centre of everything, with still pools
of shadows and a fire throwing flowers.[10]

This beautiful poem and the one that follows, both by Norman MacCaig, are
constructed from oppositions; the simple structure is stocked by brief details
which are listed as opposites. One set of opposites doesn't replace the other;
they coexist. But of course one has to come first so that we do not experience
this coexistence until the end. We are left with it; something was held in
reserve. In their small space, the contrast injects vitality – cold to heat,
unpleasant to pleasant.

Imagine the sets placed in reverse order, as follows:

Such days, when in a firelit room, mother looks
at her four seasons, at her little boy,

in the centre of everything, with still pools
of shadows and a fire throwing flowers.

– And when trees run downwind,
their arms stretched before them.

Such days, when the sun's in a drawer
and the drawer locked,

and at bus stops people retract into collars
their faces like fists.

When the meadow is dead, is a carpet,
thin and shabby, with no pattern.

Is the poem producing the same impression? Its vitality depends on contrasts,
but also on the relative positions of the scenes. In the second version, what
has happened to the poem's tone? If we reduce the number of lines about the
fire, the positive tone would be even more seriously threatened. Which scene
makes the most chilling ending?

The tone therefore, in a compact space such as this, depends on exact
arrangements of position and length. By ending with an image of vitality, the
original version reminds us that even when the scene is bleak there might
always be something to reverse our negative impression. In relation to
'Pibroch' this poem is open. It sees experience as wide, varied and surprising,
not closed, predictable and doomed. And yet both this and 'Pibroch' are
poems of great tenderness: one of pity, the other celebration.

To see these effects in action, how would it be if the two stanzas of the
next poem were printed in reverse order:

Other Self, Same Self
Such warmth in my mind
where you talk and laugh
and drink drams
and walk among mountains

– though I touched your cold brow
on that wintry morning
that went away
and took you with it.[11]

In both these poems, MacCaig's focus on the personal group – mother and child, 'I' and 'you' – attracts sympathetic attention. But by drawing attention to form and formal language, compact treatment can distance speaker and reader from the group. In the following example by W. S. Graham, the poem's subject is a storm at sea where there have been casualties, but the treatment is to weave those details into a frieze, a monument, to emphasise metaphor and likeness in a design:

Gigha
That firewood pale with salt and burning green
Outfloats its men who waved with the sound of drowning
Their saltcut hands over mazes of this rough bay.

Quietly this morning beside the subsided herds
of water I walk. The children wade in the shallows.
The sun with long legs wades into the sea.[12]

How extraordinary to make a scene out of such little detail, to make that detail stylised, formal, yet also very moving. But is the reader moved by the aesthetics or by the contents: a storm, death, no evidence, the beach and beams of sunlight indifferent to death? It becomes very difficult to know. Mazes, subsided herds, the sun with long legs – metaphors, formal devices – the very opposite of William Carlos Williams's treatment of the woman in the street removing a nail from her shoe. The objects and people in the above picture do not encounter each other or interact. And yet that is the point; that is the vision. You might have a preference for one poem over the other but both kinds are available to use; both are examples of compact treatment, and it is by no means certain that the second example will fail to engage your attention just because its treatment is impersonal, more literary, more self-consciously art-like and removed from natural speech.

Note how both stanzas in 'Gigha' are set to appeal to the eye, not to the voice. No one would ever *say* that sentence which begins 'Quietly this morning . . .' Rather than spoken it seems designed beforehand. But that again is the point – deliberate distortion: to evoke something familiar using unfamiliar language with peculiar sound qualities: to emphasise artifice, to discover new ways of constructing sentences, to find out what a sentence can do by inventing new sentences. And what they can do can be very extra-ordinary. Here is such an example. Here are the first two lines of a short poem by Ted Hughes, 'Full Moon and Little Frieda'.

> A cool small evening shrunk to a dog bark and the clank of a
> bucket –

And you listening.[13]

Are these two lines meant to sound like natural speech? The second line sounds like a brilliant afterthought, one which might naturally occur in the process of thinking aloud, but the first distorts the typically spoken use of language and it does so in order to join each thing seen and heard into one prolonged seamless length which is that moment; 'you listening' and the sounds of the evening are one thing suddenly together, one substance the evening has shrunk towards; it is that moment of the first chill of dusk.

The word 'shrunk' describes a completed action, and yet we are still waiting for action to follow. The state of completion is also one of suspense. The meaning is between, is both at once. Those two lines have somehow become alert, trance-like. What will follow? They prepare us; they tune us to the poet's, and the child's, level of attention. Poetry is not only a kind of speech; it can raise us to a level of primary attentiveness – to wonder. It is also, surprisingly, just a few words placed carefully on a page.

We have to say that poetry has the right to depart from speech just as free verse departs from regular verse, but we need to add that such departures are never quite total. All the free verse poems printed above carry vestiges of surface regularity. And all, when they do depart from speech, do so with a residual sense of words as spoken aloud. A trace is left, and even the sentence from Graham makes reference to speech by reversing the usual order. It would have been more usual to say: 'I walk quietly this morning beside . . .' instead of 'Quietly this morning beside . . . I walk.' Such departures sharpen the reader's response. In compact treatment the use of antithesis and the sound of a voice speaking in unspeech-like ways are two of the means whereby writers quicken our sense of the language of poetry and enable us to enjoy its inventiveness.

In compact treatment the writer's and reader's imagination is responding to language as form invention with an obvious inner structure. Sentence shape and length are given priority; overall structure is dominant. The impact of writing outside of speech freshens alertness to form, but speech is hardly ever wholly abandoned; in Norman MacCaig's poems it is hard to assess where speech ends and inner structure begins and which is given priority, since voice or attitude curiously depend on how the poems are shaped. Equally audible in his poems is the kind of arrangement where sets of details contrast, and this is where experiments with compact treatment might begin. The subject is firm, but approaches to it conflict. There are two sets of approach, each sharply detailed, each in focus. How should they be arranged? How will a different arrangement change the poet's voice, attitude and judgement?

METAPHORS, NARRATIVE AND PERSONAE

Metaphors

It is often claimed that the driving force of poetic language is metaphor: a likening of things normally unlike, such as in the examples above from 'February – Not Everywhere', where the meadow in February becomes a threadbare carpet, faces are 'like fists', a fire throws flowers, and the boy is 'four seasons' to his mother. Metaphor makes the strongest impact when the comparison is deliberately extravagant and unusual, as when Sylvia Plath in one of her poems likens a blank sky to 'a pig's backside'. It also succeeds, as in Norman MacCaig's poem, where the poet develops a single chain of metaphors: the seasons becoming signifiers of feeling, but in ways we don't quite expect. The metaphors here enable new ideas to grow and expand. The skill is in allowing this growth to occur, while choosing each metaphorical item so that it will freshen response to experience. If faces are like fists we notice them more. Such metaphors help to sharpen attention, and also to express feeling-reactions such as depression, excitement, joy. The mother's ordinary yet extreme pleasure in her child is expressed through a metaphor in MacCaig's poem. This metaphor from a poem by Charles Causley is divided into two statements acting together:

An iron bowl sent out stiff rays of chrysanthemums. It
grew colder.[14]

Placed together, both statements are metaphorical, while the second on its own would not be. On its own, it would be simply factual, and could just refer to the weather or a time of day. The chill in these lines is felt as strongly emotional.

Writers do not always want to express feeling-reactions, and there are instances where emotional expressiveness is not required at all. Metaphor is not necessarily appropriate in such instances. The poems by Williams and Holub manage without it. Apart from 'the whisper of decay' (Holub), in these two poems the facts themselves are enough to claim our attention. Emotional feeling, as we have seen, would be especially inappropriate in 'The Fly', which succeeds because the poetic voice is dispassionate.

To attract interest and produce surprise is the point of descriptive writing, and any means is justified, not just metaphor. Sometimes metaphors are useful quite simply for adding colour, for sharpening the focus of the writing, and here they don't need to carry an emotional charge. Thom Gunn, in his poem 'A Drive to Los Alamos' speaks of 'the burnt-out furnaces of the wilderness'. This metaphor intensifies his description of the western American desert, but without emotionalising it. It enables us to see it more clearly, and to see with that simplicity of attention which marks his particular way of approaching experience.

The best metaphors are always those which have been intensely felt and internalised by the writer, where one thing really is fused with another and strongly felt as another, and this quality ought to make us wary of using metaphors for any other purpose than to say what we have seen and felt as real. But sometimes this 'reality' effect can be found *without* metaphor. The following poem confronts this problem of style. The poet could have found a way of expressing her opening statement through metaphor – 'the green was the green of . . .' – but instead she chose not to and for good reasons. This poem is framed as a narrative; it builds up its emotional response gradually. The emotionally charged intensity of metaphor simply would not get across that sense of a gradual approach to the centre of the experience.

Swami Anand
In Kosbad during the monsoons
there are so many shades of green
your mind forgets other colors.

At that time
I am seventeen, and have just started
to wear a sari every day.
Swami Anand is eighty nine
        and almost blind.

His thick glasses don't seem to work,
they only magnify his cloudy eyes.
Mornings he summons me
        from the kitchen
and I read to him until lunch time.

One day he tells me
'you can read your poems now'
I read a few, he is silent.
Thinking he's asleep, I stop.
But he says, 'continue'.
I begin a long one
in which the Himalayas rise
        as a metaphor.

Suddenly I am ashamed

to have used the Himalayas like this,
ashamed to speak of my imaginary mountains
to a man who walked through
     the ice and snow of Gangotri
       barefoot
a man who lived close to Kangchenjanga
     and Everest clad only in summer cotton.
I pause to apologise
but he says, 'just continue'.

Later, climbing through
     the slippery green hills of Kosbad,
Swami Anand does not need to lean
on my shoulder or his umbrella.
I prod him for suggestions,
ways to improve my poems.
He is silent a long while,
then, he says
     'there's nothing I can tell you
      except continue.'[15]

In this poem each statement is definite; it says what it says clearly, without decoration. Excess literariness is stripped away so that even, for example, the effects of varying shades of green in the first stanza are stated as fact. Because it is narrative, the language of straight information is sufficient, everything becomes fact. Metaphor is questionable, and this mistrust is itself part of the narrative of the poem: her own use of the Himalayas as a metaphor embarrasses her in relation to the old man's actual lived experience – she can't share that; she can't write from the centre of *his* experience, only from her own.

Narrative

We can tell that this poem is a narrative because it describes a set of experiences in time. This happened, then this: first is the general context, the norm: 'mornings', and then the specific context: 'one day'. We sense the approach is gradual; it has stages. To move from one to the other is the narrative method. Approaching the experience here is a protagonist, in this case the speaker. What happens to her happens to us. As with Thom Gunn and William Carlos Williams, we can share her world with the same simplicity of attention she brings to it. But she doesn't start to write direct from the centre, as, for example, does Sylvia Plath in many of her poems. With 'Swami Anand' we have instead a *gradual* intensification: a narrative of *approach*.

Personae

Sometimes the speaker is obviously not the writer, or the writer is speaking, but through a persona. You, the writer, are imagining the voice of someone who could be a figure from history or myth, an animal, a stranger, or a haunting voice which exists outside any of these categories, or just someone you met once. In verse drama, the characters you invent will all be personae. The word 'mask' is often used to identify the voice style of a persona. Yeats speaks through the madwoman Crazy Jane; Geoffrey Hill speaks through the mask of Sebastian Aruruth, Eliot in the voice of Alfred Prufrock, Ted Hughes through Crow; personae devices have been the stuff of a great deal of major poetry this century. Will this form continue to be used and to survive? The choice is for the next century's writers. Why has it been so useful until now? It provides an obvious way of achieving authority through self-distancing; the writer avoids placing himself on the line: he (and it usually is a 'he') dares not risk speaking from the private self and its isolation. To do so would mean a loss of general significance and therefore of poetic authority; instead he speaks through a mask.

But these comments suggest a somewhat negative view of the device, and there may be qualities of effect for it to achieve without the constant worry about authority and evasive self-distancing. Whether it will continue or be abandoned, the problem it addresses will have to be solved in one way or another, and that involves the whole question of how far any individual writer's private experience can ever fully reach that of others. How can it find access to the equally private selves who read? Because of its tradition of being immediately and sharply focused on self as well as on world, because it deals with experiences at their source, poetry faces this problem more than any other art form. But there are still occasions when mask devices will work to reduce that distance between the reader's and the writer's self, and on some occasions the solution seems far simpler than the problem.

I shall end this section on reading with a poem by Thom Gunn. The writer's sympathy for the subject is so powerful that he loans his poetic voice completely to another speaker. In this poem he makes a voice for someone who has none, or not one usually heard. The first stanza is the voice both of the poet and the man – together and indistinguishable. Before the man speaks himself, they are a duet:

Sparrow
> Chill to the marrow
> pity poor Sparrow
> got any change Sir
> Sparrow needs change Sir

I stand here in the cold
in a loose old suit bruised and dirty

I may look fifty years old
but I'm only thirty

My feet smell bad and they ache
the wine's gone sour and stale in my pores
my throat is sand and I shake
and I live out of doors

I shelter from the rain
in a leaky doorway in leaky shoes
and all I have is pain
that's left to lose

I need some change for a drink
of sweet wine Sir a bottle of sherry
it's the sugar in it I think
will make me merry

I'll be a daredevil then
millionaire stud in my right mind
a jewel among men
if you'll be so kind

The bastard passed me by
fuck you asshole that's what I say
I hope I'll see you cry
like Sparrow one day[16]

IDEAS FOR WRITING

What is it about words that generates excitement? To write poems you need
to be able to feel that words do this, and also that they can do it in a relatively
short space. One of the truly amazing things about poems is that they can go
so far, say so much, sound like speech yet take up so little room. A poem
succeeds when it *prepares* us, when it shapes our ability to receive and think
sensuously about experience. The whole experience may not need to be there,
but the sense of being prepared and alerted – this is what readers enjoy and
what they value.

Choosing a subject

You will need to tell yourself that you will find out how to work with poetic
language only with practice. We are now at the working end, but I have not
said anything so far about how subjects for poems come to be chosen. From
my own experience of writing poems and from what I know and have read,
it is clear that even writers whose lifetime's effort is with poetry do not

themselves know, and are often inclined to say that the subject chose them. Sometimes anger or an outraged sense of justice can move you to write; sometimes a moment of lived experience you wish to preserve in a powerful and memorable form of words; sometimes an image in a film, on television, in a photograph; sometimes the subject forms slowly, is a loose combination of feelings, a drifting together of sensations, feelings and ideas which, as they approach each other, form a centre. And sometimes it comes from reading other poems, discovering a new structure, sensing an atmosphere and being curious about how the poet produced it so sensationally.

It has been said, notably by T. S. Eliot, that poetry is conceived below the level where reasoning and analysis occur, and precedes discursive or argumentative thought. It can simply involve hearing a voice in your mind, and in finding the right setting for that voice. Macbeth, for instance, does not reason with himself to commit murder; he simply turns himself into a process through which it will come about. This state of allowing oneself to become possessed of a feeling is also found in Sylvia Plath's thoughts about the sea (see Chapter 2, p.61). Other poets adopt a more sociable view of the case, write about issues already to the fore in public debates and reinvent the language of public space. But given such plurality it would be wrong to imagine that you have only one choice and must write only one kind of poem. Experimenting with subjects equally means experimenting with forms.

In listing the following suggestions, I only ask that you aim to write whole poems. You are the writer; you must must decide, and to write whole poems will enable you to experience effects and changes as you write. You will need to remember that poetry tries to deal with experience at its source; that is, before it becomes obvious what the experience is about. The struggle with words and structures is inevitable, and difficult. Will your eventual poem come through? Will readers hear it? Given these demands, there is a point in the struggle with words where commitment to the poem you are writing takes over. Simplicity of attention can help, but finding this can take several drafts, revisions, returns to the original voice and impulse. In my own case, I find myself always trying to work towards simplicity and away from confusion, but not always successfully. One certain thing is that poems follow a line towards the centre of an experience. They may start near it, as Elizabeth Bishop does in her poem. But even if they start some distance away, they move towards it. It is by going in that direction that commitment begins to be felt. The aim, ultimately, is to find that point of excitement. Once that is found, there's nothing to do but continue.

Syllabic poems

In eight or ten stanzas of four lines each, write a poem where each line contains eight syllables. If you have written eight syllables, go on to the next line. Choose your subject first. It could be an event, a portrait of a person, a setting with an encounter involving one person, yourself, or a group. It could refer to something in the present or the past, and you could use either tense. Don't worry about rhyming or sound patterns. These can happen without your having to think about them, and even if they don't it doesn't matter; you will have written a poem. Simply keep to the four-line stanza, eight-syllable rule.

I tried this method myself with two or three poems I wrote after watching children playing video games. I didn't like the effect of the games at all – life experience appeared to be a matter of zapping one adversary or problem after another and when you have zapped the lot that is success. Alex Kidd was the name of the video character. Is success a matter of luck or skill? Could you repeat the performance, even if you finish as a winner? The syllabic effect seemed to fit well with this type of rapidly shifting narrative structure.

Alex Kidd in Miracle World
Alex Kidd, he was devoured
by an eagle on a sea-cliff.
From side to side it moves across
the screen while Alex's little

ghost goes up and up and Alex
is back again with two more lives.
Skipping treacherous ledges he
drops in the sea, birds become fish,

swims down and along collecting
moneybags, and dodging the sharp
piranha. Where threat is he shifts
to reverse and negotiates

a greenish frog's killer bubbles,
a huge yo-yo fish. And this time
gets the hamburger. Lots of cheers,
but this is only zone one and

afterwards ten more. It's three he's
in now, waved at by a sucking
octopus. Another life lost.
Survival is miraculous

Alex, but where are all your friends?
Here they are and both on the safe
side, though in turn each one is you.
A skill they learn hazardously

gets you as far as you can go.
Now on a bouncy motorbike
then drowning in a lava lake
zone four is the limit so far.

Oh Alex Kidd, brave Alex Kidd,
so superiorly evolved,
see your punches coming easy.
Though in fine fettle, ghastlier

trials wait, and when you reach the
last zone, is your desired close
to know it's with a complete skill
you succeed, not from luck or by

accident? Can you be sure it
wasn't chance, impulse or a feint?
Go back Alex, try, and find you'll
defeat miracle world never.[17]

You may have noticed that in this poem I have broken the rule about ending
each line with a significant word. I did this deliberately. The only rule for a
line was a syllable count.

Questions, commands, direct address

Develop an idea by using a series of simple commands or questions – Don't
(do this, or that), Why (is this or that)? – as follows:

Don't worry about rhyming or sound patterns.
Your poem is free. It has no restrictions.
It can go anywhere and like a camera
Its lens waiting, it is not like you
Nervous of looking in certain eyes.

Commands, questions, and the use of 'You' can be developed into a narrative.
The poem 'Rape' by the American poet Adrienne Rich develops by addressing 'You' directly. Here are the first three stanzas:

Rape
There is a cop who is both prowler and father:
he comes from your block, grew up with your brothers,
had certain ideals.
You hardly know him in his boots and silver badge,
on horseback, one hand touching his gun.

You hardly know him but you have to get to know him:
he has access to machinery that could kill you.
He and his stallion clop like warlords among the trash,
his ideals stand in the air, a frozen cloud
from between his unsmiling lips.

And so, when the time comes, you have to turn to him,
the maniac's sperm still greasing your thighs,
your mind whirling like crazy. You have to confess
to him, you are guilty of the crime
of having been forced.[18]

'Rape' is a powerful poem and its address-effects are one reason for that, as well as its subject-matter. The second-person singular 'You' is moved towards the centre of the experience. Here the 'You' is clearly female, but in another poem, and another experience, the identity of 'You' could be male, black or white, or belong to any significant group you wish. This method may help you to deal with experiences without saying 'I'. It helps you to generalise while also going into some degree of detail, and to ask the questions which need to be asked.

Experiment with a poem in which you are addressing someone other than yourself as 'You', who is in danger. You have to warn them, or try to prevent them from carrying out an action. Your poem must be able to take effect immediately, therefore it must communicate instantly.

Choose a subject you are familiar with, and a 'You' who belongs to a way of life you feel you know in detail. You may wish to introduce another character, as Adrienne Rich does, someone who is a threat to 'You'. The tone will be urgent, and will carry your sense of that person and their situation.

'Rape' marks the whole experience of seeking police protection as a serious dilemma for women. It has a general relevance. Your 'You' could equally have no choice but to follow a course of action. If so, express the dangers, the conflicts. Alternatively, you might address yourself as 'You' and describe certain circumstances which cannot be managed without difficulty.

Encounter

A large number of poems describe encounters. Writers can choose to describe encounters by placing themselves in the picture, as Elizabeth Bishop does, by placing a person or creature in the picture, as Holub does, or, without any reference to an observer, by describing objects and things encountering each other. Another alternative is to imply an observer without using the words 'I' or 'he' or 'she' – as in 'February – Not Everywhere'.

Choose a photograph which illustrates an encounter. If it shows a group of people or objects, describe the scene. Or imagine you have just entered the scene. What do you see?

Walk down a street and imagine you are a stranger in the neighbourhood. Write a simple description of three things you have seen, using a stanza for each. Try rearranging your stanzas to find the most pleasing result. You may need a fourth stanza. You may wish to try and find an idea which joins them together (what kind of street is it, what does it signify, is there an observer present or not?) or to leave them unconnected. Decide which alternative you prefer.

Having experimented with this method you might then wish to expand one of the stanzas into a complete poem. The other two could disappear altogether, though possibly not entirely without trace. Experimenting with one form can lead you into another you hadn't planned but which suggests itself as you work.

Settings

Write a poem where setting is the main focus. Human beings or human feelings may or may not be present. How will you finish your poem? You could try opening out from close-up to a final wide angle shot.

On the model of 'Gigha' (p.84), describe a setting where something has just happened.

Describe a scene full of objects. Suggest that something might happen, but hasn't so far. All the objects are waiting in a kind of suspense.

You may be able to revise in the form of a poem your experiments from the 'Introductory writing exercises' on settings (p.34), and particularly on weather or climate.

Antithesis

Choose a set of two-word contrasts; for example, cold/warm; free/trapped; victim/oppressor; city/wilderness.

Find a specific event, object or situation which illustrates each word, and write a stanza for each in close-up focus.

Are the stanzas of equal length or is one shorter than the other? They could be either; again it is your decision. Experiment. If you try reversing the order does this alter the voice?

Before you begin to write, you may wish to research each of the words separately by using a spider diagram. Place the word in the middle of the page and surround it with all the impressions it suggests. See if these form particular groups: common phrases which make use of the word might be one group, negative and positive impressions another, personal feelings another. Look back. Sense which ideas attract your imagination.

You might find that one of the words carries opposite associations within itself. Colours can do this. The word *red* for example carries associations of high authority (soldiers, judges, cardinals, warnings) and revolt (blood, passion, revolution).

Narrative

Narrative happens in time. A sequence of events in time is all it requires, but there are a number of secondary considerations. 'The gas man arrived, read the meter, then left' is a narrative, but if he arrived, read the meter and then refused to leave, or changed into a rhinoceros, that would surprise most people's expectations as well as being considerably less reassuring. Poetry can deviate from the norm and produce fantasy, and therefore is particularly useful for narrative; all kinds of transformations are possible. One other point: who is the narrator of the story? What is the tone: accepting, bewildered, outraged, curious, detached? This list of attitudes might be helpful but try to avoid stating directly: 'I was bewildered/outraged/curious/ detached'. The feeling needs to come through without being named.

Write a narrative in which you are approaching an experience warily, enthusiastically, with detachment, with an attitude. But don't give this attitude a name: show it in the action, in the style, rhythm and tone.

Narrative can make use of extended treatment, as in Elizabeth Bishop's poem. Here the main focus is on the subject: what happened, but also what was it like, how did it feel? What was at the centre of the experience? You may be able to draw on a subject you have already explored either through autobiographical writing or through the introductory writing exercises. Being true to the subject and feeling quality, exploring the experience, gathering the ideas it generates, 'In the Waiting Room' narrates and explores, thinks aloud, does not worry about how long it takes, or whether the form is regular or worked out in advance. It allows itself the freedom of a looser structure, one which serves a careful slow movement, and this loose structure will help you approach the central experience gradually.

Writing from the centre. Expressionism

Your previous experiments with writing (autobiography as one instance), may have enabled you to see where the centre of an experience lies for you. You might then write directly from that centre. But if you do, you will need to think what your reader is experiencing as he or she reads your poem. They will need to know that a power of feeling is wired to those details direct. Background information will not be available whole, but only the central images and effects supplying just hints or vestiges of a background to the reader. Sylvia Plath's poems provide many examples of such effects. In her poem, 'Crossing the Water' from her collection with that title, she writes:

'Black lake, black boat, two black, cut-paper people. / Where do the black trees go that drink here? / . . . Cold worlds shake from the oar.'

Her poems often begin with a definite statement: 'Love set you going like a fat gold watch' ('Morning Song'), 'The hills step off into whiteness,' ('Sheep in Fog'). Each poem is set going by its strong opening line. The lines that follow will be flavoured and coloured by that first confident brush-stroke on the canvas. Notice the dominance of verbs in these examples. An event has taken place which will be decisive. What will be the outcome? The poet searches to discover. Ted Hughes has written about Plath's working drafts of 'Sheep in Fog'.[19] While the poem's first line suggests a foregone conclusion, it was still difficult, and painful, for the poet to continue with its suggestions of dissolution and self-effacement. The drafts show her trying to resist the implication of void, to replace it with hope and life, but unsuccessfully. At last she recovers the force of that beginning.

Expressionist writing is driven by a firmly worked consistency of texture. With its simplifying style, repetition, strong lines and suggestion of narrative, 'Crossing the Water' evokes a setting where the figures, details and angles of light are transformed briefly into a scene from myth. We feel this must be the central event in a process; its atmosphere can be sensed but not explained. The style resembles paintings by Van Gogh or Eduard Munch. It paints using bold forceful strokes. It is possible to strengthen the impact of a poem by intensifying its contrasts. To explore these effects, it may help you to look at certain paintings, and experiment with their equivalent in poetry.

Portrait

Narrative can be a way of drawing a portrait, as we saw in Sujata Bhatt's poem (p.87). It establishes time and place and moves through both in the light of a central consciousness. The portrait appears in this light. Bhatt appears to have asked herself certain questions, and these can be starting points for portrait writing:

• In what setting did you and the person concerned first meet?
• Think of an object you associate with this person.
• Think of something they often used to say.
• What other setting, outside of your experience, do you associate with them?
• Ask them one very important question: What is the question? How do they reply?

As an alternative, try to write the information you collect about this person by using their voice as a persona or mask.

Defamiliarisation. Making strange

In the following poem, Peter Redgrove has made a very strange thing even stranger. In many of his poems Peter Redgrove uses his training as a scientist, and this one is a particularly good example of how poetry can borrow its perceptions from other ways of seeing the world. What is a spider's organ of hearing? This is a scientific question, and he answers it scientifically, but then he turns the answer in the direction of poetry:

Spiderly
Specialised hairs in rows on each of eight thighs:
The spiders' ears;
On large spiders, long hairs tuned
To the wingbeats of big insects;
Small spiders have short hairs that listen,
Any sound in the correct range
Will attract a spider, such as a person humming:
Spider-charmer;
Thus to a particular tune the spider eases
Out of his crevice and stands tiptoe
With doubled claws on the piano-polish
Listening with his beards, captured by music;
But beware, there is more: night is a garden
Of winged flowers, and there are nimble spiders
Luring moths because they smell like moths;
Charmer-spider.[20]

Notice how this poem makes other things unfamiliar, not just the spiders: a piano, a person humming, a garden at night. The world of spiders is making our familiar world strange. See if you can find some facts about human beings, animals or insects which make changes to our common-sense idea of the world. Such facts will need to be very specific, so that the perception change can be realised with precision. Studying a science may already have given you ideas which will have altered your image of reality: these are the ideas you can explore.

Writing from other texts

Choose a short paragraph from a history, geography or science textbook, or a newspaper report. Find a subject that provides you with an image, a way into experience. There may be a photograph beside the text which might help. The piece you choose will probably be written as straight information, as in the following example:

In 1808 Richard Trevithick tried to capture the public's imagination by setting up a circular track near the site of the present Euston Station. On this, his latest engine, Catch-Me-Who-Can, pulled a carriage on which people could ride for the price of two shillings (10p). Unfortunately, the venture brought him no orders for locomotives and, disillusioned, he built no more. Later he sought his fortune in South America, and when Stephenson met him in Columbia in 1827, Trevithick, now known as Don Ricardo, was engineer to a shaky copper-mining company. He returned, penniless, to England and when he died in Dartford in 1833 was buried in a pauper's grave.[21]

Information tells us about the circular track near Euston, but it also inadvertently offers an image. This was one of the first public appearances of steam-driven locomotion, and in view of what Euston looks like now, the image of that toy-like track and the reception it received is heavily ironic. You could, for example, use your own knowledge of Euston as it is now (or somewhere like it) to explore that irony. You could choose another point in the story on which to focus. Underneath this conceptualised summarised life was an actual life being lived inarticulately, a journey from the city back to the wilderness. The textbook summary is helpful but the sharp focus and voice qualities of poetry are able to go much further into experience, and you won't know until you begin what you might discover by transforming your chosen text into living experience. One or two words or images from the given text can be a trigger.

The form you choose will be your own decision here, and you may not find it except by trial and error; some of the possible structures I have suggested might be what you are looking for, but there could be others. Persona might be one of them. It could be that you begin this experiment with a poem (using, as I suggest, history, geography, science) and continue it as fiction, short biography or a piece of opinion writing. The subject will be the same. You already have it as textbook information, a starting point; the end point will be to find it again through writing as art.

Chapter 4

Writing short stories

In my early sketches for this chapter, I found myself using the word 'technique' frequently. I wanted to offer not vague and sententious pleas to follow an impulse, but clear solid guidance. By technique I had in mind devices such as internal and external narration, first- and third-person narrators, trigger events, closure. These are terms often used by readers when analysing fiction. How useful are they for writers?

Instead of thinking analytically about types of perspective, narrator positions and points of view, another approach in writing fiction is to realise the thinking and behaviour patterns of a character or characters – physical build, attitude, manner of speech, direction of desire – and to see all these attributes as a *style*: a quality actualised in written style, which I will call *character-rhythm*. I use the word *rhythm* to mean those particular speech habits, attitudes and behaviours which recur, and by which we recognise one character in relation to others and to his or her surroundings and world. We know a character only through the style by which he or she is presented to us on the page. In the excerpts I have used to illustrate this approach, we can sense the writer's search for those recurrences. We can sense, too, the prose styles through which certain characters are realised.

But I didn't want to discard completely my first set of ideas. A combined objective would be to explore them both. The first approach is cool, analytic, film-like, while the second is warm, sensuous, rhythm-like, but at this stage the method I suggest is to keep both in mind while writing, and to let each one come into play as necessary. One approach may well emerge as dominant, but only through experiment will a preference become clear to the individual writer.

But first of all, in the preliminary sections below I shall raise some questions about narrative itself: What is a story? How does fictional narrative differ from that in other kinds of story-telling? For example, I shall be asking how we might compare fiction with personal narrative or anecdote, how our expectations as readers might be different when we encounter a short story from those we hold when reading a passage of autobiography. Do we expect fiction to be different in kind from verifiable report-writing, even though both make use of narrative? Do we expect fiction to be relevant to our experience of the world, and also relevant to our experience of other fiction (two kinds of relevance)? Do we assume the word 'fiction' implies a set of events which never occurred, and if so, does this mean that fiction writers always prefer *to invent*, rather than write about things that have actually happened to them? If, for example, we are going to make use of personal experiences in writing fiction, should we be aiming to present fiction as different from personal narrative?

Another question to ask at this stage concerns the difference between short stories and novels. As in the other chapters, I illustrate my comments with examples, and although most are passages from short stories I have also mixed these with excerpts from novels. The main focus of this chapter is on the art of short story writing, but the distinction novel/short story does not mean that novels should be left out. Sometimes the distinction is not that hard and fast, and certain novels or longer pieces of fiction make use of the same devices as shorter fiction. Where they do not and the differences *are* important I have made the distinction clear.

WHAT IS A STORY?

Short stories and anecdotes may show only a degree of difference, but the telling of either assumes that we can recognise in practice what a story is, how it begins and develops, how it ends. So what are stories? What are the prime constituents of a story? If a child says: tell me a story, what might she or he be expecting?

Even though we are writing for adult readers, it is worth remembering that everyone's sense of what makes a story emerges at an early age. Without being able to answer the question technically, children know by experience, as do adults. To test what writers and readers understand by *story*, look at this passage below:

> John and Mary fall in love and get married. They both have worthwhile and remunerative jobs which they find stimulating and challenging. They buy a charming house. Real estate values go up. Eventually, when they can afford live-in help, they have two children to whom they are devoted. The children turn out well. John and Mary have a stimulating and challenging sex life and worthwhile friends. They go on fun vacations together. They retire. They both have hobbies which they find stimulating and challenging. Eventually they die. This is the end of the story.[1]

Readers may disagree, but most will probably notice that if this passage is a story it lacks certain fundamental story-like features, if not all. It has a beginning – 'John and Mary fall in love' – and an end – 'Eventually they die.' It contains characters, shows the passage of time, and offers a hint, though this is debatable, that the recurring phrase 'stimulating and challenging' is typical of the characters' own way of speaking about themselves; in other words, it suggests their private opinions about their lives. But unfortunately, as Margaret Atwood no doubt calculated, the passage amounts to little more than a late twentieth-century version of the formula story ending: 'And they all lived happily ever after.' This passage, in present-day affluent societies, is what living 'happily ever after' means, or is supposed to mean, and most readers will recognise it as such whether or not they privately think it desirable.

The trouble is that we can't easily enter into its world. The gates are closed already behind 'happily ever after' and if stories only consisted of unspecific references to, or even more detailed knowledge of such 'happily ever after' states (John's hobbies, for instance, or where they went on holiday), readers would not be satisfied; that is certain. Even 'unhappily ever after' would be more compelling, and this is because readers expect conflict, disruption and a lack of immediate solution. The word 'event' conveys to us that a settled state is disrupted; a new set of values replaces the old; hence stories usually begin with a sudden and eventful change. If, one morning in their newly fitted kitchen, or listening to Mozart after their steak and claret, Mary fell out with John because she didn't want to have children at all, or if later the children did *not* 'turn out well', then readers would immediately detect story-like features. John and Mary would immediately become more interesting to us; the passage leaves us with the urge to supply disruptions not admitted to in John's (or was it Mary's?) version of their life story.

FICTION AND ANECDOTE

Many writers draw on their own experience as sources for fiction, and there are clear parallels between fiction writing, autobiography and anecdote or personal narrative, between all kinds of stories both told and written. But at some point we will need to acknowledge a distinction between the literary form short story and other literary forms of narrative, as well as between these and non-literary forms such as the anecdote. Can we discuss these forms in terms of differences of content, or should we focus instead on their different techniques? Suppose, for example, that you have just failed your driving test for the third time and are telling your friends about it. If you then used this material in a short story, would you intend to shape the narrative differently, produce a more literary style, use third-person rather than first-person narrative? Or would your aim be to change the events themselves, add to them, subtract from them? In other words, would you be altering the content?

My suspicion is that readers expecting a short story would not be wholly satisfied if they found themselves reading about your driving test, however brilliantly you expressed your version of events. The reasons behind my suspicion derive from the notion that narratives, like language itself, operate always within a social context. The social context of anecdote involves certain specific aims and conditions: the speaker is helping a known group of friends and associates to catch up on some recent information about his or her own life, on what has recently been happening to the speaker – the next instalment, as it were. The context will also suggest that those listening could follow up with anecdotes of their own if they wanted to; the context implies a continuity, not an end to communication. With anecdotes, communication continues after the telling, just as it was already established before it. Both these conditions differ from those implied by fiction writing, where communication has not been established previously, will not continue afterwards, and does not rely on the listener's or reader's prior acquaintance with the settings and characters of the narrative.

Another way of comparing fiction to anecdote is to insist that anecdote can succeed merely by describing a routine – how I passed my driving test; how I climbed Everest – whereas fiction always requires that routines are broken. So you might make use of your driving test as material for a story, but invent a scene where just as you are reversing round a corner, the examiner sees his wife with another man.

Readers are likely to associate the telling of an anecdote with speech, and although many written stories are constructed to imitate closely the sound of a speaking voice, the other conditions still operate: written fiction isn't a conversation, we aren't expected to reply, we don't know the writer beforehand, we expect the communication to come to an end, we expect routines to be broken.

But having said that, there could still be similarities between told anecdotes and written fiction. Both may contain evaluations: 'And the worst thing of all was . . .', and summaries: 'And even now that terrible examiner is still allowed to frighten the life out of people. He should be sacked.' The crisis point and conclusion can be highlighted, and implications for others, not just the speaker, can be developed into a message or judgement.

We might describe J. D. Salinger's novel *The Catcher in the Rye* as a long extended anecdote told to us by the main character Holden Caulfield as he moves from place to place around New York, expelled from school and unable to go home. But the people he meets are not anecdotal but encountered within the social context of readers reading a novel. We feel we are being introduced to them for the first time; we are not expected to exercise any prior knowledge of them, hold any pre-formed judgements or add our own information about them to his. They begin to exist as and when they are encountered. His narrative establishes them for us in close-up, in detail; we sense their immediate impact, and also meet them by way of Holden's strongly developing attitudes; hence we experience a clash of characteristics: those of Holden's character with theirs. We can still feel however, because of his tone of friendly alliance with his readers, that Holden's narrative leans towards anecdote. But he realises himself that the social context of reading fiction is usually not like that:

What really knocks me out is a book that, when you're done reading it, you wish the author who wrote it was a terrific friend of yours and you could call him up on the phone whenever you felt like it. That doesn't happen much, though.[2]

The fiction writer will inevitably be more interested in developing the message or meaning of a piece for a general reader *unknown to her or him personally*. We are speaking here of a greater *degree* of emphasis on meaning general to all, rather than saying anecdotes have no emphasis of that kind whatsoever. In fiction writing we also expect the characters to exist to a degree independently of the teller and her or his audience of friends, but again this is only a matter of degree. An anecdote could end simply by saying: 'It just goes to show what Aunty Jessica is like, aren't you convinced by what I'm saying?' A piece of fiction would need to do more; otherwise the general reader would simply respond by saying: 'So what? – I'm convinced, but I don't happen to know this lady and am not likely to; your opinion of her is of no importance to me!' It follows, therefore, that the fiction writer will be aiming to involve us with the characters independently, will enable us to feel the impact of their experiences as having a relevance wider than the scenes displayed, and that the shape of the narrative will serve those ends clearly.

We therefore come on to specific features of technique and shaping in fiction writing. Even if we are puzzled by what the phrase 'wider relevance' might mean, this can be answered partly in technical ways. Included in the appendix to this chapter is a piece of oral narrative recorded by the Irish writer J. M. Synge in his book *The Aran Islands*. This book is about the communities living in those islands just after the turn of the century when an oral culture of story-telling still thrived. At the end of the excerpt, Synge records his reactions to the story, which is told by an old fisherman to a family group.

STORY CONVENTIONS

We don't need Synge's scholarship (see p.140) to convince us that this story has strong fairy-tale elements, as well as an obvious link with Shakespeare's play *The Merchant of Venice*. The old man's story combines a large number of familiar story motifs: the marriage bargain, the meeting with a helper, the later demand that the bargain should be met, the pound (five pounds) of flesh and no blood, the reunion of the lovers. The story has little 'relevance' to its listeners in terms of their immediate environment or experience of living 'on a wet rock in the Atlantic', to fishing, small boats, rough seas. But even so, most readers will be able to understand that bargains should not be made unless they are intended to be kept, and that lovers where possible should be appeased. It has some relevance then in terms of its *content*. But it also has another type of relevance, and this consists more of the audience being able to recognise these motifs and character-types (merchants, hags, etc.) as being story-like. It has a relevance to certain established conventions.

In the present day we are not likely to read such a story in a collection of modern short stories, to tell it, write it or hear it, but the modern short story still consists of what we might call *narrative conventions*: features which produce relevance to other stories of the same type. In our case such conventions will be likely to remind us not of medieval folk-tale (though in certain cases they might) but of film.

CAMERA PERSPECTIVE

Here we come to the first type of approach in fiction writing.

The distinctions I made between *perspective narration* and *character-rhythm* will become clear as we investigate. The story below, by Anne Spillard, is a good example of a story emerging through the first type of approach, the perspective-type. The teller of the story is not present as a character in the story, and simply shows us what happens. We are enabled to see the characters from a distance, to hear their speech, to sense how a camera is moving in close to them, moving away, pausing on certain details. We visualise a scene. The story draws on the same techniques that we find in the visual media.

'No Legal Existence' by Anne Spillard
In the sluice, the nurses were looking at a mass of fibre and blood clots in a bowl behind the steriliser.

Phyllis peered over their shoulders, still holding the bedpan she had come to empty.

'What is it?' she asked, 'an abortion?' – it was just how she had imagined it would be, all that mess and blood. It didn't look a bit like a baby.

Jenny answered her: 'The afterbirth.' She went to the door and looked into the ward, to make sure no one was coming. The other nurse pulled Phyllis over to the urine-testing cupboard.

Dorothy took a crumpled white paper bag from the shelf underneath it, beside the plastic toothmugs.

'Look,' she said. She opened the bag and pulled a blue kidney dish from inside.

'A baby,' breathed Phyllis. Her eyes opened wider as she looked at the tiny foetus. Without moving her eyes she bent down and set the bedpan on the floor.

'It's perfect,' Dorothy said. They crowded round, looking at the perfection of the foetus, lying in the dish.

'Oh, look at its beautiful fingers, and its ears.'

Each fingernail was like a tiny pear, the ears waxen flaps pressed onto the skull by a hasty thumb as an afterthought. Only the eyes seemed too big. They were protuberant and staring, under lids you could see through. You could see the dark completeness of the liver through transparent skin. There was an awed pause.

'It's a girl,' said Jenny.

'Who's is it? asked Phyllis.

'Miss Hayward's.' They all turned and looked through the window in the sluice door. Miss Hayward's bed was opposite. She was thumbing through a magazine.

'Dorothy's husband used to work with this man she'd been going out with,' said Jenny.

It was the usual story: he was going to marry her, when he'd got settled in Australia. But instead he'd sent her a letter. . . .

It isn't a baby, thought Phyllis. Because a baby has to be there twenty-eight weeks. This perfect human shape is just a thing. It has no legal existence. It has never done anything, not moved or spoken, or seen anything, and no one except us will ever see it.

'What do you do with it?' she asked.

'Throw it away,' said Jenny. She made a face. 'You just wrap it up in the bag and put it in there.' She nodded her head towards the bin by the sink, with its rubber lid that didn't disturb the patients, and the white lining hanging untidily round its top.[3]

If we compare this passage with the passage by Margaret Atwood, we can see that it does present sudden change. It breaks a routine. It lifts the character Phyllis (clearly a newcomer) out of her preconceptions, educates her, and educates its readers in the process. It is not anecdotal. We can't supplement the story with any prior knowledge about this hospital and these characters; we meet them independently. But it will have *content* (as well as *technical*) relevance for a wide range of readers, even to the point where some may object to the way it chooses to make its content relevant. What, for example, might Miss Hayward's version of events have been like? She presumably knows far more about the preceding situation than do the nurses, and could be in shock even though their observation of her 'thumbing through a magazine' suggests otherwise. Her judgement of events is not available, and a more searching treatment might have presented her side of things. Instead of focusing on Miss Hayward, the characters are seen looking at the baby in the dish, and we focus wholly on them and on it: 'a girl'. In this way, the story aims to control our sympathy by leaving certain viewing positions vacant while emphasising others. We see through the eyes of selected characters, not all. What, culturally, does being a girl mean in this context? Does it mean becoming like Miss Hayward? The story doesn't explore this possibility.

But such objections imply that the story has force. What can we learn from it about technique? We need to know about some of the ways in which third-person narrative can work.

Third-person narrative

In third-person narrative, an important decision you will need to make when shaping a story is to work out the position of the camera. Are you:

1 standing far away from the characters, seeing a large section of their life history in one panoramic shot (as in the John and Mary passage)?
2 standing very close to the characters, an eye-witness watching how they behave, where they stand, what they say, what they are doing from second to second?
3 standing right inside their heads, so that you are describing the world through their eyes and in their own words?

We call the first two positions *external narration*, and the third *internal narration*. An equivalent set of terms would describe (1) and (2) as *external focalisation* and (3) as *character focalisation*. Focalisation implies a camera position. As the writer, you have a choice. You can stand away from the characters and observe them as a group, move close to the characters, occupy their viewing positions, move back to a distance. Even third-person 'she/he/they narrative' can look through the eyes of a character and show us what they see. As readers, our sympathy is usually reserved for those characters whose viewing positions we are allowed to occupy, and withheld from those we are not. Hence the writer can manipulate the direction of our sympathy. In the story above it goes towards the nurses and the foetus, and away from Miss Hayward. But the principle doesn't always work in this way. In the *Jaws* films, just before an attack, we often see victims from the shark's position. Would it be possible to produce this sinister effect in fiction?

Phrases such as 'he/she saw/felt/wondered' begin the shift from straight-forward external narration where the reader is addressed directly and given external information about scenes and characters. But when we hear a character's own reactions *in his or her own words*, we know that the shift is complete. Writers do not necessarily use these terms, but they do understand when a shift needs to occur.

In 'No Legal Existence' the first sentence shows us the nurses, while the second shows us Phyllis: each externally. The writer here is addressing the reader directly. But we soon realise that we are in the same position as Phyllis, that of a nurse 'peering over [the others'] shoulders'. We are not seeing what's there until Phyllis sees it, and like her we don't understand quite what it is we are looking at. When we get to: 'It didn't look a bit like a baby', this statement is clearly Phyllis's opinion, *and is addressed internally to herself*. These words are what Phyllis is actually thinking as she looks down at the placenta in the bowl. The shift is complete, and from then on we get hers and the nurses' reactions, but mainly Phyllis's, in a second-by-second close-up record of response.

The paragraph beginning 'Each fingernail . . .' might sound just like external narrative commentary, but it happens entirely within Phyllis's thoughts. She is the one who is seeing, thinking, reaching her final judgements. The camera is now occupying her viewpoint entirely. The story returns to external narration only at the end: 'She [Jenny] nodded her head towards the bin by the sink, with the rubber lid that didn't disturb the patients . . .' This observation may be Phyllis's, the external narrator's or both. We can't be sure whether Phyllis has noticed the lid is made from rubber; but we can be absolutely sure that the narrator intends the reader to notice. Hence this final sentence feels like external narration; it strongly appears that here the narrator is speaking to us directly about the final scene with the bin. The closing shot pauses to outline the lid. We know, now, why bins have soft lids.

The story structure has moved from external narration to internal and finally back to external; and this device reinforces our sense that the story has reached a conclusion. The story is shaped partly by these switches in narrative position, and partly by the fact that the object of focus – the baby – has now disappeared.

In third-person narrative it is very important to realise that you do possess this cinema-like power of attention to a scene and its characters; you can make decisions about where you stand, what you see, what you choose not to see, or which character's vision to inhabit. You can therefore become the story's director, deciding the angles of shots, the degree of distance and close-up, and make use of pausing slow-motion effects, montage and flashback. Your readers will see what you decide to let them, and hear what you want them to hear.

First-person narrative

If you decide to use a first-person 'I – narrator', then this 'I' will be occupying the same scene as the story characters and interacting with them. 'I' will be one of the characters.

But in some cases, the 'I' may not interact, and may observe without being part of the story. In the following passage by V. S. Pritchett, 'I' shows just enough hint of attitude to characterise him, but not enough to cause him to interfere:

> In a dead place like this town you always had to wait. I was waiting for a train, now I had to wait for a haircut. . . .
>
> I picked up a newspaper. A man had murdered an old woman, a clergyman's sister was caught stealing gloves in a shop, a man who had identified the body of his wife at an inquest on a drowning fatality met her three days later on a pier. Ten miles from this town the skeletons of men

killed in a battle eight centuries ago had been dug up on the Downs. Still, I put the paper down. I looked at the two men in the room.

The shave had finished now, the barber was cutting the man's hair. It was glossy black hair and small curls of it fell on the floor. I could see the man in the mirror. He was in his thirties. . . . The lashes were long too, and the lids when he blinked were pale. There was just a suggestion of weakness.[4]

Like Scott Fitzgerald in his novel *The Great Gatsby*, Pritchett has used a narrator who is allowed to make independent judgements while maintaining a stance of distant but careful scrutiny. The external narrating camera eye has become a human 'I' witness, present but detached.

The story that follows is then told to the 'I' narrator by the hairdresser; it concerns the customer, in the above passage, who fell in love with the hairdresser's wife. The 'I' listens while the hairdresser tells him a story – an anecdote – about how the customer once tried to slit his own throat. (The swishing razor and a mark on the customer's neck feature strongly). But the whole piece has a framework which is larger than the anecdote itself, and distances us from it. The anecdote here is told by one complete stranger to another (the narrator is a newcomer to the town), which alters the sense from continuing friendly contact to one which is sharply and finally discontinued, and both these features bring the piece a degree closer to fiction.

The first-person narrative in Pritchett's story makes use of the cool, film-like techniques we associate with perspective writing. A camera eye is recording what somebody sees. The medium is visual.

CHARACTER-RHYTHM

This alternative approach can appear more attractive to writers because for one thing it doesn't so directly involve the technical business of narration change: external to internal, control over viewing position, visualisation. Though it can be visual, the approach here is more painterly, less photographic. Words move over the page like brush-strokes, and trace with their speed, slowness and adjustment the rhythm of a character's recurrent patterns of behaviour. The reader gets to know the character from inside as well as from outside, through the character's thoughts and processes of thought – which might turn into speech or stay unspoken – as well as from matters such as physical build, gesture, typical behaviour, even from their smell, and certainly from their attitude.

In this approach, if you are using first-person 'I' narration, the narrator must be a character with strong presence. Opinions, prejudices, outrageous judgements can all be expressed by a speaker in the first person, and it will be important therefore that the reader is able to recognise these characteristic attitudes and ways of speaking and that these attitudes trigger the story's events. Character-rhythm holds clear implications for what happens in a story. It is because the characters are what they are that certain events happen to them while other events do not. Instead of writing *about* characters, the writer is producing their rhythm, and their whole life will be present in that rhythm.

A character's rhythm may change, be sometimes harmonious, sometimes discordant, and can be altered by circumstances. David Lodge's novel *Nice Work* opens with one of the main characters, Victor Wilcox, in a state of anxiety about work: a familiar enough experience especially on a Monday morning in the middle of January, which is when Victor wakes up. But Lodge does not merely give us information *about* Victor and his work, he shows it as it is happening *to* Victor. Reading this passage from the first and second paragraphs of the novel, it is not easy or even appropriate to describe it as internal or external narration, nor to think of one type of narrative shifting into another. Somehow they are dubbed and become one style. The stance of the chartacter and the style of the writer have become one thing, one substance. We see Victor lying in bed, but we also feel what it is like to be him and to have his thoughts. His actions, impressions and anxieties are stylistic features of the actual writing itself – flat, enervated; then a manic, frantic bombardment of images; muddled, fumbling reactions: all consistent with Victor's and his wife's half-wakeful state at this time in the morning:

Monday, January 13th, 1986. Victor Wilcox lies awake, in the dark bedroom, waiting for his quartz alarm-clock to bleep. It is set to do this at 6.45. How long he has to wait he doesn't know. He could easily find out by groping for the clock, lifting it to his line of vision, and pressing the button that illuminates the digital display. But he would rather not know. Supposing it is only six o'clock? Or even five? It could be five. Whatever it is, he won't be able to get to sleep again. This has become a regular occurrence lately; lying awake in the dark, waiting for the alarm to bleep, worrying.

Worries streak towards him like enemy spaceships in one of Gary's video-games. He flinches, dodges, zaps them with instant solutions, but the assault is endless: the Avco account, the Rawlinson account, the price of pig-iron, the value of the pound, the competition from Foundrax, the incompetence of his Marketing Director, the persistent breakdowns of the core blowers, the vandalising of the toilets in the fettling shop, the pressure from his divisional boss, last month's accounts, the quarterly forecast, the annual review. . . .

In an effort to escape this bombardment, perhaps even to doze awhile, he twists on to his side, burrows into the warm plump body of his wife, and throws an arm around her waist. Startled, but still asleep, drugged with Vallium, Marjorie swivels to face him. Their noses and foreheads bump against each other; there is a sudden flurry of limbs, an absurd pantomime struggle. Marjorie puts up her fists like a pugilist, groans and pushes him away. An object slides off the bed and falls to the floor with a thump. Vic knows what it is: a book entitled *Enjoy Your Menopause*.[5]

This passage can teach us so much about good writing that it's hard to know where to start. It is liberal first of all with close-up details – that list of worries in paragraph two – but it shows how they hit, how they act and what is their effect; the term 'effective' means exactly that: there are results, consequences. And these effects are present within the style's mechanical urgency. If we ask: How do we know what we know about this character? The answer is through the style and arrangements of words, in full, their rhythm. We also know it through the harsh references to finance accounts, pig-iron, the paraphernalia of items as they land plop on a desk and won't go away.

The whole rhythm of existence for Vic is determined by work and work's rhythms. And we know equally important things about Marjorie's rhythms too; she engages in a somnambulist battle with Vic which is not actually aggressive, and we recognise the topic of her book. So if we ask another question: What is it about these characters that interests this writer? What is he trying to get at? The answer is – to discover their rhythm, their style, their angle towards the world, themselves, and each other. Speech and dialogue happen as one more feature of character-rhythm. By changing their circumstances, their rhythms may change too, but not immediately. We might define fiction's style and purpose as an instrument for recording such changes, the equivalent in text of a seismic graph. At this point in *Nice Work* the fluctuations are small, but attention to detail and style will be there just as much when a large event is occurring. In one of the stories printed in the Appendix to this chapter, 'The Stone Boy', there is no way the character could have reacted other than he did; it was his rhythm; it was the rhythm of the days and of his living: he could not simply switch into the one required of him by other people.

In the passage below from the beginning of V. S. Pritchett's story 'Handsome is as Handsome Does', the writer again is trying to find the rhythms of the characters:

In the morning the Corams used to leave the Pension which was like a white box with a terra-cotta lid among the vines on the hill above the town, and walk through the dust and lavish shade to the beach. They were a couple in their forties.

He had never been out of England before but she had spent half her youth in foreign countries. She used to wear shabby saffron beach pyjamas with a navy blue top which the sun had faded. She was a short, thin woman, ugly yet attractive. Her hair was going grey, her face was clay-coloured, her nose was big and long and she had long yellowish eyes. In this beach suit she looked rat-like, with that peculiar busyness, inquisitiveness, intelligence and even charm of rats. People always came and spoke to her and were amused by her conversation. They were startled by her ugly face and her shabbiness but they liked her lazy voice, her quick mind, her graceful good manners, the look of experience and good sense in her eyes.

He was a year older. On the hottest days, when she lay bare-backed and drunk with sunlight, dozing or reading a book, he sat awkwardly beside her in a thick tweed jacket and a white hat pulled over his eyes. He was a thickset, ugly man; they were an ugly pair. Surly, blunt-speaking, big-boned, with stiff short fair hair that seemed to be struggling and alight in the sun, he sat frowning and glaring almost wistfully and tediously from his round blue eyes. He had big hands like a labourer's. When people came to speak to her, he first of all edged away. His instinct was to avoid all people. He wanted to sit there silently with her, alone. But if the people persisted then he was rude to them, rude, uncouth and quarrelsome. Then she had to smooth away his rudeness and distract attention from it.[6]

If we look at the description of these two characters, our attention is drawn to physique, attitude, dress, way of speaking – separate features that together make up this man and this woman. Through expressions such as 'thickset, surly, blunt-speaking, stiff, short, struggling, frowning, glaring, big hands, edged away, instinct to avoid, sitting silently, quarrelsome', the writer is finding words for the slow-moving, clumsy, irritable temperament that forms in all its combined aspects this man and his life. His thick fingers matter as much as his thoughts, and very often inexperienced writers do not realise how powerful and important a character's size, appearance and build are. The oddly combined, awkward rhythms of the man and the woman together will determine the direction of the story. At the end, will she still be smoothing away his rudeness? Will she have abandoned him? Which story-events will enable the writer to discover what binds her to him, or what might break the tie?

In suggesting these ideas about rhythm I suspect that I am only saying what most of us already know; characters in fiction are rhythm-like because living people are like this too. But fictional characters only exist in words. Finding a character means finding a style that fits their rhythm. The words that hit the page come with the same pace and spirit as the character who enters into being through the words – fast and sharp, or slow, warm, pleasing, cool and relaxed, sensual, ironic or irritable: character exists as style, and style as rhythm. One perhaps shows contrasting rhythms within the one personality: a dark stroke can destroy an established balance, as in Stevenson's story of Jekyll and Hyde.

With living people, we can sense that some are frenetic, fast-moving, over-active, driven, while others are slow, patient, deliberate, reticent; some are accident-prone, ironic, forgetful, others smooth as machines. Some resemble New York taxi drivers, others live their whole lives in a trance. Many have particular physical characteristics which accord with their pace of living and attitude to others. To be able to sense character in this way, without judgement, can only be an advantage for fiction writing, indeed for all forms of writing where the aim is to explore human behaviour and deepen our knowledge of it, and by the same process explore language. From the way he writes we can sense Pritchett trying to explore and imagine the rhythms of the two people he portrays, just as John Berger in Chapter 2 reviews the obscure rhythm of his mother's life; and he does it so well that we sense her whole life is there, in his portrait, even while we know little in the way of facts.

But a character is not a specimen in a bottle labelled ugly, handsome, large-boned or phlegmatic. The medieval theory of personality – that we are each mixtures of four humours – or even those of astrology – that Aries people like to get all the attention, for example – are of little use to a writer unless the characters are set free into worlds of *action*. The question is not: Who are they? What are their characteristics? It is rather, what will these character-istics make them do, make them say? Fiction's research into character depends on style *and* action. Its aim is to find the style that drives action.

In D. H. Lawrence's novel *Sons and Lovers*, the appearance of the young woman Miriam Leivers in the story produces a style of writing which is in harmony with her character: long, exploratory paragraphs, a heaviness of attitude conveyed to us by the slow tempo and pace of Lawrence's sentences. The writing associated with the eldest son, William, in the Morel family, is by contrast, fevered, impetuous, factual and sharp. We can sense that this rhythm not only fits William's character, but suggests that Lawrence wanted to speed through the episode of William's short life and death in order to get to the centre of the novel which does not concern William Morel but the younger son, Paul.

Rhythm and story structure are interdependent: one creates the other. Characters must interact with each other and the world; this or that style of action is how we know them. The writer arranges things so that they act. The writer has in mind some situation, some set of conditions, which will serve to produce the maximum revelation. If, in Melville's novel *Moby Dick*, the enraged, obsessive Captain Ahab is placed in command of a ship, there is no way he will *not* eventually encounter the white whale.

QUESTIONS AND SUMMARY

It may be then, that if fiction narratives originate in character-rhythm, then this one feature will be a clue to several problems which frequently confront writers:

Where should I start? Do I need a plot? A plot occurs when rhythms clash and the clash creates consequences. A character encounters circumstances which threaten their rhythm of living: a loss, a meeting, a sudden break of routine. Such events are called trigger events. To surround a character with chaos and change and then have them plod on stolidly as before, impervious to everything, would make an interesting story because it forces the reader to anticipate change in the character. Will the expected change actually happen? Can this character really just carry on as before? Readers look for trigger events and writers must supply them; in short stories the need is felt at once, and many stories start during, just before or after such trigger events.

Shall I write in first-person or third-person narrative? Character can be explored from the inside using both these types of narrative. (Note the use of the third-person in *Nice Work*.) But the first-person emphasises how characters form words consciously for themselves, their choice of words, slang registers, consciously expressed attitudes. But speech qualities can be significant in both types of narrative, as follows:

> You would think 'en suite' was the most beautiful phrase in the language, the lengths Marjorie went to introduce it into her conversation. If they made a perfume called 'En Suite' she would wear it.[7]

Third-person narrative can refer to speech as well as include it in dialogue. But first-person narrative shares the same aim and direction as speech throughout – the character is speaking direct to the reader.

What about external narrative, camera angle, perspective? You may begin with a range of objective statements about a person, as Pritchett does, and as Lodge is doing in the short extract above, but that process must lead as quickly as possible *into* the character. Even if you include a short life history, it can be positioned within the consciousness of one of the characters, or within a specific place-and-time setting, as when Vic Wilcox looks in his bathroom mirror:

> Wilcox: Victor Eugene. Date of birth: 19 Oct. 1940 . . . 1966–70, Senior Engineer, Vanguard Engineering . . . [The list goes on] 1978–80, Manufacturing Director, Rumcol Castings; 1980–85, Managing Director, Rumcol Castings. Present position: Managing Director, J. Pringle and Sons Casting and General Engineering.
>
> That's who I am.
>
> Vic grimaces at his own reflection, as if to say: come off it, no identity crisis, please. Somebody has to earn a living in this family.[8]

'As if to say: come off it . . .' The paragraph of facts sees Victor through a wide perspective, but in what follows we hear his voice and style, his rhythm.

What about point of view? By this phrase we mean viewing position rather than statements of opinion. In short stories particularly, one character's point of view will dominate, and we call this character the *protagonist*. We see through their eyes, get to know their speech, attitude, physique; in other words it is their rhythm which claims our attention the most; they are there, in the scene, and we hear from them and about them the most often; their judgements too will in the end try to exert most control.

How important is the setting? Settings and environments have rhythms too, and these can be just as distinctive as rhythms of character. Outdoor settings – weather, climate, the seasons, times of day – all these will stir up rhythms latent within character. The moods of the sea become the moods of the writer herself in Sylvia Plath's 'Ocean 1212W' (see p. 61).

In the following passage from 'Art Work', a story by A. S. Byatt, the rhythm belongs to a children's television programme:

> In the front room, chanting to itself, for no one is watching it, the television is full on in mid-morning. Not loudly, there are rules about noise. The noise it is making is the wilfully up-beat cheery squitter of female presenters of children's TV, accented with regular, repetitive amazement, mixed in with the grunts and cackles and high-pitched squeaks of a flock of furry puppets, a cross-eyed magenta haystack with a snout, a kingfisher blue gerbil with a whirling tail, a torpid emerald green coiled serpent with a pillar-box red dangling tongue and moveable fringed eyelids. At regular intervals, between bouts of presenter-squitter and puppet snorts and squawks, comes, analogous to the spin-cycle, the musical outbursts, a drumroll, a squeak on a woodwind, a percussion battery, a ta-ta-ta TA, for punctuation, for roseate full-frame with lime-coloured logo T-NE-TV.[9]

This description resembles that of the couple in V. S. Pritchett's story in one very important respect: it searches for rhythms; it discovers them and embodies them in its own verbal assault and battery of sounds. *The words* have it: style and rhythm are identical. The rhythm of this house is just as important to A. S. Byatt as the characters who live there. Indeed, we can only begin to understand the characters by listening to the tempo of the setting: its familiar noises, silences, routines. This extract also exposes the television programme's story-like, automatic-washing-machine-cycle structure: a musical crescendo ending – banal, of course, but it makes us wonder if the story itself will be dealing in similar effects. Will it too eventually reach spin-cycle?

What about time-management in fiction? Hemingway's 'A Very Short Story' covers a time period of two years, while Thurber's 'The Unicorn in the Garden' (see Appendix below) happens in the space of a few hours. On the page, both stories are of more or less the same length. Both describe a significant episode in the life of two characters, and the time covered simply depends on the length of that episode (two hours or two years). But texts can be any length regardless of the time period. Short stories however must focus on that time of maximum significance, that centre of maximum revelation. Novels can generally allow a preamble; short stories generally cannot.

What is the relationship between crisis and closure? One character, or a group, is forced to re-view their behaviour. A villain is removed; a hero rewarded. Lovers reunite. These are not crises but closures, and yet will rely on crisis for their development. In crises, outcomes are invisible, the future blurred, focus is fixed upon action (the present) totally. She might desert him; he might be arrested; the wolf might blow the house down. Closure ultimately converts that 'might' into 'has' or 'has not'. If you want to close a story, crisis must happen first. But you can decide to extend crisis and refuse to take the final step into closure.

GENERAL COMMENTS

Finding the characters

An exceptionally shy character finds herself in front of a class of rowdy thuggish teenagers. A retired policeman has his clothes stolen at a swimming pool. A shop assistant in a stationers is confronted by a mad tramp carrying a dog; the tramp refuses to leave until the assistant has sent a Christmas card to Saddam Hussein. During a school outing, a boy dives into a lake, pulls up a waterlily and presents it to a girl in front of her friends. A terrorist bomb detonates in a supermarket. A young boy witnesses a pig being slaughtered on his uncle's farm. All these story ideas include characters. But which characters? Do we start from nothing and invent them?

When researching a character, see if you can find someone in the street, on a bus, in a bar, or someone known to you, who acts like you imagine your character to be: what do they wear, what particular aspects of their behaviour, manner, speech, facial expressions, can you observe? Not all policemen are the same, and stereotypes will be less interesting than particular individuals, so try to find a particular person whose dress, behaviour, appearance, suits your story. There must be some of your colleagues who look like New York taxi drivers, or even like Libyan terrorists. Study them carefully, but remember they are not fixed by yours or anyone's judgement. When they act, your view of them might change. Get inside their skin as well as their thoughts. You will need to choose the protagonist. Is it the woman teacher or one of her students?

Motif

A simple motif can strengthen a story. A motif becomes visible to us when we can abstract the dominant element from a story. Such elements might be loss/recovery; gift/acceptance (or rejection); challenge; encounter; pursuit/capture (or escape). The story about the waterlily has an obvious *gift* motif, the story about the teacher a *challenge* motif.

Writing about emotions

To present an attitude forcefully, envelope it with action, show it rather than name it.

Experienced writers apply this rule for good reasons. Emotional attitudes need to be illustrated by action because, however powerful, emotional response is of itself uncertain, shifting and strongly influenced by circumstances. It cannot be easily recognised and named, especially by a character experiencing it. *Sons and Lovers* offers a good starting point once again. In the passage that follows the mother and father, Gertrude and Walter Morel, confront each other in the family's tiny kitchen:

> The kitchen was full of the scent of boiled herbs and hops. On the hob a large black saucepan steamed slowly. Mrs Morel took a panchion, a great bowl of thick red earth, streamed a heap of white sugar into the bottom, and then, straining herself to the weight, was pouring in the liquor.
>
> Just then Morel came in. He had been very jolly in the Nelson, but coming home had grown irritable. He had not quite got over the feeling of irritability and pain, after having slept on the ground when he was so hot; and a bad conscience afflicted him as he neared the house. He did not know he was angry. But when the garden-gate resisted his attempts to open it, he kicked it and broke the latch. He entered just as Mrs Morel was pouring the infusion of herbs out of the saucepan. Swaying slightly, he lurched against the table. The boiling liquor pitched, Mrs Morel started back.
>
> 'Good gracious,' she cried, 'coming home in his drunkenness!'
>
> 'Comin' home in his what?' he snarled, his hat over his eye.[10]

Because we see them in action and in the circumstances, we can sense here how the different rhythms of husband and wife clash.

A feature to avoid is the use of body states to describe an emotion. When an emotion becomes extreme, as in anger, terror, ecstasy, revulsion, inexperienced writers often decide that the most accurate way to present these is by referring to the character's inner organic body-state reactions: the pounding heartbeat, racing pulse, tears, sweat, the pit of the stomach, the sudden spinal chill. Nobody says, while being pursued by monsters, burglars, the police, an enraged parent or lover: 'My pulse was racing and I could hear my heart thumping in my chest as tears streaked down my face.' Although these features might seem rhythm-like, they will not help you to find the unique rhythm of the character's experience. Since rhythm is a function of style, as we have seen, stock cliché phrases for emotional response are not going to reveal it but obscure it. At that level one person's reaction to fear is much like another; the personal rhythm which makes a character real to us is hard to find using stock cliché-response style.

Emotion stays concealed from the mind until some chance combination of events happens to release it, and the writer's job is to focus on that unique random-seeming mixture of circumstances in the external world. How does the character react? Is the character normally anxious, easily upset, or careful, steady and meticulous? Why has he or she reacted now and not beforehand? How are the circumstances different? Emotional experience will depend on these differences. Somebody says or does something which calls forth some hidden emotional energy. Again we can see that describing that energy in the abstract will always be less effective than showing it in the circumstances.

If, for example, the narrator had introduced Phyllis to us in 'No Legal Existence' by telling us that she was a trainee nurse on her first assignment in the terminations ward and was not sure what she would find there, the impact of the story would have been lost. To say, 'Phyllis felt anxious because it was her first job; little did she know what a terrible shock it would be' would be to name her emotion with only a vague reference to circumstances, and circumstances need close-up, specific and detailed settings. Notice how in 'No Legal Existence' the writer repeatedly refers to objects suggesting waste products: the bin, bed-pan, urine-testing cupboard.

So far in this chapter we have been exploring certain devices at work in short stories, but this still leaves the most basic question open. How do writers decide what to write about? How do ideas for stories originate? You will be able to experiment with techniques: close-up and long distance shots, modes of narration, conveying an emotion without naming it, but only if you have a story idea. Here again, a knowledge of the available techniques will be useful. You will need to focus on a sudden change of state, a character or a group of characters, and a setting.

Finding a setting

Finding a setting will enable you to make certain important decisions about your story as a whole. You will need to be able to watch your characters carefully, at certain points to look through their eyes at the scene before them, to see what emotional colouring it produces in those characters and how it affects their rhythm. You will benefit from thinking of yourself as standing in a room with them, and when choosing a subject the setting could be one useful clue.

Is it a public space (a police station, a cafe, a classroom), or a private space (a kitchen, a hotel room, a car)? Is it a setting you know in detail – a workplace, a house, a place you have visited on holiday? Your story may of course alternate between these, so that the characters' behaviour changes depending on whether they are seen in private or in public. V. S. Pritchett has set a number of his stories at the hairdressers, an obvious spot for allowing one character to tell a story. Angela Carter has explored the folk-tale setting in several of her stories, as in 'The Werewolf' (Chapter 1, p.24). Joyce made use of Dublin, his home town, for a group of stories exploring a setting and a period. Settings and their implications trigger events, and rather than hoping that one will say it all, you might try exploring the potential of one setting in more than one story.

A useful exercise, especially if you are working in a group, is to make a list of objects which members of your group then try linking together into a story, but another method is to do this with settings. (See also *Story-writing exercises* below.) One group chooses three or four settings; the rest have then to produce a story which links them into a narrative, for example, *a boarding house, Alaska, the steps of the British Museum*, in any combination. Each setting has atmosphere, possibilities, and the idea here is to be as inventive as possible, both with the list and with the linking narrative. The need to be inventive in this way can help to provoke a sense that stories often make reference to wider environs than the confined one of a single limited setting, that characters can come from widely different settings or backgrounds and meet in a new setting.

But a single setting can still offer a highly potent stimulus. A confined space can allow the writer to tell us something we otherwise would not know about a setting, to make use of his or her personal knowledge, and provide both a stable background where routine events occur, and an opportunity for disrupting those settled routines. It also favours the sharpness of close-up focus. It provides a range of external circumstances which help to develop rhythm and trigger emotion.

The search for a setting can itself trigger a story: two people are walking along a street looking for a hotel room for the night (or the afternoon); or one character is seen in one place, two or more in another and at the end they manage to join forces; or the setting itself is in transit (a car, a railway carriage, an aircraft) and aimed at a destination (another setting).

Fantasy

In a short story by Woody Allen, 'The Kugelmass Episode',[11] the protagonist enters a type of time-machine which enables him to escape from his dull life into love-affairs with characters from fiction (he chooses the romantic Madame Bovary from Flaubert's novel who is herself inclined to escape from a dull life to have affairs with fiction-like characters). A similar effect is explored by Martin Amis in his story 'Let Me Count the Times',[12] where erotic fantasy is enough in itself to supply the role of a time-machine-type device. In the story 'The Beast in The Jungle' by Henry James, and the novel *Remains of the Day* by Kazuo Ishiguro, fantasy is unrealised, and the ordinary world continues undisturbed, though the characters hardly find this outcome to their liking. The point is that fantasy situations and ordinary reality are often shown as being in opposition.

Monsieur Grand in Albert Camus's novel *The Plague* is an amateur unpublished writer attempting a piece of fiction which begins: 'One fine morning in the month of May an elegant young horse woman might have been seen riding a handsome sorrel mare along the flowery avenues of the Bois de Boulogne.'[13] Its author, however, is unable to get beyond the first sentence, and is continually refining his literary prose style by making minor and trivial vocabulary adjustments. His whole aim is that the publisher who receives and reads the manuscript will stand up and say to his staff: 'Gentlemen, hats off!' Not only does this episode warn us against the idea that stories need to make picturesque, literary and elegant impressions, it also reassures us that first sentences never need to stand alone, supporting the weight of an entire story and its ultimate reception. By the end of *The Plague*, Monsieur Grand has still failed to write his novel, or even to progress beyond that first sentence. We sense he is happy with the scene as it still is, in its picturesque, elegant and undisrupted state.

His composing it in the middle of a plague-ridden city might also make us wonder about the writer's responsibility to the real and shared conditions under which other people are trying to make sense of their lives. The understood term for this responsibility is *realism*, but stories do not have to reproduce, in a slavish, uninventive way, the confining facts of the everyday and the obvious. Woody Allen's approach in his short story about Madame Bovary is to invent a bizarre *idea* which forces the otherwise dull facts into fresh and increasingly volatile combinations. The obvious plot (a married man becomes involved in an exciting and glamorous liaison, has to tell lies to his wife, increasingly finds the adventure irksome and regrets it) undergoes a self-mocking comic revival. The story contains a good deal of naturalistic detail, even while proposing an odd, inventive and clearly fictitious situation. So naturalistic details can and often do occur in stories that explore unusual worlds. Such details make them seem convincing; we engage with those worlds as if they were real and habitable.

In fantasy fiction of this sort, the rhythm can often depend on a playful, inventive let's-see-what-happens-if type of style. Character becomes stereotyped for the purpose. It would be fruitless to expose someone as dull and realistically complex as Mr Coram to a time-machine with Madame Bovary in it. But this type of fiction is just as able to research attitudes to class, sex and environment as is the kind which makes a bond with ordinary reality. Many students enjoy the chance to break away from reality. In a recent example by one of my students, a US President speaks to a Martian about Earth as Utopia; in another a woman 'wins' a customer in a supermarket trolley dash. Such fantasy can allow events which realism would resist, but to begin with the settings are often quite ordinary and recognisable.

Delay and suspense

The usual occasion for suspense is the crime story, but stories can fit that pattern without being classed as such. We might even describe 'No Legal Existence' as a crime story. First of all, Phyllis suspects a body, is proved wrong, then finds a real body. As a result she, along with the others, rather crudely imagines a crime, then a culprit (Miss Hayward), only to find that the actual deceased has no legal existence, hence the whole case is dropped. Suspense therefore has some place in the story. We know Phyllis is going to discover *something*, and her doing so is only a matter of time. Her wrong assessment will have to be followed by a right one sooner or later.

There is hardly room for delay in this story, but where there is, delay can focus attention by manipulating details which excite, but do not fulfil, our expectations. While reading the following passage, from James Herbert's novel *Lair*, we already know from the blurb, the Prologue, the paperback cover picture, and because this novel is a sequel, that the story depicts enormous voracious rats with a taste for blood. In a matter of time the rats will attack people, but when, how? In the Prologue there is also some suggestion of a deformed and hideous white rat, so we read on in expectation of its appearance:

> Woollard's weathered face was creased into deep trenches of anger as he turned the corner of an outbuilding, when suddenly he caught sight of a small white object lying in the mud. At first he thought it might be just a bird-feather, but the tinges of red along one edge aroused his curiosity. He squinted as he approached, deciding it wasn't a feather at all but a tiny, obviously dead animal. He was used to finding dead mice around the place, for the cats *usually* did their job well enough. This time, though, there was something odd about the furry corpse.
>
> Stooping to examine the body more closely, he suddenly drew in a sharp breath. He reached for the object he now knew was not a dead mouse. Blood had matted the fur at one end and two of the claws were missing. He dropped the cat's paw in disgust.[14]

Eight sentences pass and still no rat; several times we hear what the object is *not*. Only by the ninth sentence do we hear what it is – a cat slaughtered by 'something'. Delay works towards expectations already strongly implanted. At the point of reading, our expectations make us guess, and guess wrong. The writing actually prevents the knowledge we desire, and then supplies something else. So we read on, hoping that maybe the next episode will supply what we anticipated.

As a device, delay cannot operate unless readers are given some goal, some target of expectation. If they are not, the withholding of facts will instead lead to obscurity. Delay will prevent readers from reaching the goal too quickly, but they must know beforehand what it is. Suspense writing operates by telling us what to expect, and finally supplying what we expect, but in ways we couldn't have imagined. The whole of *Lair* keeps us in suspense about the white rat. We know the end of the novel before we begin, but the pleasure is in getting there, in having the horrible details spilled out. The whole effect – since we are almost told the story beforehand – is eventually to offer us what we know, but in the precise, flavourful details, so that in the final stages of suspense we don't have to guess, just relish and enjoy.

Delay occurs as a local and temporary effect: it involves careful sentence-level structuring and the planting of unspecific suggestive details, but suspense covers the whole range of a story. Both operate by driving the reader towards certain expectations and suspending their fulfilment, but the expectations must be planted first. In delay, we do not meet with the desired outcome, while with suspense we do, eventually: we know James Bond will always succeed; it is the *how* that matters, and this is suspense.

A more obvious but related type of suspense occurs when there is no actual delaying tactic but a momentary shock-effect. A door creaks, a window suddenly flies open, a potential victim is face to face with a maniac. What will happen? One event leads directly to another. But even here readers will need some target of expectation: the house is possessed; the vicar, we suspect, is a natural-born killer. Either we meet the monster and so can imagine the devastation about to happen, or we see the effects of the devastation without meeting the monster. In both cases something is withheld from us, but something we anticipate nevertheless.

Some writers, especially beginners, believe that in order to keep a reader interested the obvious facts should be left for the reader to guess; that obscurity will serve to focus desire. If I write an opening paragraph in which people are dressed in black and appear to be grieving, without actually mentioning that this is a funeral, the omission has no point. Why omit what is obvious anyway? If I then later inform the reader that the gathering was taking place on a film-set and these were actors, then the reader might think that there was a real point being made about film representation. But the reader would, quite rightly, be expecting *some* point, and not just a muddled attempt at suspense where no desire or feeling of suspense is present. Suspense needs to be felt *at the time*, not in retrospect. Thus, in the 'it was all a dream' ending, readers can feel misled and resent the change of target expectations; nor will they explode with joy when the dull truth is finally revealed.

Delay however is a valued device, and not only useful in thriller writing. In the following passage from Kate Chopin's 'The Story Of An Hour' (written in 1894) the main character, Louise, has just received the news of her husband's death. She retreats to her room and sits by an upstairs window; we expect to hear her trying to come to terms with her sudden loss:

She could see in the open square before her house the tops of trees that were all aquiver with the new spring life. The delicious breath of rain was in the air. In the street below a peddler was crying his wares. The notes of a distant song which someone was singing reached her faintly, and countless sparrows were twittering in the eaves.

There were patches of blue sky showing here and there through the clouds that had met and piled each above the other in the West facing her window.[15]

The reader anticipates grief, only to be told about a view, and a surprisingly inappropriate one at that; we know what Louise is seeing, but not what she thinks or how she responds to these signs of spring life, nor how these connect with her bereavement. Does she sense her exclusion from the life outside the window, or an involvement with it? We are uncertain. The writer deliberately withholds the desired knowledge. Delay, in this story, raises questions about feeling, not action, and marks a difference between this type of story and the mystery or thriller-type narrative where close speculation about the characters' feelings (especially when these are half-formed or confused) is less likely to influence our attention. Though both types generate desire for an outcome, Kate Chopin's story truly does project us towards that unforeseen point where stock reactions are broken with and radically re-viewed. The woman finds herself alone with reactions she could never have predicted; instead of grief she uncovers a sense of excitement, freedom, power.

Atmosphere and foregrounding

What is atmosphere? Our first idea might be that atmosphere is connected to place and time: the Mediterranean, medieval cathedrals, the twenties, Transylvania. The word implies a cultural reference point, as if by whispering *Odeon, Texas, Harris Tweed* or *Dracula*, we conjure it up. But a vampire figure who drove around Texas wearing Harris Tweed would confuse our expectations of atmosphere; the word implies a special kind of consistency.

On the other hand, our second opinion might be that such a combination of disparate details could be atmospheric, and we might therefore conclude that atmosphere depends upon the function of powerful images, images with a strong cultural resonance. New and bizarre images have atmosphere, as do those with a strongly traditional suggestiveness. Traditionally it requires very exact knowledge of a way of life, of types of places where such life will continue, its habits, its routines, and of how people have been influenced by these; it suggests long time periods, gradualness. Strangeness and menace are atmospheres, but these need an extended period of time to become prevalent.

Certain atmospheres are more suitable for stories to grow in than others: atmospheres of tension, disappointment, optimism, violence – *tenuous* stabilities. The violence is just below the surface; the optimism will lead to a disappointment; habit will absorb and kill whatever tries to escape from it. (James Joyce's *Dubliners* stories, for example, are studies in the way that habit and atmosphere constantly deaden the impulse towards new life.) But to continue the discussion about atmosphere, we need to consider a related device: *foregrounding*.

All stories aim to achieve impact, and in longer stories there may be several points where impact occurs. It occurs when a speech, image or event is *foregrounded* for us; it stands out and becomes significant and memorable. The writer wishes the reader to finish the story and carry away something: an image, a judgement, a face, a decisive speech. Writers need to imagine those points where the foregrounding will be memorable, and to keep such effects in mind. In the process of writing, new possibilities of foregrounding may suggest themselves. Foregrounding can serve to underline a story's basic motif. But such emphasis is not all it can do. It can just be there for itself, and have nothing to do with the story's basic structure. A story may contain several foregrounded images, or just one: a colour, an object, a few seconds of elation or disappointment, a mistake, a face in a window. Beginnings and endings are the usual places to find them. In the passage below by Carson McCullers, she begins her story 'The Ballad of the Sad Cafe' with an image:

> If you walk along the main street on an August afternoon there is nothing whatsoever to do. The largest building, in the very centre of the town, is boarded up completely and leans so far to the right that it seems bound to collapse at any minute. The house is very old. There is about it a curious, cracked look that is very puzzling until you suddenly realise that at one time, and long ago, the right side of the front porch had been painted, and part of the wall – but the painting was left unfinished and one portion of the house is darker and dingier than the other. The building looks completely deserted. Nevertheless, on the second floor there is one window which is not boarded; sometimes in the late afternoon when the heat is at its worst a hand will slowly open the shutter and a face will look down on the town. It is a face like the terrible dim faces known in dreams – sexless and white, with two grey crossed eyes which are turned inwards so sharply that they seem to be exchanging with each other one long and secret gaze of grief. The face lingers at the window for an hour or so, then the shutters are closed once more, and as likely as not there will not be another soul to be seen along the main street.[16]

This is a bleak picture, but sharp, atmospheric; the story that follows is haunted by it: a wrecked house, a single, abandoned occupant, a sense of derelict, half-finished restoration, a secret gaze of grief. It constitutes one foreground in a story in which there are many. It somehow has to be just where it is and just as it is, and as we move through the passage we sense the writer is turning up the current gently, determinedly; the power-surge is slight but definite, the image not overstated. In this passage, foregrounding serves the underlying atmosphere; it shows us what connects the house, the street and the face; it shows us what habits link them. Each detail has a carry-forward effect. Meaning here accumulates in the face: the decided point where atmosphere has reached its strongest expression, so that one detail counts for everything else. The rhythm is established. In this face the potential for change, for love, for contact, for a story, is dissipating, falling apart, and yet the potential was there, and in 'The Ballad of the Sad Cafe' the story that follows is about the attempt (the failed attempt) to establish a new atmosphere, new rhythms and rituals of behaviour.

McCullers succeeds in finding a dominant image which fixes at once the unbroken continuous atmosphere of this place. She discovers the human features of that atmosphere. If we decide to try to catch the atmosphere of a town or a community, it could be important to think about the kinds of people or faces uniquely coloured by its meaning or equally those whose rhythms work in opposition to it, and to make those faces the characters.

Dialogue

Character-rhythm always moves along a central line that leads to dialogue but may not reach it until circumstances make speech necessary. Dialogue occurs as one of the signs of characters interacting, so that if a short story begins, as it might, with dialogue and the interaction is stressful, then to show conflict, the writer will be relying on dialogue alone. But if, as is more likely, the opening dialogue illustrates a routine situation rather than a conflictual one – a goodbye not intended to be forever – that dialogue will still have to be significant. It must establish a style, mood or attitude.

Character-rhythm needs to hold the possibility of speech; some characters find speech easy, others not. To some it will be naturally part of their rhythm; to others it only happens when rhythm is jarred.

In her novel *To the Lighthouse*, Virginia Woolf uses several pages to explain and illustrate the conflict set up by the opening piece of dialogue. In the novel's first scene, the Ramsay family are discussing the possibility of a journey by boat to the lighthouse:

> 'Yes, of course, if it's fine tomorrow,' said Mrs Ramsay. 'But you'll have to be up with the lark,' she added.
>
> To her son, these words conveyed an extraordinary joy. . . .
>
> 'But,' said his father, stopping in front of the drawing-room window, 'it won't be fine.'[17]

In between the words 'joy' and 'But', Woolf includes a whole page of reaction and analysis of character-rhythm, and after the father's reply another page before Mrs Ramsay says:

> 'But it may be fine – I expect it will be fine.'

Barely seconds have passed, yet another page follows: three pages to excavate one hardly devastating (on the face of it) exchange (they do not reach the destined lighthouse until page 236). So in shorter fiction, dialogue has to make itself felt without the help of elaborate in-between commentary.

In a short story, dialogue cannot be wasted; it is crucial especially for conflict, but the tension therefore needs to build up *before* it can be felt through dialogue. Dialogue reserved for crisis points is usually more hard-hitting, for then the characters are likely to say something irrevocable. The excerpt from *Sons and Lovers*, where action precedes the exchange, is more like the dialogue technique of short story writing than that seen in *To the Lighthouse* above. In *Sons and Lovers* the writer has already established the character-rhythms; he then sees and expresses how they clash.

In the conversation below, the writer restricts himself to only one means – telephone dialogue – for discovering the characters. Their rhythms *speak*, and as we read we can know the characters just as though we were hearing them described:

'Why haven't you called me? I've been worried to –'

'Mother, darling, don't yell at me. I can hear you beautifully,' said the girl. 'I called you twice last night. Once just after –'

'I *told* your father you'd probably call last night. But, no, he had to – Are you alright Muriel? Tell me the truth.'

'I'm fine. Stop asking me that, please.'

'When did you get there?'

'I don't know. Wednesday morning, early.'

'Who drove?'

'He did,' said the girl. 'And don't get excited. He drove very nicely. I was amazed.'

'*He* drove? Muriel, you gave me your word of –'

'Mother,' the girl interrupted. 'I just told you. He drove *very* nicely. Under fifty the whole way, as a matter of fact.'

'Did he try any of that funny business with the trees?'

'I *said* he drove very nicely, Mother. Now, please. I asked him to stay close to the white line, and all, and he knew what I meant, and he did. He was even trying not to look at the trees – you could tell. Did Daddy get the car fixed, incidentally?'

'Not yet. They want four hundred dollars just to –'

'Mother, Seymour *told* Daddy that he'd pay for it. There's no reason for –'

'Well, we'll see. How did he behave – the car and all?'

'Alright,' said the girl.

'Did he keep calling you that awful –'

'No. He has something new now.'

'What?'

'Oh, what's the *diff*erence, Mother?'

'Muriel I want to *know*. Your father . . . talked to Dr. Sivenski.'

'Oh?' said the girl.

'He told him *every*thing. . . . The trees. That business with the window. Those horrible things he said to Granny about her plans for passing away. What he did with all those lovely pictures from Bermuda – *every*thing.'

'Well?' said the girl.[18]

Just what was it with those trees? The telephone conversation also builds up suspense. The mother and daughter both know what their conversation is about, and we are forced to construct what we can from that alone. But the target here is precise: the worrying behaviour of Seymour. We are given the scattered jigsaw pieces of a narrative which possibly won't be complete until the end of the story: 'everything' must wait.

Action sequences

The use of third-person present-tense narrative can have an effect similar to that of horse-racing commentaries on television or radio and is therefore useful for action writing. Even the slower pace of *Nice Work*, which uses this type of narrative, can move quickly into video-game sequences. In the passage below from Margaret Atwood's novel, *Bodily Harm*, two women are escaping from a scene of street-fighting during a political coup on a Carribbean island:

> 'I can't see,' says Rennie. Her sandals are muddy, the bottom of her skirt is dripping; she's more disgusted than frightened. Window-breaking, juvenile deliquency, that's all it is, this tiny riot.
> 'Come on,' says Lora. She gropes for Rennie's arm, pulls her along. 'They'll be up here in a minute. . . . We'll take the path.'
> Rennie stumbles after her. She's disoriented, she has no idea where they are, even the stars are different here. It's slow going without a moon. Branches heavy with damp flowers brush against her, the smells are still alien. She pushes through the leaves, slipping on the wet earth of the path. Below them is the road. Through the undergrowth she can see moving lights now, flashlights, torches, and hurrying figures.[19]

A racing commentary, but with the horse now and then as narrator, so that we get flash-glimpses of the world through Rennie's eyes as she runs: 'the stars are different here . . .' or, 'that's all it is, this tiny riot'. Brief efforts of self-reassurance, rushed seconds of reflection. Before it finally closes and resolves, rhythm here is pushed towards its limit. At its extreme this is automatic spin-cycle: the novel is going to end. However confused, self-questioning and listless her tempo of living might have been before this episode occurred, here it is forced into high-speed flash reaction. But no clichés are used; no pulse-rate. The focus is all external: wet earth, damp flowers, moving lights.

STORY-WRITING EXERCISES

Some, not all, of the exercises below are devised for group sessions. Not everyone will have the chance to work in groups, and many who have may prefer to write on their own. My aim with these exercises is to provide the individual writer who wants to go forward with a means of developing certain practical skills, and to build confidence by suggesting ways in which writers can work together. The kind of understanding derived from practice is worth far more than any amount of analysis and afterthought, but it will still be important to think, discuss and reflect on what happens in the writing, contribute ideas, make up new rules, sort out what makes a story.

Group stories

The group divides into smaller groups who work together; each small group is given the first sentence of a story:

1 The door opened. Miss Baker entered the classroom backwards dragging a . . .
2 He waited till she had gone out. Then . . .
3 Outside the petrol station, two men in leather jackets stood glaring at each other, both were . . .
4 She kept on glancing up at the . . .

Once your group has completed the first sentence, pass it on to the next group who adds another, and so on until the conclusion.

Each finished story must contain (in any order):

- a short speech (a word or phrase will do) or short piece of dialogue;
- details about one (or more) of the characters;
- details about the setting;
- a very unusual object;
- a surprising event;
- finally, a concluding sentence.

Apart from its amusing results, one point of this exercise is to find out what impact is produced by sudden switches of attention from character to setting to dialogue.

Settings, objects, first and last sentences

Each group chooses an object and a setting and passes this information to the next group, who then outline a story which centrally involves them both, e.g. the Tate Gallery/a glider; an oil rig/a violin; a tattoo parlour/a copy of *Wuthering Heights*.

Alternatively, you might allow yourself one word or phrase, naming a setting or object which is the title of a story. What is the story you would construct around it?

Try writing the first and last sentence of a story. Everyone then writes a story of about 500 words which joins these two sentences.

Story and anecdote

Each person in the group relates an anecdote (something which happened to them recently, however trivial). The group then discusses how this could be framed in a short story.

Possible suggestions might be:

1 Is the anecdote a routine? Are there ways of breaking the routine?
2 The group decides to retell the anecdote from another starting point, as flashback for example, or by using third-person narration, or present tense rather than past. How do these changes affect the narrative?
3 Can the anecdote be part of a longer story? Can two anecdotes be joined up? Is there a way of framing the anecdote, so that, for instance, one of the characters tells it, and another character reacts?

Character and rhythm

Writing in the first person, use slang familiar to you (Jewish-American, Geordie, Cockney). Let your main character tell the story in his or her own words. As with a poem, you need to lift that voice off the page and turn it into rhythm-like speech.

The following notes can be used as a group exercise for exploring characters in third-person narrative.

Everyone in the group is given a name: the name of their character. Each person should quickly write three things about this character and introduce him/her to the group.

Each member of the group then asks you questions about him/her, and you answer without hesitation. Such questions might be: What are his/her ambitions? What does he/she do on a Friday evening? What actions and objects do you link them with? What setting suits them particularly and makes them feel at ease? What setting would make them feel ill at ease? What words and phrases do they often use?

Now your character has a problem. Tell the group what it is. Imagine a solution and ending. Using third-person narrative, write the story remembering that the character you have invented has a rhythm. Try to let your style follow this rhythm.

Use Pritchett's opening paragraph in 'Handsome is as Handsome Does' as the basis of an experiment. See if you can invent two characters together – using the above method if you wish – whose appearance, attitude and behaviour make them incompatible. They could be partners or they could be employer and employee, doctor (or nurse) and patient, tutor and student.

Use third-person narrative (present or past), some dialogue, and quickly introduce some issue between them which is causing tension or sharp disagreement.

If you want to research these characters further, explore one of their routines: getting up; going to work; eating; expressing an opinion, writing a letter. The aim is to find their style. (See again how Victor Wilcox's routine of waking up in the morning has his style: worried, evasive, tangled up with work.)

Delay

A fire has started at night in a house on a street. Describe objectively how it begins.

Describe objectively how your main character discovers there is a fire in the house next door.

Describe he/she reaching the phone. Introduce certain irrelevant details: the television programme runs on as before, the kettle has stopped boiling in the kitchen, the washing-machine continues.

Before the fire engines arrive, describe the street, the houses, the people and faces gathered outside, but *not* under any circumstances the fire.

Is the small fire becoming an inferno? Is anyone inside? By not answering them, make the reader ask these questions.

The first page of a thriller

During a race-meeting at a famous stadium one of the trainers produces a heavy automatic pistol without warning and shoots himself. The story is told by his friend who was standing nearby when the incident happened.

Write this incident as the first page of a story, making it no more than one page (350 words) in length. Add names, place-names, delay, action, view-point, details of behaviour, reactions of the crowd, and so on.

After you have written it, you can check your version against the opening of *Nerve* by Dick Francis (see Appendix, p.135).

Attitude

A character has broken her or his arm and is waiting with a group of friends or family for the ambulance to go to casualty.

Using third-person narrative write the story showing the character's *attitude*. Choose one of the following attitudes (if you wish, pick one blind out of a hat). Make use of objects, action, dialogue, but do not use the word on the card. The idea is that the rest of the group (your readers) have to guess which attitude you are portraying. It might be one of the following: bored; terrified; optimistic; embarrassed; politically correct; accusing; childish; self-satisfied; miserable, etc.

Here is an example. See if you can name the attitude:

'So. No ambulance? So, we wait for the ambulance.'

He moved his fingers. Agony. 'No sweat,' he said.

They all gaped. He bared the length of his arm: The Terminator; flexed the separate fingers with machine precision: a cyborg.

They gaped at the U-bend of flesh in his lower arm. He felt for the kitchen knife in the side-board drawer, and prepared to expose the skeleton underneath . . .

'Stop it. John!' his mother shouted. 'Nothing ever seems to upset you, does it? You just don't care about anything!'

She sat down to cry.

He slung on his leather jacket with one arm loose, and with the other hand flicked open his shades and placed them over his eyes.

His fingers still flexed, disconnected from pain.

'Gimme five,' he said. 'Oh!'

Writing about an emotion without naming it

Choose a word for an emotion, e.g. anger, joy, fear. Writing in the third person, try to convey the emotion without naming it. Use dialogue, confrontation, monologue, setting, style, but instead of referring to internal body states, show what is visible to an observer. Write a short piece of narrative which shows rather than names or tells the emotion.

A STORY IN THREE SENTENCES

The above exercise is a useful way of engaging quickly with a situation, a character, an outcome. It may be that if you attempt this you will find yourself involved in a writing process with an obvious story-like drive to it, especially if you then experiment with some of the techniques described above.

Another way of making a start is to read two or three stories carefully, and then to write each story in your own words *but in three sentences only*.

The next step is to write your own story in three sentences, giving it characters, a trigger-event and its consequences. I have already suggested some one-sentence story outlines at the beginning of the section above – 'Finding the characters' (p.116) – and the next step will be to expand such a one-sentence idea into three sentences:

A young boy watches a pig being slaughtered on his uncle's farm. He looks through the barn door and sees the pig's eye staring at him while the two men are trying to capture it. Afterwards, for a trick, they ask him to close his eyes and open his hand for a present: it is the pig's eye.

Another example might be:

A woman leaves her baby for a few moments outside a shop. She returns from inside to find that the baby and pushchair have been taken. She searches, calls the police, and goes home only to discover her sister, who is slightly mentally handicapped, cuddling the baby and playing with him.

You may already have an idea based on a character and a setting you know and which interests you. Try out a number of three-sentence stories and decide which one appeals to you. As shown in Chapter 2, 'Autobiographical writing', one method of helping you to make your decision is to write some notes after each three-sentence story to investigate the possibilities of each. It may also be helpful to think about each story as a *motif*. Does it have one? The first of the above stories could be described as having a gift motif; the second, loss/restoration. Remember that although you have now written something, you have still not committed yourself to the ending you have planned. In the actual writing you could make several changes. But at this point you should commit yourself to making a start on the story you have chosen.

Before beginning to write the full story, you may benefit from reading out your three sentences to the group or by trying them out on a reader or your tutor. In this way you will be able to make sure that you have established a trigger-event and its consequences and moved the narrative forward towards a conclusion. It is probably best to write out your first full draft while you are alone, and work at it independently.

The three-sentence version was not produced for a reader, but your full draft will be. Look again at your three sentences. The *sequence of events* is in front of you, but the *narration* could begin at any point in that sequence, with a telephone conversation after the events have happened, or minutes before the initial event occurs, or hours or days before. You may wish to give us a panoramic shot of your characters' life histories, or begin with one of the other narrator-positions. You will need to decide whose viewpoint is going to dominate, and whether you want to include any minor characters not mentioned in your three-sentence version. You may decide to focus on the setting *before* your characters appear there. Again, try out some of these possibilities and see which of them appeals to you. You might also consider while you are writing where the foreground points are likely to appear, and what main impression of setting, character and atmosphere you intend your readers to gather from the story, and, most important, what you want your readers to enjoy: is it delay, suspense, dialogue, impact, the appearance, attitude or behaviour of certain characters?

Think about your characters and study them carefully. You are allowed to know more about them than you actually reveal to the reader, and as you research them you could try to find out what they might say to each other in a letter or postcard, or imagine a newspaper report of an incident which involved them if that is appropriate for your story. If you get stuck with the narrative, one of these letters could actually be sent. But you have to be careful here, since what people say in letters might not be what they are able to say in the circumstances of the narrative, and these circumstances will be important for triggering emotional response.

Your three-sentence version will have served you well even if you decide not to keep the original ending. As your story develops its own momentum another ending altogether might suggest itself; the initial outline could change and even be discarded. Your working imagination may find other endings, other points of foreground from those you planned, and may push beyond your initial three-sentence framework. It will certainly produce fresher and more sharply focused details than you were able to think of when planning your three-sentence version. Because there are more discoveries to be made, allow yourself to make them.

At this point you are letting the story itself take control. One of the most satisfying experiences in writing is when the writer and the story itself seem to be sharing in the act of composition; the narrative finds a momentum of its own – it makes demands of the writer, and both demands collaborate in the production of an ending.

WRITING WITHOUT A PLAN

Some writers will feel more confident with a plan to work on. Others may decide that it suits them better to work without an initial plan in mind. A character, or characters, a setting, a piece of dialogue, an image of a room or some other space with one or two characters, or an initially empty space – these may be enough. Someone will arrive; something will happen; the writer works by discovery. Only at the moment of writing is it possible to be sure what will occur, and the writing process itself produces a gradually evolving image of the story's shape.

This state of openness, provided the writer is also able to work with readers in mind and has a feel for the structure of stories, character-rhythm and narration, can release insight and dramatic force. It also places writer and reader in almost the same position: one of highly active, concentrated attention and curiosity. It also places both in the same position as the characters, who feel the impact of surroundings and events with the same degree of response as writer and reader. Did the writer of 'The Stone Boy' (see the appendix below) know beforehand how her characters would react to the event or did she start the event, and then explore?

Some writers insist on reminding us that the whole idea of real characters with real impulses and feelings, who inhabit a world similar in recognisable ways to the comprehending reader's is suspect. Such writers question the realist project fundamentally, and invent (with a conscious show of invention) alternative worlds, characters, settings, happenings. What drives this type of fiction writing is freedom of invention; the impulse behind it has the same kind of inventiveness as fantasy.

In the passage below from Angela Carter's novel *The Passion of New Eve*, the reader's pleasure is lured by an erotically charged stylistic extravaganza, an orgy of the inventive both verbal and imaginary. The sensuality of language is enlarged beyond the usual aim of representing with humble accuracy a world of ordinary perception:

> A wasted inner-city moon to which pollution lent a mauvish tinge leaked a few weak beams upon my prey as she swayed on shoes so high they took her a little way out of this world; they transformed her into a strange bird-like creature, plumed with furs, not a flying thing, not a running thing, nor creeping thing, not flesh nor fowl, some in-between thing, hovering high above the ground which was, all the same, its reluctant habitat.
>
> I could hear her wordless song above the intermittent roar of the traffic, although she sang so very softly; yet her voice was so high it seemed to operate at a different frequency from the sounds of the everyday world and it penetrated my brain like a fine wire. She wandered down the vile street, picking her way among the refuse with the rapt delight of a shepherdess in a pastoral straying among flowers in a meadow. I caught the sharp reek of musk from the furs that swung about her shoulders with a vivid life of their own, as if they were accompanying her, not as if she possessed them.
>
> Her recklessness, to saunter, singing so, so brilliantly decorated, up and down the desperate streets, appalled and enchanted me; it was infectious. I caught it. Under the dying moon, she led me on an invisible string through back streets where winos and junkies lay among rubble and excrement. Her vague song, now loud, now soft, her lascivious totter that sometimes broke into a stumbling dance for a few seconds, the hot, animal perfume she exuded – all these were the palpable manifestations of seduction.[20]

The figure we see is like the style of Angela Carter's prose, which 'saunters brilliantly', which transforms with 'a different frequency the sounds of the everyday world', but does not quite make a convincing transformation. We can't quite be sure about dismissing this creature from the recognisable and allowing her to inhabit only the strange. She falls between the two. Is she an object of admiration and desire ('brilliantly decorated'), or of pity ('her lascivious totter')? Is she artificial or animal? Stylish or clumsy and out of place? Is the narrator enchanted or appalled? Carter mixes elements which we usually experience as opposites.

This is a novel, but its style effects are just as available to a writer of short stories. Does this recklessly sauntering prose know where it is going? Does it have an immediate or far-sighted plan? Could it be that it has not, and that its attraction lies in *not* knowing where it will go next? The nature of its seduction is its unpredictability for readers, possibly too for the writer.

This passage from Angela Carter keeps us guessing about the character it presents. But suppose for the writer too there is no plan, only a shadowy character to contend with? Imagine the following scene: one evening you have dozed off in front of the fire and wake to find a person sitting in the armchair opposite. If you call the police they do not arrive. If you phone your friends the lines are engaged. There is no way of blocking this encounter or bringing it to a tidy and quick end. What follows will be the story of the whole episode.

You begin to write the story without knowing whether this person will turn out to be threatening, worth welcoming, manipulative, in need, honest, devious, shy, joyful or wise, or even someone you did know once, maybe a long time ago. You simply do not know, any more than the 'you' waking up knows. How will their rhythm become visible? What will they do? You really are entering the unknown, without a map. The sense of urgency (what happens next?) may actually help you to write. As you begin, try to accept the first thoughts that come to you.

APPENDIX: MORE SHORT STORIES

From 'Nerve', by Dick Francis

Art Matthews shot himself, loudly and messily, in the centre of the parade ring at Dunstable races.

I was standing only six feet away from him, but he did it so quickly that had it been only six inches I would not have had time to stop him.

He had walked out of the changing-room ahead of me, his narrow shoulders hunched inside the khaki jerkin he had put on over his racing colours, and his head down on his chest as if he were deep in thought. I noticed him stumble slightly down the two steps from the weighing-room to the path; and when someone spoke to him on the short walk to the parade ring, he gave absolutely no sign of having heard. But it was just another walk from the weighing-room to the parade ring, just another race like a hundred others. There was nothing to suggest that when he had stood talking for two or three minutes with the owner and trainer of the horse he was due to ride, he would take off his jerkin, produce from under it as he dropped it to the ground a large automatic pistol, place the barrel against his temple and squeeze the trigger.

Unhesitating. No pause for a final weighing-up. No goodbyes. The casualness of his movement was as shocking as its effect.

He hadn't even shut his eyes, and they were still open as he fell forwards to the ground, his face hitting the grass with an audible thud and his helmet rolling off. The bullet had passed straight through his skull, and the exit wound lay open to the sky, a tangled, bloody mess of skin and hair and brain, with splinters of bone sticking out.

The crack of the gunshot echoed round the paddock, amplified by the high back wall of the stands. Heads turned searchingly and the busy buzz and hum of conversation from the the deep railside racegoers grew hushed and finally silent as they took in the appalling, unbelievable, indisputable fact that what remained of Art Matthews lay face downwards on the bright green turf.[21]

From 'The Unicorn in the Garden' by James Thurber

Once upon a sunny morning a man who sat in a breakfast nook looked up from his scrambled eggs to see a white unicorn with a gold horn quietly cropping the roses in the garden. The man went up to the bedroom where his wife was still asleep and woke her. 'There's a unicorn in the garden,' he said. 'Eating roses.' She opened one unfriendly eye and looked at him. 'The unicorn is a mythical beast,' she said, and turned her back on him. The man walked slowly downstairs and out into the garden. The unicorn was still there; he was now browsing among the tulips. 'Here, unicorn,' said the man, and he pulled up a lily and gave it to him. The unicorn ate it gravely. With a high heart, because there was a unicorn in his garden, the man went upstairs and roused his wife again. 'The unicorn,' he said, 'ate a lily.' His wife sat up in bed and looked at him, coldly. 'You are a booby,' she said, 'and I am going to have you put in the booby-hatch.' The man, who had never liked the words 'booby' and 'booby-hatch', and who liked them even less on a shining morning when there was a unicorn in the garden, thought for a moment. 'We'll see about that,' he said. He walked over to the door. 'He has a golden horn in the middle of his forehead,' he told her. Then he went back to the garden to watch the unicorn; but the unicorn had gone away. The man sat down among the roses and went to sleep.

As soon as the husband had gone out of the house, the wife got up and dressed as fast as she could. She was very excited and there was a gloat in her eye. She telephoned the police and she telephoned a psychiatrist; she told them to hurry to her house and bring a straitjacket. When the police and the psychiatrist arrived they sat down in chairs and looked at her, with great interest. 'My husband,' she said, 'saw a unicorn this morning.' The police looked at the psychiatrist and the psychiatrist looked at the police. 'He told me it ate a lily,' she said. The psychiatrist looked at the police and the police looked at the psychiatrist. 'He told me it had a golden horn in the middle of its forehead,' she said. At a solemn signal from the psychiatrist, the police leaped from their chairs and seized the wife. They had a hard time subduing her, for she put up a terrific struggle, but they finally subdued her. Just as they got her into the straitjacket, the husband came back into the house.

'Did you tell your wife you saw a unicorn?' asked the police. 'Of course not,' said the husband. 'The unicorn is a mythical beast.' 'That's all I wanted to know,' said the psychiatrist. 'Take her away. I'm sorry, sir, but your wife is as crazy as a jay bird.' So they took her away, cursing and screaming, and shut her up in an institution. The husband lived happily ever after.[22]

From 'The Aran Islands' by J. M. Synge

When I was going out this morning to walk round the island with Michael, the boy who is teaching me Irish, I met an old man making his way down to the cottage. He was dressed in miserable black clothes which seemed to have come from the mainland, and was so bent with rheumatism that, at a little distance, he looked more like a spider than a human being.

Michael told me it was Pat Dirane, the storyteller old Mourteen had spoken of on the other island. I wished to turn back, as he appeared to be on his way to visit me, but Michael would not hear of it.

'He will be sitting by the fire when we come in,' he said, 'let you not be afraid, there will be time enough to be talking to him by and by.'

He was right. As I came down into the kitchen some hours later old Pat was still in the chimney-corner, blinking with the turf smoke.

He spoke English with remarkable aptness and fluency, due, I believe, to the months he spent in the English provinces working at the harvest when he was a young man.

After a few formal compliments he told me how he had been crippled by an attack of the 'old hin' (i.e. the influenza), and had been complaining ever since in addition to his rheumatism.

While the old woman was cooking my dinner he asked me if I liked stories, and offered to tell one in English, though he added, it would be much better if I could follow the Gaelic. Then he began:-

There were two farmers in County Clare. One had a son, and the other, a fine rich man, had a daughter.

The young man was wishing to marry the girl, and his father told him to try and get her if he thought well, though a power of gold would be wanting to get the like of her.

'I will try,' said the young man.

He put all his gold into a bag. Then he went over to the other farm, and threw in the gold in front of him.

'Is that all gold?' said the father of the girl.

'All gold,' said O'Conor (the young man's name was O'Conor).

'It will not weigh down my daughter,' said the father.

'We'll see that,' said O'Conor.

Then they put them in the scales, the daughter in one side and the gold in the other. The girl went down against the ground, so O'Conor took his bag and went out on the road.

As he was going along he came to where there was a little man, and he standing with his back against the wall.

'Where are you going with the bag?' said the little man.

'Going home,' said O'Conor.

'Is it gold you might be wanting?' said the man.

'It is, surely,' said O'Conor.

'I'll give you what you are wanting,' said the man, 'and we can bargain in this way – you'll pay me back in a year the gold I give you, or you'll pay me with five pounds cut off your own flesh.'

That bargain was made between them. The man gave a bag of gold to O'Conor, and he went back with it, and was married to the young woman.

They were rich people, and he built her a grand castle on the cliffs of Clare, with a window that looked out straightly over the wild ocean.

One day when he went up with his wife to look out over the wild ocean, he saw a ship coming in on the rocks, and no sails on her at all. She was wrecked on the rocks, and it was tea that was in her, and fine silk.

O'Conor and his wife went down to look at the wreck, and when the lady O'Conor saw the silk she said she wished a dress of it.

They got the silk from the sailors, and when the Captain came up to get the money for it, O'Conor asked him to come again and take his dinner with them. They had a grand dinner, and they drank after it, and the Captain was tipsy. While they were still drinking, a letter came to O'Conor, and it was in the letter that a friend of his was dead, and that he would have to go away on a long journey. As he was getting ready the Captain came to him.

'Are you fond of your wife?' said the Captain.

'I am fond of her,' said O'Conor.

'Will you make me a bet of twenty guineas no man comes near her while you'll be away on the journey?' said the Captain.

'I will bet it,' said O'Conor; and he went away.

There was an old hag who sold small things on the road near the castle, and the lady O'Conor allowed her to sleep up in her room in a big box. The Captain went down on the road to the old hag.

'For how much will you let me sleep one night in your box?' said the Captain.

'For no money at all would I do such a thing,' said the hag.

'For ten guineas?' said the Captain.

'Not for ten guineas,' said the hag.

'For twelve guineas?' said the Captain.

'Not for twelve guineas,' said the hag.

'For fifteen guineas,' said the Captain.

'For fifteen I will do it,' said the hag.

Then she took him up and hid him in the box. When night came the lady O'Conor walked up into her room, and the Captain watched her through a hole that was in the box. He saw her take off her two rings and put them on a kind of a board that was over her head like a chimney-piece, and take off her clothes, except her shift, and go up into her bed.

As soon as she was asleep the Captain came out of his box, and he had some means of making a light, for he lit the candle. He went over to the bed where she was sleeping without disturbing her at all, or doing any bad thing, and he took the two rings off the board, and blew out the light, and went down again into the box.

He paused for a moment, and a deep sigh of relief rose from the men and women who had crowded in while the story was going on, till the kitchen was filled with people.

As the Captain was coming out of his box the girls, who had appeared to know no English, stopped their spinning and held their breath with expectation. The old man went on –

When O'Conor came back the Captain met him, and told him that he had been a night in his wife's room, and gave him the two rings.

O'Conor gave him the twenty guineas of the bet. Then he went up into the castle, and he took his wife up to look out of the window over the wild ocean. While she was looking he pushed her from behind, and she fell down over the cliff into the sea.

An old woman was on the shore, and she saw her falling. She went down then to the surf and pulled her out all wet and in great disorder, and she took the wet clothes off of her, and put on some old rags belonging to herself.

When O'Conor had pushed his wife from the window he went away into the land.

After a while the lady O'Conor went out searching for him, and when she had gone here and there a long time in the country, she heard that he was reaping in a field with sixty men.

She came to the field and she wanted to go in, but the gate-man would not open the gate for her. Then the owner came by, and she told him her story. He brought her in, and her husband was there, reaping, but he never gave any sign of knowing her. She showed him to the owner, and he made the man come out and go with his wife.

Then the lady O'Conor took him out on the road where there were horses, and they rode away.

When they came to the place where O'Conor had met the little man, he was there on the road before them.

'Have you my gold on you?' said the man.

'I have not,' said O'Conor.

'Then you'll pay me the flesh off your body,' said the man. They went into a house, and a knife was brought, and a clean white cloth was put on the table, and O'Conor was put upon the cloth.

Then the little man was going to strike the lancet into him, when says lady O'Conor –

'Have you bargained for five pounds of flesh?'

'For five pounds of flesh,' said the man.

'Have you bargained for any drop of his blood?' said lady O'Conor.

'For no blood,' said the man.

'Cut out the flesh,' said lady O'Conor, 'but if you spill one drop of his blood I'll put that through you.' And she put a pistol to his head.

The little man went away and they saw no more of him.

When they got home to their castle they made a great supper, and they invited the Captain and the old hag, and the old woman that had pulled the lady O'Conor out of the sea.

After they had eaten well the lady O'Conor began, and she said they would all tell their stories. Then she told how she had been saved from the sea, and how she had found her husband.

Then the old woman told her story, the way she had found the lady O'Conor wet, and in great disorder, and had brought her in and put on her some old rags of her own.

The lady O'Conor asked the Captain for his story, but he said they would get no story from him. Then she took her pistol out of her pocket, and she put it on the edge of the table, and she said that any one that would not tell his story would get a bullet into him.

Then the Captain told the way he had got into the box, and come over to her bed without touching her at all, and had taken away the rings.

Then the Lady O'Conor took the pistol and shot the hag through the body, and they threw her over the cliff into the sea.

That is my story.

It gave me a strange feeling of wonder to hear this illiterate native of a wet rock in the Atlantic telling a story that is so full of European associations.

The incident of the faithful wife takes us beyond Cymbeline to the sunshine on the Arno, and the gay company who went out from Florence to tell narratives of love. It takes us again to the low vineyards of Wurzburg on the Main, where the same tale was told in the middle ages, of the 'Two Merchants and the Faithful Wife of Ruprecht von Wurzburg.'

The other portion, dealing with the pound of flesh, has a still wider distribution, reaching from Persia and Egypt to the Gesta Romanorum, and the Pecorone of Ser Giovanni, a Florentine notary.

The present union of the two tales has already been found among the Gaels, and there is a somewhat similar version in Campbell's Popular Tales of the Western Highlands.[23]

'The Stone Boy' by Gina Berriault

Arnold drew his overalls and raveling gray sweater over his naked body. In the other narrow bed his brother Eugene went on sleeping, undisturbed by the alarm clock's rusty ring. Arnold, watching his brother sleeping, felt a peculiar dismay — he was nine, six years younger than Eugie, and in their waking hours it was he who was subordinate. To dispel emphatically his uneasy advantage over his sleeping brother, he threw himself on the hump of Eugie's body.

'Get up! Get up!' he cried.

Arnold felt his brother twist away and saw the blankets lifted in a great wing, and, all in an instant, he was lying on his back under the covers with only his face showing, like a baby, and Eugie was sprawled on top of him.

'Whassa matter with you?' asked Eugie in sleepy anger, his face hanging close.

'Get up,' Arnold repeated. 'You said you'd pick peas with me.'

Stupidly, Eugie gazed around the room as if to see if morning had come into it yet. Arnold began to laugh derisively, making soft, snorting noises, and was thrown off the bed. He got up from the floor and went down the stairs, the laughter continuing, like hiccups, against his will. But when he opened the staircase door and entered the parlor, he hunched up his shoulders and was quiet because his parents slept in the bedroom downstairs.

Arnold lifted his .22-caliber rifle from the rack on the kitchen wall. It was an old lever-action Winchester that his father had given him because nobody else used it any more. On their way down to the garden he and Eugie would go by the lake, and if there were any ducks on it he'd take a shot at them. Standing on the stool before the cupboard, he searched on the top shelf in the confusion of medicines and ointments for man and beast and found a small yellow box of .22 cartridges. Then he sat down on the stool and began to load his gun.

It was cold in the kitchen so early, but later in the day when his mother canned the peas, the heat from the wood stove would be almost unbearable. Yesterday she had finished preserving the huckleberries that the family had picked along the mountain, and before that she had canned all the cherries his father had brought from the warehouse in Corinth. Sometimes, on these summer days, Arnold would deliberately come out from the shade where he was playing and make himself as uncomfortable as his mother was in the kitchen by standing in the sun until the sweat ran down his body.

Eugie came clomping down the stairs and into the kitchen, his head drooping with sleepiness. From his perch on the stool Arnold watched Eugie slip on his green knit cap. Eugie didn't really need a cap; he hadn't had a haircut in a long time and his brown curls grew thick and matted, close around his ears and down his neck, tapering there to a small whorl. Eugie passed his left hand through his hair before he set his cap down with his right. The very way he slipped his cap on was an announcement of his status – almost everything he did was a reminder that he was eldest – first he then Nora, then Arnold – and called attention to how tall he was (almost as tall as his father), how long his legs were, how small he was in the hips, and what a neat dip above his buttocks his thick-soled logger's boots gave him. Arnold never tired of watching Eugie offer silent praise unto himself. He wondered, as he sat enthralled, if when he got to be Eugie's age he would still be undersized and his hair still straight.

Eugie eyed the gun. 'Don't you know this ain't duck season?' he asked gruffly, as if he were the sheriff.

'No, I don't know,' Arnold said with a snigger.

Eugie picked up the tin washtub for the peas, unbolted the door with his free hand and kicked it open. Then, lifting the tub to his head, he went clomping down the back steps. Arnold followed, closing the door behind him.

The sky was faintly gray, almost white. The mountains behind the farm made the sun climb a long way to show itself. Several miles to the south, where the range opened up, hung an orange mist, but the valley in which the farm lay was still cold and colorless.

Eugie opened the gate to the yard and the boys passed between the barn and the row of chicken houses, their feet stirring up the carpet of brown feathers dropped by the molting chickens. They paused before going down the slope to the lake. A fluky morning wind ran among the shocks of wheat that covered the slope. It sent a shimmer northward across the lake, gently moving the rushes that formed an island in the center. Killdeer, their white markings flashing, skimmed the water, crying their shrill, sweet cry. And there at the south end of the lake were four wild ducks, swimming out from the willows into open water.

Arnold followed Eugie down the slope, stealing, as his brother did, from one shock of wheat to another. Eugie paused before climbing through the wire fence that divided the wheatfield from the marshy pasture around the lake. They were screened from the ducks by the willows along the lake's edge.

'If you hit your duck, you want me to go in after it?' Eugie said.

'If you want,' Arnold said.

Eugie lowered his eyelids, leaving slits of mocking blue. 'You'd drown 'fore you got to it, them legs of yours are so puny,' he said.

He shoved the tub under the fence and, pressing down the center wire, climbed through into the pasture.

Arnold pressed down the bottom wire, thrust a leg through and leaned forward to bring the other leg after. His rifle caught on the wire and he jerked at it. The air was rocked by the sound of the shot. Feeling foolish, he lifted his face, baring it to an expected shower of derision from his brother. But Eugie did not turn around. Instead, from his crouching position, he fell to his knees and then pitched forward onto his face. The ducks rose up crying from the lake, cleared the mountain background and beat away northward across the pale sky.

Arnold squatted beside his brother. Eugie seemed to be climbing the earth, as if the earth ran up and down, and when he found he couldn't scale it he lay still.

'Eugie?'

Then Arnold saw it, under the tendril of hair at the nape of the neck – a slow rising of bright blood. It had an obnoxious movement, like that of a parasite.

'Hey, Eugie,' he said again. He was feeling the same discomfort he had felt when he had watched Eugie sleeping; his brother didn't know that he was lying face down in the pasture.

Again he said, 'Hey, Eugie,' an anxious nudge in his voice. But Eugie was as still as the morning about them.

Arnold set his rifle on the ground and stood up. He picked up the tub and, dragging it behind him, walked along by the willows to the garden fence and climbed through. He went down on his knees among the tangled lines. The pods were cold with the night, but his hands were strange to him, and not until some time had passed did he realize that the pods were numbing his fingers. He picked from the top of the vine first, then lifted the vine to look underneath for pods and then moved on to the next.

It was a warmth on his back, like a large hand laid firmly there, that made him raise his head. Way up the slope the gray farmhouse was struck by the sun. While his head had been bent the land had grown bright around him.

When he got up his legs were so stiff that he had to go down on his knees again to ease the pain. Then, walking sideways, he dragged the tub, half full of peas, up the slope.

The kitchen was warm now; a fire was roaring in the stove with a closed-up, rushing sound. His mother was spooning eggs from a pot of boiling water and putting them into a bowl. Her short brown hair was uncombed and fell forward across her eyes as she bent her head. Nora was lifting a frying pan full of trout from the stove, holding the handle with a dish towel. His father had just come in from bringing the cows from the north pasture to the barn, and was sitting on the stool, unbuttoning his red plaid Mackinaw.

'Did you boys fill the tub?' his mother asked.

'They ought of by now,' his father said. 'They went out of the house an hour ago. Eugie woke me up comin' downstairs. I heard you shootin' – did you get a duck?'

'No,' Arnold said. They would want to know why Eugie wasn't coming in for breakfast, he thought. 'Eugie's dead,' he told them.

They stared at him. The pitch cracked in the stove.

'You kids playin' a joke?' his father asked.

'Where's Eugene?' his mother asked scoldingly. She wanted, Arnold knew, to see his eyes, and when he had glanced at her she put the bowl and spoon down on the stove and walked past him. His father stood up and went out the door after her. Nora followed them with little skipping steps, as if afraid to be left alone.

Arnold went into the barn, down along the foddering passage past the cows waiting to be milked, and climbed into the loft. After a few minutes he heard a terrifying sound coming toward the house. His parents and Nora were returning from the willows, and sounds sharp as knives were rising from his mother's breast and carrying over the sloping fields. In a short while he heard his father go down the back steps, slam the car door and drive away.

Arnold lay still as a fugitive, listening to the cows eating close by. If his parents never called him, he thought, he would stay up in the loft forever, out of the way. In the night he would sneak down for a drink of water from the faucet over the trough and for whatever food they left for him by the barn.

The rattle of his father's car as it turned down the lane recalled him to the present. He heard voices of his Uncle Andy and Aunt Alice as they and his father went past the barn to the lake. He could feel the morning growing heavier with sun. Someone, probably Nora, had let the chickens out of their coops and they were cackling in the yard.

After a while another car turned down the road off the highway. The car drew to a stop and he heard the voices of strange men. The men also went past the barn and down to the lake. The undertakers, whom his father must have phoned from Uncle Andy's house, had arrived from Corinth. Then he heard everybody come back and heard the car turn around and leave.

'Arnold!' It was his father calling from the yard.

He climbed down the ladder and went out into the sun, picking wisps of hay from his overalls.

Corinth, nine miles away, was the county seat. Arnold sat in the front seat of the old Ford between his father, who was driving, and Uncle Andy; no one spoke. Uncle Andy was his mother's brother, and he had been fond of Eugie because Eugie had resembled him. Andy had taken Eugie hunting and had given him a knife and a lot of things, and now Andy, his eyes narrowed, sat tall and stiff beside Arnold.

Arnold's father parked the car before the courthouse. It was a two-story brick building with a lamp on each side of the bottom step. They went up the wide stone steps, Arnold and his father going first, and entered the darkly paneled hallway. The shirt-sleeved man in the sheriff's office said that the sheriff was at Carlson's Parlor examining the Curwing boy.

Andy went off to get the sheriff while Arnold and his father waited on a bench in the corridor. Arnold felt his father watching him, and he lifted his eyes with painful casualness to the announcement, on the opposite wall, of the Corinth County Annual Rodeo, and then to the clock with its loudly ducking pendulum. After he had come down from the loft his father and Uncle Andy had stood in the yard with him and asked him to tell them everything, and he had explained to them how the gun had caught on the wire. But when they had asked him why he hadn't run back to the house to tell his parents he had had no answer – all he could say was that he had gone down into the garden to pick the peas. His father had stared at him in a pale, puzzled way, and it was then that he had felt his father and the others set their cold, turbulent silence against him. Arnold shifted on the bench, his only feeling a small one of compunction imposed by his father's eyes.

At a quarter past nine Andy and the sheriff came in. They all went into the sheriff's private office, and Arnold was sent forward to sit in the chair by the sheriff's desk; his father and Andy sat down on the bench against the wall.

The sheriff lumped down into his swivel chair and swung toward Arnold. He was an old man with white hair like wheat stubble. His restless green eyes made him seem not to be in his office but to be hurrying and bobbing around somewhere else.

'What did you say your name was?' the sheriff asked.

'Arnold,' he replied; but he could not remember telling the sheriff his name before.

'Curwing?'

'Yes.'

'What were you doing with a .22, Arnold?'

'It's mine,' he said.

'Okay. What were you going to shoot?'

'Some ducks,' he replied.

'Out of season?'

He nodded.

'That's bad,' said the sheriff. 'Were you and your brother good friends?'

What did he mean – good friends? Eugie was his brother. That was different from a friend, Arnold thought. A best friend was your own age, but Eugie was almost a man. Eugie had had a way of looking at him, slyly and mockingly and yet confidentially, that had summed up how they both felt about being brothers. Arnold had wanted to be with Eugie more than with anybody else but he couldn't say they had been good friends.

'Did they ever quarrel?' the sheriff asked his father.

'Not that I know,' his father replied. 'It seemed to me that Arnold cared a lot for Eugie.'

'Did you?' the sheriff asked Arnold.

If it seemed so to his father, then it was so. Arnold nodded.

'Were you mad at him this morning?'

'No.'

'How did you happen to shoot him?'

'We was crawlin' through the fence.'

'Yes?'

'An' the gun got caught on the wire.'

'Seems the hammer must of caught,' his father put in.

'All right, that's what happened,' said the sheriff. 'But what I want you to tell me is this. Why didn't you go back to the house and tell your father right away? Why did you go and pick peas for an hour?'

Arnold gazed over his shoulder at his father, expecting his father to have an answer for this also. But his father's eyes, larger and even lighter blue than usual, were fixed upon him curiously. Arnold picked at a callus in his right palm. It seemed odd now that he had not run back to the house and wakened his father, but he could not remember why he had not. They were all waiting for him to answer.

'I come down to pick peas,' he said.

'Didn't you think,' asked the sheriff, stepping carefully from word to word, 'that it was more important for you to go tell your parents what had happened?'

'The sun was gonna come up,' Arnold said.

'What's that got to do with it?'

'It's better to pick peas while they're cool.'

The sheriff swung away from him, laid both hands flat on his desk. 'Well, all I can say is,' he said across to Arnold's father and Uncle Andy, 'he's either a moron or he's so reasonable that he's way ahead of us.' He gave a challenging snort. 'It's come to my notice that the most reasonable guys are mean ones. They don't feel nothing.'

For a moment the three men sat still. Then the sheriff lifted his hand like a man taking an oath. 'Take him home,' he said.

Andy uncrossed his legs. 'You don't want him?'

'Not now,' replied the sheriff. 'Maybe in a few years.'

Arnold's father stood up. He held his hat against his chest. 'The gun ain't his no more,' he said wanly.

Arnold went first through the hallway, hearing behind him the heels of his father and Uncle Andy striking the boards. He went down the steps ahead of them and climbed into the back seat of the car. Andy paused as he was getting into the front seat and gazed back at Arnold, and Arnold saw that his uncle's eyes had absorbed the knowingness from the sheriff's eyes. Andy and his father and the sheriff had discovered what made him go down into the garden. It was because he was cruel, the sheriff had said, and didn't care about his brother. Was that the reason? Arnold lowered his eyelids meekly against his uncle's stare.

The rest of the day he did his tasks around the farm, keeping apart from the family. At evening, when he saw his father stomp tiredly into the house, Arnold did not put down the hammer and leave the chicken coop he was repairing. He was afraid that they did not want him to eat supper with them. But in a few minutes another fear that they would go to the trouble of calling him and that he would be made conspicuous by his tardiness made him follow his father into the house. As he went through the kitchen he saw the jars of peas standing in rows on the work bench, a reproach to him.

No one spoke at supper, and his mother, who sat next to him, leaned her head in her hand all through the meal, curving her fingers over her eyes so as not to see him. They were finishing their small, silent supper when the visitors began to arrive, knocking hard on the back door. The men were coming from their farms now that it was growing dark and they could not work any more.

Old Man Matthews, gray and stocky, came first, with his two sons, Orion, the elder, and Clint, who was Eugie's age.

As the callers entered the parlor, where the family ate, Arnold sat down in a rocking chair. Even as he had been undecided before supper whether to remain outside or take his place at the table, he now thought that he should go upstairs, and yet he stayed to avoid being conspicuous by his absence. If he stayed, he thought, as he always stayed and listened when visitors came, they would see that he was only Arnold and not the person the sheriff thought he was. He sat with his arms crossed and his hands tucked into his armpits and did not lift his eyes.

The Matthews men had hardly settled down around the table, after Arnold's mother and Nora had cleared away the dishes, when another car rattled down the road and someone else rapped on the back door. This time it was Sullivan, a spare and sandy man, so nimble of gesture and expression that Arnold had never been able to catch more than a few of his meanings. Sullivan, in dusty jeans, sat down in the other rocker, shot out his skinny legs and began to talk in his fast way, recalling everything that Eugene had ever said to him. The other men interrupted to tell of occasions they remembered, and after a time Clint's young voice, hoarse like Eugene's had been, broke in to tell about the time Eugene had beat him in a wrestling match.

Out in the kitchen the voices of Orion's wife and of Mrs. Sullivan mingled with Nora's voice but not, Arnold noticed, his mother's. Then dry little Mr. Cram came, leaving large Mrs. Cram in the kitchen, and there was no chair left for Mr. Cram to sit in. No one asked Arnold to get up and he was unable to rise. He knew that the story had got around to them during the day about how he had gone and picked peas after he had shot his brother, and he knew that although they were talking only about Eugie they were thinking about him and if he got up, if he moved even his foot, they would all be alerted. Then Uncle Andy arrived and leaned his tall, lanky body against the doorjamb and there were two men standing.

Presently Arnold was aware that the talk had stopped. He knew without looking up that the men were watching him.

'Not a tear in his eye,' said Andy, and Arnold knew that it was his uncle who had gestured the men to attention.

'He don't give a hoot, is that how it goes?' asked Sullivan, trippingly.

'He's a reasonable fellow,' Andy explained. 'That's what the sheriff said. It's us who ain't reasonable. If we'd of shot our brother, we'd of come running – back to the house, cryin' like a baby. Well, we'd of been unreasonable. What would of been the use of actin' like that? If your brother is shot dead, he's shot dead. What's the use of gettin' emotional about it? The thing to do is go down to the garden and pick peas. Am I right?'

The men around the room shifted their heavy, satisfying weight of unreasonableness.

Matthews' son Orion said: 'If I'd of done what he done, pa would've hung my pelt by the side of that big coyote's in the barn.'

Arnold sat in the rocker until the last man had filed out. While his family was out in the kitchen bidding the callers good night and the cars were driving away down the dirt lane to the highway, he picked up one of the kerosene lamps and slipped quickly up the stairs. In his room he undressed by lamplight, although he and Eugie had always undressed in the dark, and not until he was lying in his bed did he blow out the flame. He felt nothing, not any grief. There was only the same immense silence and crawling inside of him; it was the way the house and fields felt under a merciless sun.

He awoke suddenly. He knew that his father was out in the yard, closing the doors of the chicken houses so that the chickens could not roam out too early and fall prey to the coyotes that came down from the mountains at daybreak. The sound that had wakened him was the step of his father as he got up from the rocker and went down the back steps. And he knew that his mother was awake in her bed.

Throwing off the covers, he rose swiftly, went down the stairs and across the dark parlor to his parents' room. He rapped on the door.

'Mother?'

From the closed room her voice rose to him, a seeking and retreating voice. 'Yes?'

'Mother?' he asked insistently. He had expected her to realize that he wanted to go down on his knees by her bed and tell her that Eugie was dead. She did not know it yet, nobody knew it, and yet she was sitting up in bed, waiting, to be told, waiting for him to confirm her dread. He had expected her to tell him to come in, to allow him to dig his head into her blankets and tell her about the terror he had felt when he had knelt beside Eugie. He had come to clasp her in his arms and, in his terror, to pommel her breasts with his head. He put his hand upon the knob.

'Go back to bed, Arnold,' she called sharply.

But he waited.

'Go back! Is night when you get afraid?'

At first he did not understand. Then, silently, he left the door and for a stricken moment stood by the rocker. Outside everything was still. The fences, the shocks of wheat seen through the window before him were so still it was as if they moved and breathed in the daytime and had fallen silent with the lateness of the hour. It was a silence that seemed to observe his father, a figure moving alone around the yard, his lantern casting a circle of light by his feet. In a few minutes his father would enter the dark house, the lantern still lighting his way.

Arnold was suddenly aware that he was naked. He had thrown off his blankets and come down the stairs to tell bis mother how he felt about Eugie, but she had refused to listen to him and his nakedness had become unpardonable. At once he went back up the stairs, fleeing from his father's lantern.

At breakfast he kept his eyelids lowered as if to deny the humiliating night. Nora, sitting at his left, did not pass the pitcher of milk to him and he did not ask for it. He would never again, he vowed, ask them for anything, and he ate his fried eggs and potatoes only because everybody ate meals – the cattle ate, and the cats; it was customary for everybody to eat.

'Nora, you gonna keep that pitcher for yourself?' his father asked.

Nora lowered her head unsurely.

'Pass it on to Arnold,' his father said.

Nora put her hands in her lap.

His father picked up the metal pitcher and set it down at Arnold's plate.

Arnold, pretending to be deaf to the discord, did not glance up but relief rained over his shoulders at the thought that his parents recognized him again. They must have lain awake after his father had come in from the yard: had they realized together why he had come down the stairs and knocked at their door?

'Bessie's missing this morning,' his father called out to his mother, who had gone into the kitchen. 'She went up the mountain last night and had her calf, most likely. Somebody's got to go up and find her 'fore the coyotes get the calf.'

That had been Eugie's job, Arnold thought. Eugie would climb the cattle trails in search of a newborn calf and come down the mountain carrying the calf across his back, with the cow running down along behind him, mooing in alarm.

Arnold ate the few more forkfuls of his breakfast, put his hands on the edge of the table and pushed back his chair. If he went for the calf he'd be away from the farm all morning. He could switch the cow down the mountain slowly, and the calf would run along at its mother's side.

When he passed through the kitchen his mother was setting a kettle of water on the stove. 'Where you going?' she asked awkwardly.

'Up to get the calf,' he replied, averting his face.

'Arnold.'

At the door he paused reluctantly, his back to her, knowing that she was seeking him out, as his father was doing, and he called upon his pride to protect him from them.

'Was you knocking at my door last night?'

He looked over his shoulder at her, his eyes narrow and dry.

'What'd you want?' she asked humbly.

'I didn't want nothing,' he said flatly.

Then he went out the door and down the back steps, his legs trembling from the fright his answer gave him.[24]

Chapter 5

Theatre

In the previous chapter I was exploring the question of what makes a story. A story happens when a routine is broken; stories move quickly towards the disruptive event. Do plays follow this pattern? I went on to talk about characters, but again, do playwrights create characters in the same way as writers of stories? At the end of the chapter I described a scene where a stranger arrives and the writer has no knowledge of what will happen. If you decided to write this scene as the opening of a play, would you be asking: What does this stranger look like? Whose eyes are we allowed to see through? Who is the narrator? At least the first problem is easily solved; the audience will see a live and visible actor. The character will be a creation of the actor and the director, as well as of the writer. In answer to the second question, the characters look at each other, and the audience looks at them both. Both characters are equal before the audience. In answer to the third question, unless there is a third member of the cast called 'The Narrator' present, there will be no narrator at all; the audience will be trying to make out the story from what they see happening on the stage. Nobody knows the story – not the characters, not the audience, because it hasn't happened yet. It is actually taking place before our eyes.

In the theatre, characters do tell stories, characters do look back and reflect on experience, but they never do this silently or secretly or even semi-consciously, as they can in fiction. The consequences of their story-telling on stage are visible and instant. Not even Hamlet, the great soliloquiser, can easily find space where no one at all is listening. With poetry and fiction, readers can have complete, privileged access to a character's secret, interior reflections without any other characters present. But in the theatre, every speech is an action involving somebody else instantly. Often, too, body movements and silences communicate in place of spoken words; a silence can be an action. An action, in the theatre, is something done to one character by another. Words are actions. One word can be an embrace, a touch, a shrug, a fist in the air. A silence too can be any of these. Action of some kind is inescapable. And again, all this is because the story is taking place, now, as we watch.

Types of play

Writers in the theatre need to know how to communicate with audiences, and writers and audiences make distinctions between types of play. Even if you are experimenting with a script and are aiming to write only a short scene or piece of action, you will be able to do this more confidently if you have some sense beforehand of the conventions and possibilities in different types of play. Such differences are not new. Most of us are familiar with terms such as farce, comedy, tragedy, mystery play. More recently we have soaps, sitcoms, comedy sketches, drama documentaries, serial dramas and adaptations; many of these use locations and film sets rather than a stage, but circus acts, music hall and puppet shows are also part of the very broad and inclusive term 'theatre'.

In shaping this chapter I have divided my comments under three main sections: 'Personal Theatre', 'Issues Theatre' and 'Experimental Theatre'. I see these as the primary colours of the form. As we shall find out almost at once, most plays are mixtures of these colours, but with writing in mind it helps if, to begin with, we can mark the distinctions clearly.

PERSONAL THEATRE

In 1984 I directed a play with a group of English and Drama undergraduate students. Firsthand experience of acting and production is not essential for writing but it undoubtedly helps, and any book on writing plays should not omit this advice. Just as reading stories and poems stimulates the development of writing, so the experience of making theatre, as well as watching plays regularly, adds to your store of practical knowledge. So I want to begin by talking about an experience of directing for the stage. The subject of Pinter's short play *Family Voices* is exactly what we might find in a play where personal theatre predominates. Even though its use of language and treatment of its subject is unusual, its centre is the space where routines of living are experienced, where characters struggle for personal expression, and define themselves by what they call 'home'. Because the play was originally written for radio, it contains no instructions about pauses, silences, or a set, and even though it was staged in London as well as produced on radio, none of us had seen the stage production. With this play, the lack of stage instructions offered a challenge, and we had to work out how to control its impact on a live audience.

Pinter's text was written for three voices. Voice One, a young man aged about twenty, has left home. He sits in his lodgings writing a letter to his mother. His mother, Voice Two, is present on stage in the place he has abandoned. His father, Voice Three, is dead. When he speaks, therefore, it is from the ultimate point of distance and separation. The other two are closer to each other, but still miles apart (she sits and waits for a letter; it never arrives), so should the stage be divided: mother in sitting-room/son in lodging house? She sits at home perched on a large settee thinking mournfully of her son, he at a desk in his room in a large city. But almost as soon as the son begins to speak the audience knows he is writing a letter; they know to whom, and they also know this isn't the kind of letter he could send. All this distance might be fine for radio. How could it work on stage?

In rehearsals we began to experiment with the space. The mother remains fixed; the son moves about. With the mother locked in her sitting-still position, the son moves out of his space and into hers and even sits down next to her. While he describes the strange routine of life in his present, she describes what life was like in their past – her son at home, her husband and son going for walks together. He strides, gesticulates, recreates in full view of the audience the strange inhabitants of the house where he now lives and acts out his encounters. She only sits, marginal and defeated.

He sits beside her. Do they look at each other? Does he make physical contact, touch her hand? He looks at her, but she only gazes away. If he touched her that would be an act requiring a response. But he doesn't need her response. He has escaped. By his behaviour the audience can see this. To sit by her side when she doesn't know where he is is cruel, calculated, but his speaking tone sounds anything but cruel. He has shed all the restrictions of her protective, parental gaze, and yet his tone sounds friendly and innocent of the break even while he describes things which have nothing at all to do with her possessive maternal interests. The audience can see he is teasing her, depositing her in the margins of his life. The routines which occupied that sitting-room have been broken. Instead he describes other routines, other rooms, other people – a gay ex-policeman called Riley; a Mrs Withers; a schoolgirl called Jane 'who does her homework'; an old man, Mr Withers; a woman 'who wears red dresses'. His text hints that the house is some sort of brothel. What is his mother thinking?

VOICE TWO: Have you made friends with anyone? A nice boy? Or a nice girl?

There are so many nice boys and nice girls about. But please don't get mixed up with the other sort. They can land you in such terrible trouble. And you'd hate it so. You're so scrupulous, so particular. . . .

Darling, I miss you. I gave birth to you. Where are you?[1]

Such desperation might seem poignant, but it is also a barely concealed attempt at repossessing him. In saying 'scrupulous . . . particular', and saying that last line, she looks at him: it is just what she wants him to be, just what she wants him to hear. Her maximum expressions move him not at all.

In the last few minutes of the play, the father arrives (Voice Three). He died, we are told, not knowing where his son was. Now he comes back. We decided he should reach the stage by walking towards it out of the auditorium.

His presence gains full control of all the available space; in other words he
steals it back from the son. The son has been winning the audience over and
entertaining them by acting out the alarming, amusing, bewildering encounters with Jane, Riley, and the landlady Mrs Withers:

> She was in the Women's Air Force in the Second World War. Don't drop
> a bollock, Charlie, she's fond of saying. Call him Flight sergeant and he'll
> be happy as a pig in shit.
>
> You'd really like her, mother.[2]

and old Mr Withers:

> VOICE ONE: Mother, mother, I've had the most unpleasant, the most
> mystifying encounter, with the man who calls himself Mr Withers. Will
> you give me your advice?
>
> Come in here, son, he called. Don't mess about. I haven't got all night.
> I went in. A jug. A basin. A bicycle.
>
> You know where you are? he said. You're in my room. It's not Euston
> Station. Get me? It's a true oasis. . . .
>
> My name's Withers. I'm here or thereabouts. Follow? Embargo on all
> duff terminology. With me?. . . You're in a disease-ridden land, boxer.
> Keep your weight on all the left feet you can lay your hands on. Keep
> dancing. The old foxtrot is the classical response. . . . Up the slaves. Get
> me? This is a place of creatures, up and down stairs. Creatures of the
> rhythmic splits, the rhythmic sideswipes, the rums and roulettes, the
> macaroni tatters, the dumplings in jam mayonnaise, a catapulting ordure
> of gross and ramshackle shenanagins, open-ended paraphernalia. . . .
> Mind how you go. Look sharp. Get my drift? Don't let it get too mouldy.
> Watch the mould. Get the feel of it, sonny. Get the density. Look at me.
>
> And I did.
>
> VOICE TWO: I am ill.
>
> VOICE ONE: It was like looking into a pit of molten lava, mother. One look
> was enough for me.[3]

Any audience must surely think this bizarre. 'Open-ended paraphernalia' for
sure. But is it open-ended? It is, but also it is anything but. The jumbled
rubbish of old Mr Withers's speech can be heard, and seen, as the old male
chauvinist advice mechanism, springing into action with any passing youth
who gets in its way. The emblem of it is: 'Look at me, *and respect me*', the
act of a substitute parent – a command the son can't take seriously at all. To
him, Mr Withers is just another old josser doing his stuff. The son's response
in telling this story is a shrug.

But male advice revives again with the father. He appears, the judge, admonitory. He sits down between mother and son on the family settee. He speaks to each of them with avenging playfulness, but his threat is serious; it has to be felt as such both by them *and* by the audience. Will the son's response be another shrug?

> VOICE THREE: I know your mother has written to you to tell you that I am dead. I am not dead. I am very far from being dead, although lots of people have wished me dead, from time immemorial, you especially. It is you who have prayed for my death, from time immemorial. I have heard your prayers. They ring in my ears. Prayers yearning for my death. But I am not dead.
>
> Well, that's not entirely true, not entirely the case. I'm lying. I'm leading you up the garden path. I'm playing about. I'm having my bit of fun, that's what. Because I am dead. As dead as a doornail. I'm writing to you from my grave. A quick word for old time's sake. Just to keep in touch. An old hullo out of the dark. A last kiss from Dad.
>
> I'll probably call it a day after this canter. Not much more to say. All a bit of a sweat. Why am I taking the trouble? Because of you, I suppose, because you were such a loving son. I'm smiling as I lie in this glassy grave.
>
> Do you know why I use the word glassy? Because I can see out of it . . .[4]

How does the son react? Respectfully this time? How does the mother? Turning directly to her, her dead husband articulates the words: 'Not much more to say. All a bit of a sweat.' It hurts her, is intended to. Facing her, he stares into her eyes.

We wanted the audience to feel his gesture as making a repulsive comment on his marriage. She submits, looks down. But with the father the son is unsubmissive. His tactic is to ignore him and talk about his new family in place of the old one: a shrug *in supremis* and unanswerable:

> VOICE ONE: They have decided on a name for me. They call me Bobo. Good morning, Bobo, they say, or See you in the morning, Bobo, or, Don't drop a goolie, Bobo, or, Don't forget the diver, Bobo, or, Keep your eye on the ball, Bobo, or, keep this side of the tramlines, Bobo, or, How's the lead in your pencil, Bobo, or, How's tricks in the sticks, Bobo, or, Don't get too much gum in your gumboots, Bobo.
>
> The only person who does not call me Bobo is the old man. He calls me nothing. I call him nothing. I don't see him. He keeps to his room. I don't go near it. He is old and will die soon.[5]

During the second part of this speech the son stares at the father, lowers his voice not his eyes. They are standing up and facing each other across the space of the stage. The comic attitude of the son's speech gives way to another in the final paragraph. The audience must be able to sense that change, and to make a connection between old Mr Withers and the father.

With this speech the son succeeds in putting his father down and humiliating him, and hence in regaining the space. Those prayers truly were immemorial; the audience must feel the change of tone and the deadly aim of the new tone of defiance.

Arranging this play for the stage had tested our inventiveness. We had to make our own decisions about movements, gestures, actions, tones of voice and use of the stage space. We had learned and developed a kind of code which we and the audience somehow understood. But it wasn't until later that I found myself reading a book which explained this code to me.

Two years after directing this play an American friend lent me a copy of *Impro*, by Keith Johnstone. Johnstone had developed his ideas while working with actors and writers at the Royal Court in the early 1960s, and afterwards at theatre schools in Britain and North America. A point he makes is that once they have learned the rules of status transaction actors can improvise without the inhibiting pressure to be original. His next point is that status transactions happen all the time in life. We recognise low and high status behaviour instinctively, but we can also train ourselves to observe it:

Low status (submissive)
Breaking eye contact then glancing back
Turning the body – hands, feet – inward
Sitting or shrinking while others stand
Keeping in one place while others move about
Moving the head and shoulders while speaking
Touching the face or mouth while speaking
Speaking quickly and in broken sentences
Introducing 'er' in mid-sentence (self-interruption)

High status (dominant)
Holding eye contact, breaking it, not glancing back
Stretching the body to fill space
Standing while others sit or shrink
Moving into unoccupied space
Detecting the centre of the space and occupying it
Keeping the head and shoulders still while speaking
Occupying space with hand gestures
Speaking slowly in coherent sentences
Introducing 'er' at the beginning of sentences (interrupting others)

When practising improvisation, the effort to manage gesture, eye contact, positioning, can feel crude and unwieldy at first, but these effects will quickly free the actors by giving them certain sure and reliable rules. If the gardener plays high status towards the duchess, the effect will be a dramatic reversal, convention overturned, and audiences enjoy it when status positions change or become uncertain. The tutor–student relationship obviously implies a fixed status position, but one that may also be flexible. Students like it if I ask them to try and change this status relationship in a formal setting such as a lecture-room. They move about, throw things, try to leave; the lecturer, like the mother in *Family Voices*, is deposited on the margins and ignored. If I try to join in their conversations then my status becomes uncertain and that makes them uneasy.

Status transactions operate in all forms of theatre, but in personal theatre, writers, directors and actors are exploring its effects in conditions where the struggle for dominance happens between characters who belong to the same closely related group. On stage, *Family Voices* became a play about occupying the space, making eye contact, breaking it, lowering the voice and using a voice-tone inappropriate to the words being said. A conciliatory tone, a loving gesture, clashes with meanings and words which are effectively mocking, unfriendly, cruel. Through this *inappropriateness*, father and son challenge each other's status, and the son teases his mother's sincere utterances by imitating them. While the mother can only speak with an appropriate tone, father and son have become what Johnstone calls 'status experts', able to play high or low in a game of pretence and imitative mockery. The play ends with the father's cryptic statement:

> VOICE THREE: I have so much to say to you, but I am quite dead. What I have to say to you will never be said.[6]

Is his tone here one of defeated withdrawal (low status)? Or the verbal equivalent of breaking eye contact – indeed all contact – deliberately (high status)? The text will not say, and its impact may depend entirely on how the actors are feeling at that precise moment, on how their status behaviour has influenced them up to that last moment of the performance.

In writing for the theatre, an important idea is to learn from every play you are involved with as actors, directors and audiences. The writer needs to imagine the text in their hands. He or she has a mixed role: writer, director, actor, stage manager and audience, all at once. He or she will need to sense how the space is used, how tones are inflected, how even minor actions express attitude, to think about the images given to the audience, what information the audience needs, and when it should be provided. This multiple responsibility can seem difficult to control, but of course ideally a real director and real actors will take the text away with them and do what they like with it. Even so, such control is rather more than just a nominal one; a scene needs to be sensed as it is written, and sensed in terms of sound, space, action and audience response. Writers wanting to retain control will often include elaborate stage directions, as Becket does in *Waiting for Godot*, or Arthur Miller and Tennessee Williams do in their play-texts. Pinter, on the other hand, often provides texts with minimal directions; this method allows powerful elements of the creative process to continue after the text has been written; the actors and director explore the text and develop it through experiment.

In personal theatre, audiences will usually expect a group of characters who have already formed closely bonded relationships. It is highly likely that these relationships will undergo a change: the bonds will be reviewed, reaffirmed or broken. Small actions of acceptance or rejection will speak powerfully. The focus is in close-up and occupies the characters' present experiences, even though we might hear from the characters about certain important events in their past. The audience may also anticipate a set with which the characters are familiar, a domestic space, a work-place, and one which the audience will themselves recognise as familiar. But the set itself may also speak powerfully by signifying a particular epoch, decade or social group. In Shelagh Delaney's play *A Taste of Honey* the district buildings outside the window, 'cemetery, tenements, slaughterhouse', sum up the play's gloomy urban background. Suburbia too has its own groups of signifiers, as audiences of Alan Ayckbourn's plays will surely have noticed. Naturalistic settings inevitably contain objects, dress, decor, types of behaviour, and these will communicate a social image, a style, and the possibility therefore of certain issues: single parenthood, divorce, poverty, affluence.

In Act One of David Mamet's play *Oleanna*, a college tutor is playing high status with one of his female students. When she confesses her problems with his course, he comes out from behind his desk and tells her he 'understands'. He moves about, occupies all of the space, acts with increasing confidence while she shrinks even further into herself. She feels humiliated by not being able to learn properly or understand the concepts in a book he has written. He sympathises, offers support, tries to break out of his high status as tutor to reach her as an equal. But is he really able to change his high status position? Having moved out of his formal role, the audience, and the student, don't know where he is or how to react. His words say one thing, his behaviour another. Is he really being friendly, an equal, or patronising? His status therefore is not low, or high, but uncertain, and this uncertainty generates the drama. In important ways drama is uncertainty.

Personal theatre can't easily be steered clear of issues: close groups don't operate in sealed units; families are exposed to social pressures; social issues develop and are visible in that intimacy; attitudes from the world outside seep in; conflict follows. *Oleanna* too is a play not just about conflict but the politics of conflict, the politics of status.

WRITING EXERCISES: ONE

Before we go on to explore the Issues theatre, here are some plans for writing that will help you to investigate status transactions.

1 Write a dialogue between two characters which contains no obvious status play. Deliberately make it as dull and ordinary as possible. If you wish, insert pauses and silences in the dialogue. It could be in a shop, on a bus, in a queue, in the park. The characters might know each other; they could be members of the same family-group, or they could be strangers: it's up to you.

   Act out the scene in your group and inject status play into it: one character plays high, the other low. Then act it again and reverse the relationship. Try to explore how quite ordinary dialogue can be played out on stage in contrasting ways.

   Write the same dialogue twice, each time with different stage directions. Look back at the list of Low and High features (p.156). Use the stage directions to make clear the alternative ways of interpreting the dialogue.

2 Choose two characters, one of whom writes a letter to the other. The letter must give clues to the audience about the relationship as it was, *and* reveal how time and distance have changed it. *But while one character refers to these changes directly, the other refuses and talks about something else.*

   Imagine them on stage in the same space. How do they use the space?

   Act out the scene, and develop it. The actors may want to make suggestions and additions too. Working together, try to develop the scene towards a crisis.

   As you write and revise the scene, think carefully about *speech as action*. Many speeches, perhaps not all, should have action equivalents; what are these? A shrug, a sneer, a possessive embrace or attempt to touch, a blow, a movement towards or away?

   In *Family Voices*, a speech of endearment can have an action that is the very opposite of what is said. 'An old hullo out of the dark' is definitely not intended to be comforting. But even then there could be alternative ways of playing the line. A warm, friendly father could make this speech sound even more menacing than one who deliberately sets out to attack.

Further exercises

The aim of these exercises is to choose a scene which deliberately involves something impossible happening. The technique is to make that thing (a complete status reversal) actually take place. The emphasis here is on inventiveness of dialogue, where one character goads, persuades, bribes or threatens another into submission. Ideas such as, 'If you don't, I'll. . . . Wouldn't it be wonderful if . . . ? Why don't you give it a try . . . ? Just who do you think you are?', are appropriate here.

1 Interview

Cast: Two interviewers: A, B.
Interviewee: C.
Secretary: D.

Director.
Script co-ordinator.

Plot: In their office, A and B gang up to intimidate C. A and B play high, C low. D enters and plays off A against B, embarrasses and intimidates them and supports C. C + D dismiss A + B, and assume their position as employers.

2 Invasion

Cast: Teacher: A.
Students in class: B, C, D, E.
Students at the door: E, F.

Director.
Script co-ordinator.

Plot: A introduces topic via a dull monologue; this is the class's first meeting this term. After three or four minutes, a knock on the door. E and F enter, 'looking for a course to join'. B and C say (loudly), 'You can have our place on this course. We don't like it. (They describe it as if it were a bad deal package holiday with no perks.) You can swap with us.' A objects, becomes violent. Complete mayhem erupts.

3 Shop assistant

Cast: Shop assistant: A.
Customer one: B.
Customer two: C.
Customer three: D.

Director.
Script co-ordinator.

Plot: B meekly arrives to buy something. A asks B to take over the shop while A goes out for a lunch-break. B naturally refuses. A then becomes dominant, manipulates or persuades or blackmails or bribes B to take over. B gives in. A leaves B with instructions. (These are complicated: the shop sells advanced stereo equipment + computers; or meat; or vegetarian + health products, etc.)

B is now in charge. C enters and asks questions which B can't answer. B is in utter confusion. D then enters with even more outrageous demands. B is completely unable to cope with these two customers and panics.

Finally A returns, pretending to be yet another difficult customer. B, previously meek, becomes violent.

4   Messenger

Cast: Boss: A.
        Worker: B.
        Messenger: C.

        Director.
        Script co-ordinator.

Plot: A sends C to B with a message: 'Your children are starving. Come and work for me, I'll pay you a good wage.' C turns this into an imperious demand: 'Work here for next to nothing or starve', and returns with an abusive message from B. Further messages are sent, each one distorted by the messenger. A sends C to B with an even more attractive message: 'You can have a share of the profits, a big house, free booze, a car.' C goes back to B with worse threats, the offer of an even lower pittance, and returns with an even more abusive message from B. What happens?

Extra characters could be B's wife, children, fellow workers.

This is a complex exercise using a divided stage space. It can make use of a realistic looking domestic set, naturalistic actions and dialogue; or it can be played in a stylised manner which approaches mime.

5   Alternative letter exercise

Cast: Writer of letter: A.
        Second speaker: B.

        Scriptwriter.
        Director.

Plot: A duologue. The letter which A composes aloud to B contains references to A and B's past relationship and longs for its renewal.

B does not hear it, and refuses to be involved. B describes all kinds of new things, people and events which A would not understand. The letter arrives. B describes an event where he shows it to some new friends who laugh and make fun of it. It becomes a sign of contempt and complete ridicule, but B only hints at this.

Will there be a reply? A grows increasingly unconvinced, even though desperate to receive one. Finally A becomes accusing and bitter.

Finally B begins to write the text of a reply – one of reconciliation – but we don't know whether to believe in it. Or whether it will be sent.

All of these exercises can be developed into a piece of theatre of short play length, or can make use of short scenes with minimal dialogue. In each case I have left out directions for a completed ending, assuming that several different endings are possible.

ISSUES THEATRE

Many plays are rich in issues rather than dominated by just one. Social realism in the theatre, because it often depicts family relationships in difficult conditions, deals with a range of hopes, disappointments, disintegrating ambitions, plans and deceptions, simply because its aim is to show an image of a group in all aspects of its living. But issues theatre makes one issue its subject, and the characters, instead of being identified in part for his or her individual qualities, are made to represent a single viewpoint or value. If you include this type of character you will be moving your text in the direction of this type of theatre even though it may contain individualised characters as well. As an example, Arthur Miller's *The Crucible* presents both the individualised character, John Proctor, victim of the Salem witch-hunts in seventeenth-century Massachusetts, and the more stereotyped character, Reverend Hale, the church's regional expert on devil-worship. Later we meet the even more stereotyped character, Judge Danforth, who assumes all accused are guilty till proved innocent.

Uniformed officials, representatives of established institutions, judges, civil servants, often perform roles which act more like functions than characters, and yet the awareness of individualised characters turns the audience's sympathy away from institutions and their lip-servers and towards the men and women they tyrannise. Certain scenes in *The Crucible* focus on John Proctor and his wife. These scene are personal theatre in an issues play. Miller has mixed these primary colours deliberately, but has done it so that the resulting shade carries very strong traces of issue.

At a further extreme in issues theatre, characters might wear masks, carry placards or even become placard-like in their speech. Status transactions occur between rival groups. Instead of a familiar domestic enclosure, the stage becomes a platform, a public space. Mime replaces private spontaneous action. Songs and chants disturb the surface of naturalistic speech. Performance is choreographed, gesture and timing predicable. Image rather than plot stands in the foreground.

One exception to this list of principles for issues theatre is Samuel Beckett's use of stylised effects in action and speech. In his plays he makes use of such devices but raises no obvious issues which the audience would see as specific.

In Peter Brook's corporate production of the Vietnam War protest play *US* (the title signifies 'Us' the audience as well as 'United States', and both are under attack), the effect of napalm bombing is symbolised by the play's last sequence. One actor removes a butterfly from a matchbox, holds it between his fingers, strikes a match and sets fire to its wings. (A paper butterfly was used, but the point was that it could have been a real living creature tortured pointlessly.) The cast then refuses to leave the stage. The audience must make its own walk-out, an action which cannot help but seem like calculated indifference. In the text of the play the actors' own names are given. (GLENDA = Glenda Jackson, etc.). Of the 'characters' below, HUGH represents the views of the Vietcong military against the US, and BOB the US military fighting the Vietcong. But the point is that both are saying the same things; both justify war in the same words. Nationalism expressed from one side is identical to nationalism from the other.

Most of the actors gather behind HUGH, marching like zombies. A few gather behind BOB, holding parts of crushed aeroplanes, taken from the garbage heap. Both HUGH and BOB have microphones. The two groups face each other.

HUGH: We want to tell the U.S. Imperialists once again that the vast ocean of several hundred million Chinese people in arms will be more than enough to submerge your few million aggressor troops. Your atom bomb cannot intimidate the Chinese people. If you want to send your troops, go ahead, the more the better. We will annihilate as many as you can send, and can even bring you receipts. We know that war brings destruction, sacrifice and suffering on the people. The sacrifice of a small number of people in revolutionary wars is repaid by security for whole nations, whole countries, and even the whole of mankind. Temporary suffering is repaid by lasting and even perpetual peace and happiness. War can temper the people and push history forward. In this sense war is a great school!

BOB: We know that war brings destruction, sacrifice and suffering on the people. The sacrifice of a small number of people in war is repaid by security for whole nations, whole countries, and even the whole of mankind. Temporary suffering is repaid by lasting and even perpetual peace and happiness.

HUGH turns to his group, BOB to his, and both conduct their respective 'choirs' in ritual songs:

BOB	HUGH
We know what we're doing	Found we were growing weaker every day
We know what we're doing it for	Always felt about to die Something was draining our blood away
We know what we're doing	Something has sucked us dry. It was the leech, it was the
We ought to know for	landlord leech,

Out of the way

Or you know what we do

Or we'll do it to you![7]

It was bulging with blood, and its
jaws were made of steel.
We tore it off
Threw it down
Crushed it under our heel.

The point of this scene is that neither side meet; neither communicate. The
issue is the gap, and the similarity. Each side mirrors the other. Peter Brook,
director of *US*, commented in the play's Preface:

US used a multitude of contradictory techniques to change direction and
to change levels. It aimed to put the incompatible side by side. But this
wasn't drama. This was in a way seduction – it used a contemporary, highly
perishable fun-language to woo and annoy the spectator into joining in the
turning-over of basically repellent themes. All was this preparation, like
all the many phases of a bull-fight which precedes the kill. We aimed not
at a kill, but at what bull-fighters call the moment of truth. The moment of
truth was also our one moment of drama, the one moment perhaps of
tragedy, the one and only confrontation. This was when the very end of all
pretences of play-acting ceased and the actor and audience together paused,
at a moment when they and Vietnam were looking one another in the face.
   I am writing this preface just after doing a production of *Oedipus*. It
seems the opposite pole from *US* and yet to me the two pieces of theatre
are strongly related. There is nothing in common in their idiom, but the
subject matter is almost identical. The struggle to avoid facing the truth.
Whatever the cost a man marshals everything at his disposal to skid away
from the simple recognition of how things are. What is this extraordinary
phenomenon at the very root of our way of existing? Is any other subject
so urgent, so vital for us to understand now, today? Is Oedipus' dilemma
something to do with the past?
   Out of the two experiences I am left with one vast unresolved query of
my own. If the theatre touches a current issue so burning and so uncomfortable as Vietnam it cannot fail to touch off powerful and immediate
reactions. This seems a good thing, because we want our theatre to be
powerful and immediate. However, when the trigger is so light, when the
ejaculation comes so soon, when the first reaction is so strong, it is not
possible to go very deep. The shutters fall fast.[8]

So the danger with an issues play is that the audience will get the point well
enough, but too quickly. The problem is one of moving the play forward so
that it triggers a deeper set of reactions in the audience – responses they could
not possibly have anticipated. The key word therefore with issues plays is to
explore the issue to its fullest. The cast, director and writer, therefore, may
have to search out and challenge not just the audience's but their own

preconceptions. Or they may have to find a more shocking image for what is unjust or intolerable.

Propaganda

Issues theatre at its most extreme becomes propaganda: we hear one side only. The Nazi rallies at Nuremburg could be counted as theatre of this type. But there are ways of presenting issues which do not see audiences as compliant, suggestible victims of the tyranny of the stage.

Treating this subject of Nazi tyranny, Brecht's issues play, *Arturo Ui*, typifies Hitler as head of a gang of mafia-like criminals in Chicago. But the audience already knows what it thinks of the issue of Hitler's tyranny, and although we certainly do need reminding about its destructive effects and violent terror, the message in its Chicago form has little immediate relevance to audiences now. In 1940, when it was first performed, the case may have been otherwise. The images of war would have clashed starkly with those in the black and white movies of the period, and Brecht's play was bringing these together in the same set.

Both images were immediate to that audience in a way they are not now. Chicago violence has now acquired a kind of fictionlike nostalgic underworld glamour. It no longer carries the same kind of immediacy as threats posed by established modern governments, hence it is difficult for Brecht's play to persuade us to accept Arturo Ui (Hitler) as a figure wielding real establishment power. Issues plays need to be continually rewritten and re-invented, otherwise they stultify the relevance of their message. To watch the overthrow of yet one more Hitler-like character or tyrant or prime minister can bore an audience, unless the source of his or her appeal is explored too. Another danger in issues plays is that action and plot become predictable and preachy, however worthy the message. If the first scene already suggests a cut-and-dried ending, what is the point of staying beyond the interval?

Brook's comments also raise this point. If first reactions are served up to audiences, the shutters will definitely fall on what happens next. In the case of *US*, if sides of a battle are going to sing separate songs, and if that is all we hear, what is the point? In *Arturo Ui*, if all we expect is the rise and fall of a tyrant, again what is the point? If first reactions are all the audience is offered, why stay? Issues theatre becomes powerful only when the audiences' reactions are changed, are forced to a deeper level of confrontation with the issues than the one they came into the theatre with. *US* began as an issues play, but developed towards experiment and research into this very problem: How do you get audiences to respond to *how things are* and to *how things should be*, while showing those things as changing, fluid, immediate, unresolved, possibly unresolvable? Will issues plays be most dramatic when they dip towards the tragic, the unresolved?

Preconceptions challenged

One of the aims of this type of theatre is to raise issues, to educate, but to educate to the point where audience preconceptions are challenged, where the issue is stripped of familiarity and made fresh. In *US*, as well as presenting scenes from the war, the actors deliver straight information about Vietnamese history. In a lighter vein though no less pointed, *Oh What A Lovely War*, a play assembled by Joan Littlewood's Theatre Workshop, contains music-hall characters, a news panel across which messages are flashed during the action, a band, admirals, generals, and business men, as well as a Master of Ceremonies who tells jokes. Some of the characters are countries: Germany, France, Britain. The point is to make the audience aware that such a complex phenomenon as a nation can be imagined as speaking with one voice. How are we supposed to react? Is one nation's voice wiser than another? In the play the answer to that is No.

The issue from both sides

Another alternative is to present an issue from both sides of a debate employing the techniques described above, but to use them so that the audience acts as judge. Such a play might well make use of private and domestic settings as well as public stage space, and conversational dialogue of personal theatre as well as group demonstration, song and mime. Issues plays mix theatre forms to suit their purpose. An issue such as 'Should Britain become a Republic?' would suit that treatment because not all the audience would have made up their minds on the issue, and those who have may not have done so conclusively; the questions are still open and unresolved. An issues play on that subject could aim to make the audience face that truth: the truth of our indecision. If the subject leaves us feeling uneasy, the play then might help us face that unease.

Caryl Churchill's play *Top Girls* constructs a forum for debating feminist issues. It begins with an imaginary dinner party attended by significant women from past literature and history. In a final scene it revives the issues but in the domestic setting of a small back kitchen of a council house in East Anglia. Historical figures are public property; they come to us with large simplified 'issues' already attached, but can still be viewed in terms of a private perspective: What were they really like? Plays such as Brecht's *Galileo* and Alan Bennett's *The Madness of George III* re-examine the characters which history has stereotyped. Churchill's play suggests the more intimate perspective in the opening scene by making these stereotyped figures speak about major subjects that traverse history, while their *manner* of speaking resembles that of normal people at dinner parties, interrupting each other, trying hard to hold on to one topic, two or three speaking at once. Her written dialogues indicate interruption using a stroke. The next speaker interrupts at the point where a stroke (/) appears:

DULL GRET arrives
ISABELLA: I tried to do what my father wanted.
MARLENE: Gret, good. Nijo. Gret. / I know Griselda's going to be late, but
   should we wait for Joan? / Let's get you a drink.
ISABELLA: Hello Gret! [*continues to Nijo*] I tried to be a clergyman's
   daughter. Needlework, music, charitable schemes. I had a tumour
   removed from my spine and spent a great deal of time on a sofa. I studied
   the metaphysical poets and hymnology. / I thought I enjoyed intellectual
   pursuits.
NIJO: Ah, you like poetry. I come of a line of eight generations of poets. /
   Father had a poem in the anthology.
ISABELLA: My father taught me Latin although I was a girl. / But
MARLENE: They didn't have Latin at my school.[9]

By interjecting themselves and their own experience, high status is still
something they play for. Have they learned this trick from those dominant
fathers they keep mentioning? Haven't they learned anything from feminism?
No, because of course they come from the past – history, literature: all except
Marlene who is our contemporary.

Private and public

In later scenes in *Top Girls*, the private perspective widens; public debates
are engaged in a private setting. However successful in business Marlene is,
her relationship with her sister in that small kitchen will never form part of
her public image. The private self is complex, baffling. When exposed, an
apparently shadowless character has shadows; there are issues she cannot
confront, losses untraced in her self-image of power. What character is and
who constructs it becomes an issue itself.

Facing the truth

Facing the truth is a major theme which joins together both types of theatre,
but in issues theatre the *audience* is the target: evidence and a charge will be
aimed at them: *Find the truth. Face it. Failing to will carry consequences.
Or: This issue must be understood; it matters*. Clearly then, issues theatre
can be a medium of great social value to its audiences.
   Personal theatre's targets suggest a more personal set of truths: *Who am
I? Where am I going? What is the price: to myself, to others?* questions which
characters ask of themselves as well as about each other. These alternatives,
as we have seen, mix in specific plays but not in all. In *Oh What A Lovely
War*, for example, the destructive effects of the First World War are
dramatised using all the conventions of issues theatre and fewer of the
personal theatre type. In Pinter's *Family Voices* by contrast, no clear issue

emerges from the text. In Miller's *Death of a Salesman*, there is a mixture. The questions Willie Loman confronts are relevant to audiences who, like him, live in cultures shaped by capitalist materialism and its key rules for success. The audience too is the target along with the character. Even so, Miller is not framing the play as a message delivered point blank at the audience. We watch the character facing painful questions in the surroundings of his family. We feel his problems are partly self-inflicted and partly his responsibility to solve.

SUMMARY AND QUESTIONS

Before we go on to explore the third area, let us summarise the main points arising from the first two:

Personal theatre

1 The setting is familiar, often domestic, the stage space contains objects, furniture, decor, clues of locality, and these give clues to social, racial background and class.
2 Characters are individuals with personal names and belong to a closely bound group, usually a family. A small cast.
3 The dialogue resembles spontaneous conversation and makes reference to private lives: their desires, their pasts, their achievements, their disappointments. It also suggests hesitations, conversation overlaps, status battles happening in close-up.
4 The problems and conflicts arising are to be solved by individuals. The truths to be faced are confronted, or evaded, by individuals. The plot moves towards those central moments of confrontation.
5 The audience absorbs information about the characters, and observes the problems, confrontations and status battles, but from a safe distance of observation. This safe distance can be broken (as Brook says about Oedipus) when a character faces the truth.
6 In most cases, writers, directors and actors all have different responsibilities which gradually link up, but the writer when constructing the text needs to be able to imagine it being performed, and particularly its impact on the audience.

Issues theatre

1 The stage space is a platform. It might for example contain a screen for video or still pictures. It presents many types of action, is versatile and accommodates a large cast. Its function is to present a performance, not to enclose it.
2 Characters are group representatives. They wear dress which signifies their

function. Uniformed officials or members of business or military organisations are typical because they are masked by their function. They don't need to be sinister. They could be clowns, dancers, music-hall entertainers, mime artists, figures from history or just members of the public.

3 As well as dialogue, the text contains songs, chants, mimes, on-stage music, or stylised speeches which present information or viewpoint. Status battles are fought between groups or their representative speakers.

4 The conflicts arising are real, not imaginary. The issue is real, not fictional. The plot, if there is one, presents events which have happened or could happen. Individuals are powerless to solve conflicts; instead they become the victims of masked forces.

5 The audience absorbs evidence about the issue, and observes the problems, confrontations and status battles, but from an unsafe distance where expected attitudes might change and familiar, obvious solutions are not available.

6 Writers, directors and actors work together to produce the script, which develops through rehearsal and co-operative experiment. A decisive factor, as above, is impact on audiences.

As I have said, these alternatives simplify a complex mixture of theatres, and plays can be made by choosing features from both. A powerful scene will never leave the audience feeling wholly safe and inviolable. Equally, no writer need be restricted to working alone, though some might prefer that. The next section addresses this very point because, to an even greater extent than in issues theatre, in experimental theatre the writer's and actor's roles begin to merge.

Before we move on to the next section, here are some questions that may arise while making an issues theatre play.

Who is our audience? If you are performing as a group to a local audience, your play might well be concerned with a local issue. You will need to assess how much the audience knows about it already and how far they have made up their minds about it. Will your audience share a consensus opinion before they arrive?

Should we present one side or both sides of an issue? If you present one side only, the shutters will fall. You might believe in one side only, but the audience won't feel challenged and respected unless you show the evidence from both. An issue can have more than two sides to it of course. But you have to keep things simple, and not let the audience get confused.

Do we want the audience to see sense and end up sharing our view? You probably do. So make the issue as real to them as you can, but make it at its most real just before they leave the theatre. Points of view and opinions carry consequences, but so does the failure to hold an opinion. This could be your message. If the audience wants to sit on the fence, make it as uncomfortable a fence as possible.

What does 'mixing the two types' mean in practical terms? If you write a scene of the personal theatre type, and introduce characters who represent an establishment – the Church, the law, the government, the council – you will be able to push your play towards an issue. Or, if you begin with issues-type characters – princess, dragon, workforce, council, student, teacher, supermarket manager, businessman, squatter, landlady – you can still make these characters speak in a naturalistic manner as they would in personal theatre: princess to dragon, for example. Or, you can introduce a variety of textures: songs, mimes, tableaux, as well as intimate personal exchanges, and mix sets: the stage as domestic set, then as platform.

EXPERIMENTAL THEATRE

Over the past half-century, experimental developments in the theatre have been rapid. The first signs, soon after the Second World War, began with a question about the writer/audience relationship. When writers such as Beckett, Ionesco, Albee, Pinter and N. F. Simpson began to experiment with dramatic language as diversion, distraction and threat, audiences were confused by what seemed a deliberate rejection of the contract all writers supposedly have with their audiences: to communicate at the level of ordinary speech about secure and normally recognised action. In drama of the Absurd, as it came to be known, ordinary speech suddenly appeared treacherously extraordinary. The 'evolving and compulsive dramatic image', as Pinter describes a play, produced characters buried up to their necks in sand; a corpse growing through the wall of a room and inflating like a balloon; a plot to end the world by teaching speaking weighing-machines to sing the Hallelujia Chorus at the North Pole and so cause ice-caps to break up with the weight of massing spectators; a mad professor who knifes his pupil while teaching her neo-Spanish.

The images evolving in absurd drama, comic, extravagant, but negative, show characters lacking motivation set upon by their blind unconscious drives or giving way to futility. By contrast, however, a parallel development in theatre workshops and co-operative theatre laboratories had begun to affirm a more positive vision of existence. Standing amidst the vision of sickening collapse was the actor's disciplined wholeness. Instead of action stemming from disruption and the breakup of routines, experimental theatre assumed a break and sought a healing reaction. The need for wholeness, both for individuals as well as communities, was being revived. Within his Paris company, Peter Brook has assembled actors from a range of racial backgrounds and cultural traditions, each with its own route to the inner world. Western traditions are not excluded, but African, Persian and Indian actors made this theatre a new experiment in multicultural art. An idea central to it is *affirmation*, as Brook has emphasised, but equal with it is a sense of primary response, *invention*: the opposite of cliché or fossilised expression.

There have been times in theatre history when the actor's work has been based on certain accepted gestures and expressions: there have been frozen systems of attitudes which we reject today. It is perhaps less obvious than the opposite pole, the Method Actor's freedom in choosing anything whatsoever from the gestures of everyday life is equally restricted, for in basing his gestures on his observations or on his own spontaneity the actor is not drawing on any deep creativity. He is reaching inside himself for an alphabet that is also fossilised, for the language of signs from life that he knows is the language not of invention but of his conditioning. His observations of behaviour are often observations of projections of himself. What he thinks to be spontaneous is filtered and monitored many times over. . . .

We experimented for instance with an actor opening a door and finding something unexpected. He had to react to the unexpected sometimes in gesture, sometimes in sound, sometimes with paint. He was encouraged to express the first gesture, cry or splash that came to him. At first all this showed was the actor's stock of similes. The open mouth of surprise, the step back in horror . . . the hair's-breadth of terror before the blankness, and then the reassuring ready-made idea coming to the rescue.[10]

Do you notice the emphasis here on 'the actor'? What has happened to 'the writer'? And yet what Brook says of actors applies to writers just as well. His experiment here is not very different from the stranger sitting in the room when you wake up. He encourages the actor to find something other than the stock cliché reactions: 'the open mouth of surprise, the step back in horror'. He believes that that 'something else' liberates inventiveness and may even develop into affirmation. What does he mean by this? We don't know, and maybe he doesn't know until it happens. But place a writer in that position and he or she will be facing the same unknown as that actor. Nobody knows the story of a response. We are watching it as it happens.

In such experiments, the once solid distinctions start to dissolve: that between actor and writer, that between audience space and stage space. Does that mean that writers have no place, or that written texts are eroded and redundant? It might seem so, but the answer depends on what is meant fundamentally by the term 'writer'. If an actor's task is to add to the store of knowledge about experience, to rediscover its roots, to re-examine theatre as encounter, drama as ritual, to find those images that release imagination, then writer and actor may indeed become one. Both face the unknown; both are responsible.

In his book *Experimental Theatre*, James Roose-Evans makes a short reference to the Kathakali dance theatre. Its ancient traditions closely resemble the way art generates meaning from plain objects:

In the Kathakali Tradition an actor will take a bench, and, by his varying use of it, appeal to our imagination to complete the picture. If he crouches behind the bench, rising up slowly, and finally steps onto it, he has climbed the Himalayas; if he lies down to sleep on it, then it has become his bed; if he sits in lotus position before it, it is his altar: if he turns it upside down and sits in it, he is paddling his canoe down the rapids; if he upends it and climbs it, it has become the tallest tree in the forest. Always it is a bench, but he pretends, and we pretend, that it is a mountain range, a bed, an altar, a canoe, a tree.[11]

Reading this passage, it seems to me that an actor performing these simple movements qualifies as a symbol of the writer's imagination at work. It may be that experimental theatre of this simple kind can teach us how to focus imagination and make it defamiliarise what we see. It can teach writers how to transform objects into meanings, how to see objects not just in functional terms. The texts that result, whether they are theatre or poems or fiction or commentary, whether read in private or performed, will induce that kind of attention which art attracts. But what is the point of writing if a non-verbal performance such as that above can do so much without needing to use words? At this point we might have to say that imagination communicates its power through a range of means, and that verbal language is simply one of those. Theatre passes beyond it to find others, but what is found can stimulate writing in forms other than theatre. One imaginative form produces another: dance can stimulate music, music words; photographs and paintings inspire poems. Alertness to other forms has that advantage; it teaches that the imagination is one.

And yet, we could ask: does experimental theatre now only aim towards that wholeness where the actor discovers new rituals, affirms centres of strength, heals what is broken? What is to be done with those destructive elements in experience? Don't those need investigating more than ever? We only have to listen to an average day's news to be almost sure that the coming week will produce stories and images of mutilation by bombs, of plundered cities with people driven out of their homes or shot down in the streets, and though most of us don't understand the thinking behind such acts, we receive it as part of reality: this is what the world is; how long before the tide reaches us here and sweeps away everything familiar, everything that seems safe? As we have seen, theatre has responded to such negative images before, and the healing affirmations described above are themselves a statement in the face of such catastrophes. The other way is to make catastrophe present, and to use the stage as a promontory-extension which connects it more directly with our present experience. The audience will be shocked, not without good reason. Here is one critic's reaction to the play *Blasted* which opened at the Royal Court Theatre in 1995:

It made me feel sick, and giggly with shock. After the press night, strangers were talking to each other. Sarah Kane [the young dramatist, aged twenty-three] will hope that this is an inverted tribute to the piece. I see it more as the sudden solidarity that descends when people have been involved in the same calamity. Cate is a retarded teenager who has got involved with Ian, a tabloid journalist. It's clear from the start that Ian is a sicko: bigoted, sadistic, a boozer and an abuser of everyone, including himself. His one remaining lung is riddled with cancer. He wears a gun sling over his unbuttoned nylon shirt at all times. He rapes Cate in a soul-destroying hotel room in Leeds. . . . In the second half, the play turns into a war-torn fantasy in which Leeds is, inexplicably, under seige. A foreign soldier breaks into the hotel room. He buggers and blinds Ian and then eats his eyeballs. Cate comes in with a dying baby. She offers up a redundant prayer that the baby will not come to any harm. Ian picks up the baby and starts to eat it. If the play has any message it is that death is preferable to life.[12]

Am I recommending this type of plot to someone thinking of writing for the theatre? One reason for keeping my comments to points of technique in this and the previous chapters is that I want to leave the subject and matter of writing to the writers. The point has been: if you want to write about this or that subject, here is a way you might think of going about it, here are some of the ways it has been done. To recommend ideas, topics and themes for writing runs the risk of taking away their energy, of making a curriculum plan of them. Writers need to discover ideas for themselves, not be dictated to, and so I can't make a push for the plot of *Blasted*. I don't actually know whether I would support it or argue forcefully against it, but whether or not it succeeds as a play would depend first on the power and skill of the writing. The plot and violent content of this play is a serious option, and shock is and must be a serious option, but shock cannot be achieved by content entirely; it needs something else: a writer who understands how to make it felt, how to make theatre of it.

But if I were writing a play of my own I would have to answer the question. I might feel this play was challenging me to do something similar, to get inside that terrible ugliness. But if I did accept the challenge I might also feel an equally strong challenge from the other direction, and want to follow the impulse towards healing, reconstruction, discovery: broadly speaking the way of Peter Brook's theatre experiments. How to meet these two challenges is a profound problem, and at my best I would sense that it wasn't just mine. It is very possible that I would find myself turning the question over to see what lay underneath. Could I be sure that the play I would write would provoke understanding and add to the store of knowledge of human experience? Would it be – to ask a Brook-type question – theatre research? But if the voices of the characters were real enough to me I would begin writing them down whatever type of play they turned up in; ultimately their voices would carry the strongest argument for letting them exist.

Hearing the characters

Of the two plays I have written, one was commissioned; I was shown the stage at the Cottesloe Theatre and told to get going on the text: rehearsals in three weeks time. The next one came by itself, and I haven't yet seen it in performance. With the second play I started by hearing the characters' voices and seeing the stage in my mind. Because I could hear them I felt that I was committing myself to them. It could be that Sarah Kane like any dramatist could hear her characters and simply wrote down what they were saying. It could be that characters and subjects choose the writer, that out of the mass of pondered ideas, something selects itself and becomes audible, even shocking. If the characters are there: frightened, abusive, grovelling, defiant; or compassionate, sane, generous, there they will be, in that form. The writer will be encountering them as well as bringing them into dramatic existence, so that writing and acting again begin to look like the same process. But as a writer I would be hoping to grow through that encounter even if in the first instance they reduced both dramatist and audience to pointless disgust. I would have to believe that the risk was worth taking.

BUILDING A PLAY

Plot and desire

A plot suggests we are now beginning to think about whole plays rather than short exploratory scenes, but if we define it differently, each scene can have a plot. A plot occurs when the audience has begun to discover that there is a story inside all this fast moving dialogue and puzzling exchange. Also, do issues plays have plots? Does the audience want to know what happens to Bob or Hugh, Glenda or 'Germany'? They may want to know what is actually happening to the groups these characters represent, otherwise the characters will seem to be talking from outside of the issue rather than from within it.

Most audiences like to discover a plot as soon as possible. A plot depends on desire: somebody wants something; a group of characters wants something – they want to destroy this and replace it with that. It might be replacing war with victory; destruction, torture and poverty with survival; ignorance with knowledge; lack of love with love; it could be that they want to enjoy the party without getting too drunk. To have a plot, a play must set up desire as soon as it can. The audience likes some time to settle down. They will notice that some people in the same room are behaving noisily and agitatedly while they themselves are silent, and this phenomenon needs adjusting to. But their way of adjusting will be to find out who wants what from whom among these people on the stage, and this demand can be supplied by all types of theatre. The need for a plot also means that when a new act or scene begins, it must either introduce a new desire or continue with the ones generated before. Desire can be produced by an outside event: someone is now in danger and must be saved, or something happens which rearranges desire.

By 'desire' do we mean fantasy, lust, distant ideals? Does a first scene have to contain these elements? In *Oleanna*, the student simply wants 'to understand', while in the first seconds of Alan Ayckbourn's play *Just Between Ourselves*, the husband, Dennis, simply wants to mend an electric kettle. But it soon turns out that this is a house where 'mending things' is a way of avoiding the more important failures and breakdowns. The 'desire' here finally is evasion. A simple desire subsides to expose another more complex one.

Developing a structure

As with fiction writing, you may need to research your characters before you write about them, but an easier way is to do this while you are actually writing the scenes, and this method has implications for the structure of a play. If you have three characters, that suggests that you potentially have *four* sets of relationships: A with B, A with C, B with C and A, B and C together. These relationships can be explored in a way that in the end produces symmetry. You don't let them go until you have explored everything, which means you move them around in relationship to each other.

A series of scenes will have the potential to explore all four sets. If you see them together in an early scene, that suggests that you could bring them together in a later scene. What has happened? How have they changed? By this method you can research these questions, rather than plan the answer in advance.

The method is to shift through the potential. Groups of characters can be researched by letting them interact as a group, then letting them meet with another group or with individual main characters later. As *opportunities* for action, certain scenes must be there, but you may not know exactly what the action will feel like in its complete form until it happens.

At the end of the previous chapter I also made the point that a writer is finding the point of maximum revelation, the centre where the characters' styles and rhythms are most active and in conflict. Theatre research, like fiction research, can hardly avoid the attraction of such a centre: the core of the play is there, and is found usually just before the play ends. The tutor attacks the student (*Oleanna*), the Lomans challenge each other with the truth (*Death of a Salesman*), Aston evicts Davies (*The Caretaker*). So how do you move your characters into the centre?

Finding the centre

Tutors don't normally attack students because they can't understand something in class. In *Oleanna* the tutor attacks because the student has formally accused him of molesting her and because, as a result, he has lost his job. Given this new situation between them, the slightest word from her could cause him to lost control of himself. The point is that *something new has happened*.

The structure of plays rarely depends on dialogue alone. Something needs to happen to readjust relationships and raise potential conflict to its maximum. This could be the entrance of a new character, a drastic change of status for one character, a revelation of something that has happened in the past, or the characters have taken some action and now face the consequences.

It is by means of this new situation that characters are pushed into the play's centre.

Often there might actually be a whole series of centres, arranged like concentric circles. The characters start on the outside, in a relatively safe position; then they either move or are driven inward. In Ibsen's play *Ghosts*, Mrs Alving reaches the first circle: the fact of her husband's promiscuity. Then she reaches the second: the fact that her son is in love with his half-sister (unknown to him an offspring of his father). Then the third: the fact that her son has an inherited syphilitic insanity. Then the fourth, and worst: that he is about to go incurably insane and wants her to give him a fatal dose of morphia. The son has also moved inward through these circles. In the scene below, mother and son stand together at the centre; now he is about to tell her everything:

MRS ALVING: What is it that's so terrible?

OSVALD: Now listen, you mustn't scream – promise me you won't. We'll sit and talk it over quite quietly. Promise me, Mother.

MRS ALVING: Yes yes. I promise – but what is it?

OSVALD: Well, you must understand that this tiredness of mine, and this not being able to think about my work – that's not the actual illness. . . .

MRS ALVING: What is the actual illness, then?

OSVALD: The disease that I've inherited – [*he points to his forehead and goes on very softly*] – is seated here.

MRS ALVING: [*almost speechless*] Osvald. No, no!

OSVALD: Don't scream, I couldn't bear it. Yes, it sits here and waits. And it may break out any day, any minute.

MRS ALVING: But that's terrible . . . !

OVSALD: Now keep quiet. That's how things are with me.

MRS ALVING: [*starting up*] It isn't true, Osvald. It's not possible – it *can't* be!

OSVALD: I had one attack when I was abroad. It was soon over – but when I found out how it had been, I began to be haunted by this ghastly fear, and I hurried home to you as quickly as I could.[13]

Although the structure does not depend on dialogue, it is of course through dialogue that the audience receives the impact of what happens in the centre. 'This tiredness of mine . . . when I was abroad . . . haunted by this ghastly fear' – these sharp references are specific, short close-ups of stretches of time, points of rooted experience, and they anchor this scene in time-sequence experience. Without them it would just be a declaration, but realism must rely on them for its impact. As I explained in the opening paragraphs of this chapter, in theatre dialogue, words are not just spoken; the most effective will have an equivalent action, and this *action-equivalent* could be a gentle or passionate embrace, a touch of the hand, a punch or a spit in the face. In this scene from *Ghosts*, while the son tells his mother about his disease, his words *are* action: they are trying to put a hand over her mouth; they are trying to hold her down. This scene shows Ibsen at his most brilliant and his darkest. Soon after this point, the play must end. The mother and son are confronting their family's past, and their own present and future. Osvald is trying to stifle the impact of what he is saying even while he is saying it. He can't speak until she first promises not to scream.

The world turned upside down

In the first section I referred to the technique of *inappropriateness*. Whether or not it carries a serious purpose, one of its more striking effects is comedy. The following sketch, The Reporter, by Victoria Wood, is a black-comic counterpart to the scene from Ibsen:

REPORTER: Widow Smith? I'm from the Herald and Argus. I believe your husband's just died and he was quite well known or something?
WIDOW: Yes.
REPORTER: We thought we'd just do a little piece on him, just a few inches.
WIDOW: I'm not sure.
REPORTER: It's just that there haven't been any jumble sales this week – we're a bit strapped.
WIDOW: Come in then, I haven't done any tidying up since. . . .

[*They go in.*]

REPORTER: Good excuse, a death isn't it, to bunk off the housework? If somebody dropped dead in our house, I'd be quite pleased.
WIDOW: Would you like a drink?
REPORTER: Depends what he died of. If it's anything catching I won't bother, ta.
WIDOW: It was his heart. It was very sudden. Biscuit?
REPORTER: No, ta. Tried my bikini on last night, nearly had a heart attack.

[*She picks up a photo.*]

This him? He looks quite sick on this actually, doesn't he?

[*Tears from the widow.*]

He looks a dead nice bloke though. So – he did what exactly, drop dead?[14]

In this scene the widow is the *defender* of a position (that of the situation's appropriate rules: what can be said, what must not be said), while the reporter is the *invader* (breaking the rules). Because it all happens in the widow's house, there's no escape; the widow is trapped; the invasion goes on relentlessly getting worse; the audience is delighted.

The point is to keep an invasion coming on and on until the defender gives in. The widow gives in and finally breaks her own rules. When Butch, the local photographer, enters, he asks the widow to pose. The husband collapsed, it turned out, while watching a *Carry On* film:

> BUTCH: . . . you'll have to crouch down a bit for me, just cup your chin, sort of 'me husband's popped his clogs but life goes on' kind of thing. Can you stop crying? I'm getting a bounce-off.
>
> REPORTER: We could call it 'Carry On Crying', Butch.
>
> BUTCH: Great, fabulous. Thanks very much love, if you want any prints, just pop in to the office.
>
> [*The Reporter and Butch leave. The Widow begins to take an overdose. The Reporter comes back in.*]
>
> REPORTER: Did I leave my . . . stop, don't take any more. Butch! Quickly!
>
> [*Butch comes back in.*]
>
> BUTCH: Oh that's smashing, love. Just turn the bottle round to me, love, then I can see the label, that's fabulous. Now hold me a pill up, and can you look sort of 'I'm topping myself but I can still have a laugh about it' kind of thing. Now take another and hitch your skirt up . . .[15]

The rules of privacy are notoriously ineffective, and the Press are notorious for breaking them. But it makes good theatre. Audiences love unacceptable behaviour, insensitivity, inappropriateness, characters with a licence to be crass, brutal, who are able to break the rules. But of course, such effects depend on there being a situation where rules definitely would apply and on characters like the widow who definitely would not break them. By the end, the other two are asking her to step outside her role, skirt hitched up, with a mocking grimace while she commits suicide. In other words, they want her to be like them, detached, inappropriate, unacceptable, which doubles the outrage into tremendous comedy for the audience. To a perhaps less obvious extent, *Family Voices* also has this comic spirit, detached, facetious, transforming all it touches from high to low, a kind of reverse alchemy, and it is interesting to wonder, especially for our purposes, how much dramatic writing springs from it.

WRITING EXERCISES: TWO

1 In your group, make a list of situations, such as the above, where people conform to rules, and discuss how these might be broken. Make use of defenders and invaders.

To work in a group means that you will be making collective decisions about the script all the time, and later about the action. Aim to move the action through two or more scenes, as above. The script can be changed as you develop the scenes you have chosen; if you decide to, improvise for parts of the action, but write out the results as a whole script.

2 In this scene, one character is clearly very distressed. The second character tries to find out why: What has happened? and tries to push the first into a revelation. She/he refuses to be pushed, and will only make scrambled, disconnected, but sometimes evocative statements that leave the audience completely on edge. The aim is to write so that their interest is held but not rewarded. In this scene, something has happened, but also, something *is* happening.

3 A slow-pace version of the above. Here a character has been through a transforming experience and is visited by a friend who asks a lot of questions. Some of these are answered but most are blocked. The experience may have been a very positive one. The character is not distressed but calm.

4 Transcribe a scene from a short story. This could be one you have read or one you have written yourself. The characters are standing in the centre of the experience, in a state of crisis action. Something has happened. The focus is on the present. What will happen next? Explore the new situation through the dialogue and using stage directions.

The following first-scene outlines are variations on the desire motif and suggest some further possibilities for writing. They could form a basis for either issues or personal theatre. Here the audience is made to desire an outcome:

1 A group of people in authority (parents, teachers, police) are behaving to their inferiors in a way which is unfair, cruel, unreasonable, unbalanced. The audience see it, the characters do not. They accept it.

2 In among a group of prisoners is one who is treated worse than all the others, in small and hurtful ways, by the authorities. Do the others ignore this prisoner, bully him, or protect him?

   Here the audience will not necessarily desire any single outcome, but only witness the desires of the characters in conflict.

3 John and Mary both have remunerative jobs, a stimulating and challenging sex life and worthwhile friends. Real estate values have gone up. But one day, Mary tells John that she wants to leave him and go to live with an actor in an experimental theatre group.

4 (Not for those with a nervous disposition.) John and Mary fall in love and get married. But then Mary turns out to be a cannibal. They quarrel, but eventually she succeeds in persuading John to indulge with her. Real estate values go up.

5 A teenage boy wants to leave home, give up school and live rough with a

group of friends in the city. His mother and sister object. In his rage he picks up a framed photograph of his dead father and smashes it.

GENERAL COMMENTS

Presence and visibility

As in fiction writing it is valuable to be able to find a rhythm for each character: they cannot exist in prose without a style. In the theatre, however, they exist physically. Physical contrasts will be visually important. Rhythm can be constructed through action without a word being said. But when they are heard, the words will need a style that makes the visible presence more visible. A haggard Cleopatra who talks constantly of intense passion is more interesting than the beauty she imagines herself to be. Characters who rush about, speak quickly and never use up their energy are more visible if sharing a scene with one who is their opposite. In *The Caretaker*, the filthy tramp Davies has a self-image of scrupulousness and pride; hence when he is told that he stinks he becomes violent. So because of their self-image and its contrast with the reality, there will be certain opinions and words that characters fear. Their self-image might, in the course of a play, begin to collapse, and then we see only the physical presence. They are alone; and the space they are in can reveal that isolation. Also, the tempo of a scene can be slowed down or speeded up by the verbal and physical behaviour of the characters, so that while writing, it helps to think of their words as verbal *behaviour* rather than just as messages with information value.

Stage space and set

The average small proscenium arch stage is thirty feet wide and thirty feet deep from front to back. The first location of the Traverse Theatre in Edinburgh was no bigger than a large room and housed about twenty members of an audience. Theatres in the round surround the actors with audience, but can be large enough to distance the action, though the distance is not so marked as it is with proscenium arch stages. If you are writing for a particular stage that you know and will be using, then you must think carefully about its size as well as its relationship to the audience. How far away is the furthest part of the audience? How close is the nearest? Is the stage flat or sloped? If you are planning a large cast, backstage arrangements will be important. Is the play intended to fit the stage, or is the stage going to be altered to fit the play, made smaller, enclosed within fixed or moveable sets?

In an enclosed set, will the characters be aware of, and refer to, the space beyond the set, out of a window, on the other side of a door? In an open set, will you be able to take advantage of all that available space? Even in personal theatre most sets are larger than the average room, so that movement of characters towards or away from each other will be exaggerated. Characters who would normally be bunched together at close quarters will have more space to express their nearness or distance from each other. The audience, like nature, abhors a vacuum, and will not feel satisfied unless the action occupies the whole available stage. There will be areas of security and insecurity. Doors, windows, telephones suggest the latter; chairs, tables, inert objects the former. One chair placed centre stage immediately implies a circle of security and beyond that a surrounding insecurity. In a proscenium arch theatre, two chairs facing towards the audience are a gateway. Centre stage facing each other their occupants will be equal. If one occupant turns her chair to face the audience, what will be the impact of that gesture?

Objects, furniture, decor are cultural symbols, so that unexpected or inappropriate objects focus attention. In the section of introductory writing exercises (p.33), I suggested listing objects which you see as contemporary icons and making them your focus for writing. The results of that exercise could influence your decisions about objects in a setting. Dress too is significant: the T-shirt with a slogan, the uniform; but colour has a more complex suggestive power. Objects will gain meaning in a play by being among characters whose reactions to them are appropriately powerful. (An example of this is the father's photograph in the fifth first-scene outline given above.) Their significance to characters may derive from a wider cultural significance. What does the image of a close relative who has died mean to people in present-day culture? An object can mean what a character chooses it to mean, but it can still have a general meaning which influences that choice. Control of it can express a desire to control the other characters. Its destruction, equally, will mean something. Or an object can just be part of the atmosphere through which the characters pass, and represent a world which continues beyond the play's action, as if the whole play were an episode in the history of those small objects.

Certain sets mirror theatre-like events found elsewhere than on a stage: churches, law courts, areas reserved for rituals, festivals, tournaments. In these public settings, access is limited but permitted, restricting rules of behaviour will operate and can be broken. Offices, lecture rooms and platforms for public speeches also imply formalities of behaviour, and in the theatre all that weight of convention can start to slide – it can be made unsafe. But the stage can also act as a substitute for those formalised types of space *without* letting chaos in through the door.

Experiment in issues theatre

In issues theatre, characters must be clearly identifiable as types with predictable roles. If seven characters are representing the Seven Deadly Sins, for instance, the audience will be able to predict their behaviour. But predictableness is not enough in itself. In one play devised by a student group,

Wrath refused to play her role or learn her lines, and behaved very irritably and disruptively, 'wrathfully' in effect. So the play was about a play that failed to take place because of Wrath's un-cooperative attitude. But the audience would understand this intriguing development; in one way she was still behaving in role.

Issues theatre might equally begin with a song outlining an issue. This form of beginning, or a similar one, would stress the type of play by exercising the right, early on, to use a range of techniques, by introducing as much *variety* as possible without straining the audience's need for clarity. An authorities versus subordinates scene (see p.179) could then be brought in to illustrate an issue in close-up. But an issues play that stays within its outline takes risks with an audience's willingness to continue being interested. Developing an issues play beyond audience predictions will increase and sharpen its insight and hence its expressive power.

Researching an issue

Reading newspaper articles for stories and viewpoints, collecting photographs from newspapers and magazines, talking to people about the opinions they hold: all of these will stimulate your awareness of the full issue as well as provide exact information from which you can then select.

How is the issue presented in the other media? Do you aim to consolidate or dislodge that presentation? Alternatively, an issues play can explore a topic from the past (and revive its relevance to the present). Community plays often do this by researching a local incident and dramatising it with the support of a huge cast. The present community, with everyone involved, mirrors that which occupied that location in the past. A smaller group could still work with the same source material, but without involving the huge quantity of time, funding and organisation that community plays demand. Anne Jellicoe's book on community plays argues an excellent case for this type of theatre.

Researching for dialogue

Although, as I explained at the start of this section, the best research takes place in the writing itself, some of it may be going on all the time. You could well benefit by listening carefully when people are speaking in unusual situations such as on the telephone or in a car. Catching the habits produced by those conditions will impress an audience by signalling your ability to handle precise detail. A car can be represented by two seats and appropriate speech habits. It also allows the audience to experience off-stage environments: a street, a traffic jam, countryside, the scene of an accident.

By focusing your attention on how subjects in conversations change, you will be able to decide which person in a group is the dominant one. He or she is usually the one who succeeds in changing the subject. You can try doing this yourself. Steal a minor detail from somebody else's anecdote and start one of your own before they have finished telling theirs. See what happens.

Sometimes people will allow themselves to be interrupted and are quite happy about it; hence conversations slide through a range of subjects in a pleasant but aimless manner. The reason is that no one is trying to be dominant. At other times, a subject takes hold because one person success-fully insists on retrieving it. She or he might keep on steering other subjects towards it. The other speakers may or may not be aware that someone is taking control in this way. Finishing other people's sentences for them may indicate a less subtle form of dominance if it happens two or three times, but it may indicate other kinds of relationship: the two speakers are sharing a passionate interest in the subject they are discussing; the thinking rhythm of one is slower than that of the other so one tries to dominate for that reason. At other times, dominant behaviour can demonstrate insecurity. The domin-ant figure who is also insecure will attract attention because of his or her uncertain status role.

FINDING AN ENDING

The way to learn about writing plays is to write a full-length play in three acts (or an equivalent number of scenes), lasting not less than one-and-three-quarter hours. The writer will in most cases know where each scene is going, will know roughly the potentials to be explored, but may not know how the play is going to end. The aim will be to *find* the ending. In the last seconds of Stravinsky's *The Rite Of Spring*, we can feel the music trying to find a way of fracturing its rhythm. It tries, fails to break out of the cycle, tries again, fails, tries, succeeds.

If the first phase is finding the potential for conflict, the middle phase is to show that conflict in action, but the last is to avoid repeating the second. Your characters will start to go round in a circle; the old conflicts will go on inventing fresh displays of action and reaction, *unless* you can find a way through. But the effort is not just yours. Your characters will also want to escape the cycle. Their conflicts will have become a routine. In a random sample of endings from Shakespeare's plays, one character strangles another then kills himself; an absent character returns and restores justice; disguises and masks have started to cause more problems than they can solve – hence they are stripped off; conflict has led to the worst event imaginable – the death of the King's beloved daughter; the lovers die by accident; the King's rule collapses and is succeeded; new generations of lovers marry: wife and husband are restored to each other; the exiled return to their homeland. In each of these endings the conflict subsides: its perpetrators are dead; its victims have either perished or escaped; a new ruler succeeds.

Mythical dramas enact the ancient rhythm of sacrifice and renewal: a death for a life. The sacred person is sacrificed to the cycle that regenerates itself through spring, and communities are dependent upon this rhythm for their survival. Tragedies produce for us the anguished consciousness of the doomed sacred person and end with their death, while the endings of comedies move the cycle forward into the future. In some contemporary drama, this poetic serial of action is twisted by a view that sees suffering not as part of ritual but as routine: it has no meaning, therefore it can have no end. Beckett's plays suggest this view powerfully. But others of the absurd tradition do manage to find a sense of renewal by blocking off the characters' bad faith and reducing their illusions: 'Now we know, now we can start again.'

One possible reading of Edward Albee's *Who's Afraid of Virginia Woolf*, for example, is that suffering and conflict can be gone through, that they are exhaustible. A fundamental decision with any play is sensing whether it can in fact end. If no end to the reiteration of conflict can be found, then that will be the ending without an end. But that will still have to be made clear to an audience. In *Waiting for Godot*, Beckett introduces a new character, a boy with knowledge of Godot, at the end of each of the play's two acts. But is it the same boy? Is it the same Godot he speaks about? Beckett is experimenting with his play to see how it *might* end.

In the ideas I have suggested for writing, the point has been to establish an outline and then allow something to happen beyond it. To actors, writers and audiences this process of *something happening beyond* is mysterious but compulsive. In the theatre, everyone making and watching plays will recognise this experience. We feel the play's structure as something organic and inevitable but also surprising and unfamiliar. The sense is of an experience being lived through; it develops its own momentum; it looks and sounds like expert improvisation: artificial, yet not. It feels both static and fluid together, and in this way it contrasts with lived and therefore unresolved experience. In the structure of a play, it may be the echoes of mythical structure we are hearing, even if the playwright consciously would avoid such a suggestion and fills the play with everything contemporary and urban. But all plays have structures, even when the structures are fractured. All plays do end. There must be a way through to the final silence.

Where do these structures come from? Is there a way of teaching them to writers? Are there rules: digressions followed by returns, subversion by synthesis? Does all drama turn the world upside down, leave it there, or try to get it back? How available to understanding is this mysterious *body* of a work of art, this making familiar things unfamiliar again? I began this book by asserting that we shroud the creative process in too much mystery, and that technical learning need not embarrass us quite as much as it does. But finally I can see why we want to defend that attitude. We want to feel that the artist does not wholly know what he or she is doing, that the drive is not subject to conscious control, that the source of ideas is elsewhere and independent, and will not appear on demand. But it hardly needs arguing that artists are experts in technical mastery; they understand their medium and research it exhaustively. They can perhaps never reach a complete under-standing; that is why they research and why they experiment. For the writer, the best research is done within the medium itself, and the first steps can reveal as much as those which happen later.

Chapter 6

Writing to persuade

Articles, essays and reports have two main aims: (1) to hold their reader's attention, and (2) to argue persuasively. Of these, the first one is essential while the second might be modified. You will always have to persuade your reader that the topic you are writing about is interesting and significant, but instead of presenting a single, strong argument, you may intend to offer a broad survey. How to hold your reader's attention comes first, but after that you can either take them on a well-planned guided tour of the topic, or straight to the point you are arguing.

WRITING AN ESSAY

I shall start with a discussion of writing essays. At school and university, almost everyone will have some experience of this type of project, but most are aware of it only as writers. Few people know it from the reading experience end. In order to write, this might seem an advantage, but in practice it means that not many will be able to tell how essays sound to the ear. Good writing possesses a strong sound-quality, and if you were to imagine your essay as a radio script, would you listen or reach for the off button? Achievement certainly at the higher levels of the education system is measured by how effectively you can write. Everyone enrolled on a course is presumed to be engaged in writing for part of the time, but in spite of the obvious necessity, many essays are written not to be read, and lack any clear idea of a reader.

If I ask students: Who is your reader? Who are you writing for? many of them think of their reader as wearing some ogrish mask when essays are due to arrive. Their real tutor is buried inside an obese image of authority which inflates at the sight of their struggling puny ideas. Their ideas may be fine but the hideous apparition will not think so, and will always suspect that they could have done very much better. This situation does not apply in every case, but where it does there are strategies for avoiding that sense of preconceived humiliation. To write well you need confidence, and be able to trust your reader. You might need to ask questions about your topic, to explore as well as explain, and to think of your reader as someone who is intelligent (we must assume) and curious, who appreciates the care you take to present useful ideas, not just clever ones. It might help to think of your reader not as an expert but as an equal, as someone you are teaching as you write. In other words, your reader is someone like you, who needs to have everything fully and carefully explained so that they don't get it wrong, and whose mind at the end should be filled with *memorable* ideas, not timid confusions and slack ambiguity.

Preliminary comments

1.   Before writing an essay, it is worth thinking about the reasons why you have been asked to write the essay. You are being asked to demonstrate your interest in some aspect of the academic course you have chosen. You may be asked to write on a set topic, choose a topic from a list or make up your own title. Not everything on your course will appeal to you with the same level of interest, but there will usually be something which attracts your attention. If you can find nothing which you can get interested in enough to write about then you do have a problem but not a *writing* problem necessarily. You may be given a chance to speak to your tutor about your essay before you begin, but whether you do or not, the essay will be a record of your commitment to some part of your course. Let us assume that you are genuinely keen to explore a chosen topic but unsure how to go about it.

2.   Writing an essay involves four basic stages: research, planning, writing and redrafting or final revision. Because everyone has their own way of working, the advice given below is not intended as a strict guide. Even so, it offers some strategies which may help you to move more quickly and efficiently from stage to stage.

Researching your topic. Pre-writing

Once you have chosen your topic, begin straight away to use your time effectively. You will be thinking about it, and reading. You should be the one who controls what you read, so rather than read everything, try to make some preliminary decisions about what you want to look for, and note down any quotations which might be useful. Your thinking and your reading will need a structure. Think about how you intend to guide your reader through the material so that he or she will not feel that you have got helplessly lost in it. Your reader must benefit, just as you must. If there are areas of the topic which are difficult for you to grasp, you can note these at this point. To frame some question about the problems will help you; you might be able to include these in your essay, along with some trial answers.

Think particularly about the impact you want to achieve, the most important points you want to make, or the most significant questions you want to ask. Ideally, your reader should come away from the essay with a clear sense of its main impact and argument, its central points of debate and your conclusion. To achieve this effect you will need to find a firm direction for your thoughts and your research.

Thinking about your reader's response will help your research and planning. But do remember that readers aren't impressed with an amount of knowledge; they need direction and impact.

If you have to deal with a large section of reading, decide on five or six points you want to make in your essay, and which of these is going to be the most significant. Work out how one point relates to another. Read with these points in mind, making notes on the connections. Information isn't enough in itself; you need *evidence*. Some facts will be information, but evidence is going to help you argue and persuade.

Planning and 'introduction': the topic statement

Plan your essay by working on a *topic statement* which will act as the drive of your essay and your main point. An essay plan can be constructed out of one single statement, contained in one or two sentences in your own words, and you may if you wish include these in your introduction. Whether you decide to or not, you should keep the topic statement by you as a firm guide. It represents the result of your thoughts and research at this stage.

Here is an example of a topic statement:

It was because of Hitler's desire for adulation that Germany lost the war. Had he placed more trust in his armed forces, Germany might have succeeded.

This statement makes a definite point. It uses the word 'because . . .' It develops cause and effect and links them clearly. It offers no evidence as yet but evidence will follow, and will not just be data about the war. It should not aim to bring out the evidence but to state a definite case: this it does. Composing a topic statement is not easy. It takes time. You should not write it unless you are prepared to stand by it. Later on you might explore other less obvious reasons for Hitler's defeat. Some people might say that Hitler was defeated, not Germany – does 'Hitler' equal 'Germany'? There will be time to consider that question later in your essay.

This topic statement can be broken down into two central concepts:

Adulation of Hitler: His speeches, politics in the depression, rise to Chancellor, refusal to share power, appeal to the masses, single-handed attempt to control the war, Nazi mythology, hero worship, belief in the right to power of the Ayrian races, attraction to tyranny, out of touch with direct operations, unwilling to concede defeat.

The armed forces: A successful military and industrial organisation aware of the strength of the allied opposition, in touch with direct operations, willingness to concede partial defeat.

The aim of the essay would be to explain the details which lie behind the concepts, by moving from left to right: from concepts towards details. A loose and unfocused essay would merely refer to the abstract ideas (on the left) without actualising them or offering evidence. If you always keep in mind what your concepts actually refer to, move in that direction, and keep your reader informed of the detailed content, the argument you construct will be persuasive and substantiable. Having constructed your topic statement, you can then decide how to inform your reader fully about what lies behind the concepts, and go into detail.

The two main concepts draw others up behind them. But here again the same principle applies.

You can set these up on the page, thus:

Speeches	What he said (quotation?).
Depression	Worse in Germany than elsewhere.
Nazi mythology	Evidence of its strength over the people, lack of humour encouraged in the popular imagination, extreme views permitted.
Refusal to share power	Specific evidence. Quote a source from letters.
Out of touch	Last days in the bunker, evidence.

And so on. Again by moving from the left to the right you will be able to say exactly what you mean by each idea, and so keep your reader from being faced by concepts without evidence.

Your topic statement could be included in your first paragraph, but in your final paragraphs you might want to modify it a little. Some other thought might have occurred to you, along with some more questions. If you end with some further problems that arise when interpreting this period of history, your reader will feel invited to ponder them too. As well as being honest, you will then be treating your reader on equal terms.

Here are some other examples of topic statements:

Good management depends on fitting resources to need.

Out of context, this sentence does not mean very much; it could be referring to stage management, polar exploration, geography fieldwork, or several other topics. But let's assume your topic is the Health Service. Having thought about the issues and researched the subject carefully, you have arrived at this statement: you believe it and are able to produce an argument with evidence to support it. Now write out the statement, and add in the specific details alongside each concept in the statement, thus:

Resources   Nursing and medical personnel, finance, equipment, medication, accommodation, beds, auxiliary support, working hours.

Needs   Patient care, staff satisfaction, care of relatives, shorter waiting lists, prompt admissions, follow-up counselling, continuing supply of resources, expansion of patient care to specialist areas: premature babies, infertility.

In your essay you need to work from concepts towards specifics so that you and the reader know precisely what you mean by 'resources' and 'needs'. Having informed them, with concrete examples and references from other commentaries as available, you will be able to initiate discussion and draw your conclusions. You may wish to highlight certain consequences, for example, that patient care takes precedence over staff satisfaction, given limited resources. You will be able to organise your material because you know exactly what your introductory concepts refer to. And because you know your reader also knows, you will be able to conduct your argument more confidently.

A topic statement which merely states, 'Good management depends on many different factors' would not give you enough scope for development, so it is obviously important, whatever you are writing about, that you construct an introductory topic statement useful to your essay; that is, one that takes the risk of saying something definite, and one you are prepared to expand on and defend.

Look at the two topic statements below, and decide which, as a reader, you think, has the more scope for expansion:

1 In *Death of a Salesman* Willie Loman is preoccupied with his sons being a success.
2 *Death of a Salesman* confronts the audience with two ideals of success: physical prowess and enterprise in business, but the impact of the play endorses neither.

Clearly (2) has several concepts which can be filled out – audience, physical prowess, enterprise, impact – and leaves open the question (to be answered later) of what the play does endorse or commmend, and how. (1) offers no concepts and instead merely leads to a retelling of the story; it avoids making any topic statement at all.

Writing the introduction

'In this essay I plan to write about a very interesting topic which I will refer to later.' Of course no one would think of beginning like this, but some introductions come close to it. In preference, you could begin by telling the reader something definite, a piece of evidence which you know leads directly to your topic statement. 'Three days before his suicide on 1 May 1945, Hitler made the following remark to his secretary . . .' Aim to introduce your topic statement in ways which will capture and hold your reader's attention. In your introduction you need to begin to *involve* the reader in thinking about the topic of your essay.

Introductions are danger zones because of the embarrassment of establishing your first contact with a reader. But such embarrassment at least implies that you know there *is* a reader. Can you make use of this knowledge? Try to establish a mood of honest enquiry. Assume a shared interest, a confidence to define the area that holds your topic statement, and a confidence to ask questions. If, when revising your essay, you read your introduction and find it says very little and sounds embarrassed, see if you can omit it altogether. The best introductions often happen in the second, third or fourth paragraph of an essay.

Writing: first draft

You now know the extent of your essay, the points it needs to raise, the concepts, related details, and its overall aim. Avoid repetition. Don't use the words in your topic statement too often. Move quickly towards detailed commentary. Keep writing until you have covered your range. You will probably revise as you go on, especially if using a word processor. Don't start writing at the last minute. You'll need at least two full days or three evenings, and then some time for revision of your draft.

If you feel your essay is becoming dull, stop, and try to see how to inject some zest into it. At this stage you may wish to introduce some of the related points or a sense of debate. As you explore the details and concepts test out if you want to modify your topic statement by taking into account some new angle.

Write for the reader. Anticipate the reader's questions and ask them. Imagine your script really is on the radio. Can you make the dull and factual passages come more alive? Your topic statement, if it is a good one, will have an argument. Keep this argument fully in mind and use it to expand your topic.

Your conclusions might not be seriously at odds with your first ideas, but they may require you to add some modifications. Don't worry. This is progress. If your explorations have been searching and genuine this could well happen.

Aim to make a complete first draft. Doing so will lift your confidence so that you feel you have something substantial to work on.

Writing: revision

Developing the content

This activity takes up far less time than writing a first draft. Although you will have found a way of organising most of your evidence and ideas, there will be items that occur to you subsequently, small improvements, perhaps an extra paragraph to cover something you only sketched out before. Equally, there could be parts of your first draft that seemed important at the time but which actually sound confusing now, and irrelevant. And then there is that quotation which, in your rush to finish, you left out completely. If you are using a notebook, carry it with you to jot down any extra ideas which occur to you, and build them into your essay as soon as you are able.

Style

You can also make small but effective style changes: check spelling; change the word order to make it more concise; improve the construction of a sentence; find a better word; try different punctuation. Keep your sentences short, and check any long paragraphs that drift away from the points you are making in them. Test your style by reading a section of your essay out loud. Rate its sound-quality. Imagine that your reader is physically present in the room and is hearing your writing for the first time. Will they be able to receive your meaning clearly without looking at your script? Will they fidget and yawn? Listen closely for puzzling, vague and obscure sentence constructions. You are allowed to keep your sense of humour. If you feel you are surrounding yourself with dull, solemn, monotonous clouds of words, remind yourself that you will be doing this to your reader too.

Check organisation

Finally, take care that any extra thoughts or pieces of evidence are fitted in the right place and will not cause confusion. The gaps between separate parts of your essay must be bridged. If you think your reader will have problems following a point, can you find ways of helping them? A signpost sentence: 'The evidence X might not look very substantial on its own, but it becomes so if we also add Z.'

Further notes on writing essays

Avoid using the passive mood of the verb: 'It can be seen that. . . . It could be reasonably argued that . . .' If it could, see it and argue it. Try out a direct statement of what you want to say, and if you still feel nervous about it, frame it as a question or say something else. Aim at the topic and convince yourself that it is indeed a target that can be hit, as follows:

> At that time, support for Clinton was secure. The arguments opposing him were too diffuse to achieve any strong and unified opposition. They had to resort to the scandal-factor. Why was this?

A strong statement followed by a question opens up the space for detailed evidence – which you will need in order to support your claim. Writing like this will challenge you to find the persuasive evidence. But writing in the passive mood allows you to avoid taking firm possession of your ideas; they belong, you are implying, to someone else, and therefore it is not your place to defend them.

If you quote from a secondary source, a critic or published commentary, use the quotation, comment on it, ask yourself how it relates to your main point. Make sure your reader reads it in the way you want them to.

Don't merely abandon it to the reader as a stand-in for your ideas. Make it work for you.

Always make sure your quotations are introduced with grammatical accuracy and support the sentence structure of your text.

Vary quotations using different types of source: a critical commentary, a quoted letter, a newspaper article, a primary source text. It is not necessary to do this, but beware of using just one source (or type of source) exclusively.

Your own discipline area (History, Cultural Studies, English, Art, Linguistics) may want you to follow certain formal procedures in writing, such as the citing of sources and secondary reading using a particular format. Make sure you know what your discipline area demands in terms of presentation and style.

OPINION ARTICLES

Choosing a topic

The aim of this section is to help you to express your opinion persuasively. You are writing either for the general reader or for a group of readers who already share an interest in the topic, though not necessarily your viewpoint. Whether you write for the general reader or a specific group will depend on the kind of topic you choose.

Let us assume that you are writing for the general reader. This target has advantages for writing because it means you will have to attract their interest; you will not be able to reel off details that would mean little or nothing to the uninformed, as would be the case if your reader already knew a lot about advanced stereo systems or clay-pigeon shooting. As I write, certain topics are prevalent; some will change and be replaced by others as the months pass;

some however may persist. In listing them, I am trying to reflect the current preoccupations we hear about on the news, in newspapers and journals, rather than just my own particular interests.

In Britain in late January/February 1995, current topics were: the export of live animals abroad; the decline of the royal family; the question of European unity; nationalism, in particular Irish nationalism and the Unionist perspective, as well as nationalism in Eastern and Central Europe; floods in North-western Europe; the issue of private as opposed to public transport; the related issue of mass pollution and large-scale environmental damage; climate change; nuclear power; lottery winners; school governors in rebellion about the funding of schools; the proposed abolition of religious worship in schools; legalisation of certain illegal substances; what to do about Eric Cantona; the genius of Peter Cook; television violence and its influence on children; reform of the CSA; the diet industry; the liberation of Auschwitz; the discovery of prehistoric cave paintings at Vallon-Pont-d'Arc; an iceberg the size of Oxfordshire splits off Antarctica.

The topics you list will depend on which year, the time of year, and which part of the world you are living in, and may indeed reflect your personal interests and those of your age group, racial or social background, your gender, sense of belonging to a dominant or marginalised group, religious beliefs or lack of them, or which newspapers you read. In other words, your viewpoints, along with the whole atmosphere of experience which forms them, will not be a matter entirely of our own individual choice but of the many environments which surround you, including television and computers. But to guard against the feeling of being swamped, it is worth making up a list as a first step. Your list will not be like this one; new items will have arrived on the scene and many of the above will have been forgotten, while some will still be with us and some may have assumed major proportions. Your own list, equally, may contain none of the above.

Your list will tell you something about the cultural directions, trends and ideas that are occupying people's minds in April 1996, July 1997, or whenever you are writing, and this will be interesting as a record in itself. I wish I could see from here what it would include. When you have made up your own list, try and see if any items on it specifically trigger your interest. It will help if you browse through newspapers and magazines and give some extra attention to one or two topics as they are represented here and there, including those seen on television. At the time of writing, I am completely unable to predict what your list will be, but am not wholly guessing when I envisage that climate change will become an increasingly visible feature of our lives as we move beyond the year 2000, but I don't feel this is a particularly eccentric view; I wish it were.

Look back at the list I made for February 1995. Your own might contain one or two items that seem trivial, as mine does (Eric Cantona, for instance?). But some viewpoints, some admittedly with tongues in their cheeks, are inclined to make more of this item than the mere mention of it suggests and to see it as connecting with more serious ones: the imbalance produced by exceptional talent, or, as in the example below, how the male brain structure is different from the female brain structure:

Men are reptiles when it comes to expressing their emotions whereas women are like monkeys, they sit down and chat about it, according to a study of brain differences between the sexes.

Brain scans of a group of young men and women have revealed significant distinctions in the activity of part of the brain – the lymbic system – associated with emotions such as pleasure, fear and happiness.

The results support other research showing that the biological differences between the sexes seems to extend to differences within the brain which may account for the stereotypical behaviours observed in men and women.

Eric Cantona's emotional outburst at a football match on Wednesday night, where he attacked a man in the crowd who was hurling abuse, is a classic example of how men lash out. 'Men often express their emotions through overt aggression,' says Ruben Gur, professor of neuropsychology at the University of Pennsylvania, Philadelphia.

'Women deal with their emotions more symbolically by talking about their feelings more than men, who often sulk, and say "what's there to talk about?" . . . The temporal limbic region deals with more basic responses, for instance like an angry crocodile lashing out in a rage.' Men are more likely to take the lizard's way out in dealing with emotionally charged situations, he said.

Professor Gur, in common with a growing number of psychologists and behavioural researchers, believes the stereotypical differences between men and women are the results of fundamental biological distinctions laid down at birth, rather than in the way boys and girls are brought up.[1]

This piece is not of course an example of opinion writing as such but a report/survey intended to arouse opinion. But if a comparatively small item in the news attracts such a lot of attention, it might be worth investigating some underlying reasons for it. Small issues can trigger larger issues. In this case, was it because the media is simply interested in things which interest the media, or because in watching a certain incident on television millions were suddenly faced with their limbic drive? Is violence not violence but a valid form of expression, particularly for men, and sex stereotype behaviour justifiable? (These seem to be the underlying questions.) Below this article are two small photographs with the footballer on one side and a crocodile on the other.

In terms of interest, minor items can generate ideas, and possibly even more ideas than those with heavy coverage. But another way of using your list is to see if anything on it has involved you personally now or in the past, or influences your sense of your own identity.

Public and personal

In the following piece the writer uses her sense of personal involvement at several points.

'Republican Virtues' by Sue Townsend

When I was a child at county junior school we were still taught that the Queen was ordained by God. You could see her everywhere – her portrait hung in every classroom, in the post office, in banks and every other public building. It was just like when I went to Russia for the first time and saw ubiquitous pictures of Lenin.

I've never seen the point of the royal family. They have had a subliminal effect on us all, particularly people in my age group. When I was growing up we were bombarded by propaganda because we had television. The coronation was the first time you were able to see a big public occasion.

When I hear unquestioning fawning it is one of the few forms of behaviour guaranteed to make me irritable. But what annoys me most are thinking people who want to water down the monarchy. Labour politicians included. To chip away at it is no good at all. Take the idea of putting them on a bike. Apart from the fact that the suggestion is an embarrassment, it would be so cruel. A sure way of killing them off one by one: a bus here, a taxi there. . . .

To rid the country of the royals altogether would be an enormous psychological boost for everyone in this country. Change in itself would be one of the republican virtues, something that would enthuse and excite people.

Republicanism is always spoken about between gritted teeth, as if it were a fearful thing: 'Britain is a conservative country that is allergic to rapid change; we prefer to evolve,' is the common clarion call.

But I think that is missing the point. They told us the Berlin Wall was indestructible and that there would be no end to the troubles in Northern Ireland. Look, too at what has happened in the Soviet Union and South Africa.

There is a whole undercurrent in British society of people who are craving change, who are willing to face it. Certainly, most of the people I talk to would gladly embrace it.

Republicanism is not about change just for change's sake. It would bring other virtues to this country, by encouraging us to rethink our institutions.

We certainly need to. People accept their lot and trust institutions because they are tired and cynical. But we cannot afford to put our trust in bodies that, if not actively corrupt, are outmoded or self-serving.

A republican constitution would have the virtue of opening doors that will allow us to know our rights, which is something that I most certainly do not. To be a citizen in full knowledge of her rights would be a wonderful gift: it would definitely make me feel better about myself.

In turn, government would have to learn to be more respectful of the people. . . . Once the British have acquired a taste for life under a republic they would grow less timid and lose some of the awe in which they hold politicians . . . a gross imbalance would be redressed: politicians would be afraid of the people, rather than the reverse. Then they would damn well listen to us.

There is one final republican virtue. I have a private theory that if they were given half a chance the royals would pack it in tomorrow. Cutting the ribbon at factory openings is ultimately demeaning. I am convinced the Queen and her family crave an end to this sorry charade.[2]

This type of article is likely to sort readers into opposing camps but the battlefield could still hold groups who wander this way and that, not sure where they belong. Another group might be those who agree with the ideas while remaining less than happy about Sue Townsend's persuasion techniques. What factors might help us assess her persuasion rating? Here are some suggestions.

The points in this checklist could be applied to any piece of opinion writing.

1 Does the piece have a strong main stem? (The title here is 'Republican Virtues', so does it fulfil its promise and offer a list of such virtues?)
2 Is its main target of attack clear? (The royal family? People who support the monarchy? Politicians? Timid attitudes?)
3 Does it anticipate counter-arguments and deal with them successfully?
4 Does it compare an old picture with a new picture? (See below, p.201.)
5 Does it succeed in making one picture more attractive than the other? If it does, how does it succeed? If not, what's wrong?

Each question will need discussion, and reactions will differ. But together they make a list of points which must be considered when attempting opinion writing.

Further notes and questions

Sue Townsend introduces the topic through her own experience: 'When I was a child . . . .' She paints a picture, the old picture, using personal narrative. Although this device may not always work, it is used very often in newspaper articles and has advantages: it draws the reader in, affirms the writer's authority to hold an opinion, establishes common ground, and reminds us of the importance of firsthand knowledge – 'this was what it was really like'; it informs by recreating, and the information it gives is concrete and credible, or aims to be.

In what other ways does Sue Townsend place herself in the (old and new) picture?

When writing, do you aim to convince your reader completely, or to half-persuade them by making them pause and re-examine their attitudes? Sometimes the second aim will be just as valid and probably more easily attainable.

Do you want to attack, rubbish and insult readers who hold the opposing view? If you do you might well alienate them, so how are you going to get them over to your side? Think again about who and what Sue Townsend is attacking. Does she produce this alienation effect, or manage to avoid it?

Does her colloquial, speaking style work in her favour? Should she have chosen a more formal register? Does she make use of her status as a well-known writer, or address the topic as an equal with her readers?

Humour

In the following extracts (both by Americans) the writers turn colloquial style into comedy. Humour itself becomes a means of persuasion. But does it trivialise? It takes that risk, but as with Victoria Wood's sketch in Chapter 5, it exaggerates, but only slightly. The serious topic is still there:

From 'The View from Abroad' by Roxanne Roberts
No Monarchy? How democratic . . . how boring.
Republics are wonderful institutions but they have this nasty habit of electing the dullest people to power. All American politicians, for example, have the same dreadful Elvis hair-do and wear jogging shorts. It's not a pretty sight, and we've got no one to blame but ourselves.

Monarchies, on the other hand, have an unfortunate habit of thrusting the most appalling people to the throne but their subjects have the luxury of feeling righteously indignant instead of just plain stupid. They didn't vote for them, after all, and can blame the royals for every bad thing that ever happened.

But boring it's not. The British monarchy is America's favourite soap-opera, a real-life Dynasty. If the hysterics and adultery and ball-gowns weren't enough, now there's drilling for oil in the grounds of Windsor Castle. If you kick them out of London, they'd feel right at home in Dallas.

And we'd love to have them.[3]

From 'Hate Sandwich' by Will Durst
Hey guys, you know what's wrong with America? There's no one left to hate any more – that's what's wrong with America. Remember the good old days when the Russians were bad and red meat was good? Now everything's turned around.

In order to be a super-power, you need a super-enemy. For instance, without Lex Luther, Superman is a freak in a cape and tights with abnormally good vision. For 40 years the US feasted off the bountiful banquet of the Evil Empire; now we're forced to snack on the low-maintenance likes of Hussein and Noriego and Cedras, tasteless toy food much resembling Cheez Whiz on Ritz. We're a land of junkies used to maintaining speed trying to get by on decaf – just a wee mite cranky, and consuming many sugar products. So, who will it be?

The French? C'mon, you can't hate the French. Everybody hates the French. The freaking French hate the French: 'Get out of my way you smelly peasant. You are interfering with my opportunity to abuse an Italian'. . . . Can't hate Canada. Sure you could try, but it's like hating vanilla ice cream – kind of hard to work up a good loathing for.[4]

The big eat and the big hate are the same: consumerism. As well as humour and *because* of it this passage is full of insight. It sends up the Big Theme – *What's wrong with America?* – while nervelessly addressing it head-on.

Narrative

The following extract begins with personal narrative and moves from there to thinking about television and children:

From 'Where Have All the Children Gone' by Joshua Meyrowitz (1982)
About six years ago I was eating lunch in a diner in New York City when a woman and a young boy sat down in the next booth. I couldn't help overhearing parts of their conversation. At one point the woman asked: 'So, how have you been?' And the boy – who could not have been more than seven or eight years old – replied, 'Frankly, I've been feeling a little depressed lately.'

This incident stuck in my mind because it confirmed my growing belief that children are changing. As far as I can remember, my friends and I didn't find out we were 'depressed' until we were in high school.

The evidence of a change in children has increased steadily in recent years. Children don't seem childlike anymore. Children speak more like adults, dress more like adults and behave more like adults than they used to. The reverse is also true: adults have begun to speak, dress and act more like overgrown children.

It is not unusual to see children wearing three-piece suits or designer dresses, or adults in Mickey Mouse T shirts, jeans and sneakers. Adults now wear what were once considered play clothes to many work locations, including the White House.[5]

As the argument develops we are back again with Cantona and the crocodiles, but this time not as the creatures but as civilised human onlookers:

Human development is based not only on innate biological states, but also on patterns of access to social knowledge. Movement from one social role to another usually involves learning the secrets of the new status. Children have always been taught adult secrets, but slowly and in stages. . . .

In the last 30 years, however, a secret-revelation machine has been installed in 98% of homes. It is called the television.

Communication through print allows for a great deal of control over the social information to which children have access. Reading and writing involve a complex code of symbols that must be memorised and practised. Children must read simple books before they can read adult books.

On TV however, there is no complex code to exclude young viewers. . . . They watch over 27 hours a week.

The world of children's books can be insulated to present kids with an idealised view of adulthood. But television news and entertainment presents children with images of adults who lie, drink, cheat and murder.

Reading skill no longer determines the sequence in which social information is revealed to children. Through books, adults could communicate with themselves without being overheard by children. Advisory warnings on television often have a boomerang effect by *increasing* children's interest in what follows. . . . Certain programmes portray adults behaving in one way in front of the children and another way when alone. 'Father Knows Best' for example reveals to the child viewer the ways in which father hides his doubts and manipulates his behaviour to make it appear to his children that he knows best.

Television undermines behavioural distinctions because it encompasses both children and adults in a single informational sphere or environment. [Therefore] in the shared environment of television, children and adults know a great deal about each other's behaviour and social knowledge – too much in fact for them to play out the traditional complementary roles of innocence versus omnipotence.[6]

This extract is comparing an old picture with a new picture and barely disguising its preference for the old one. I include it because its analysis is unusual and provocative. Nobody wants 'innocence versus omnipotence', but nor do they want its opposite: no sense of transition from child to adult and a world full of omnipotent children. I also include it because, although 'Father Knows Best' is unfamiliar to most of us, there could be programmes that do either refute or support certain of these viewpoints, and watching television is something most of us know about: references to it are likely to be recognised by readers; details of its output can be used easily as evidence – not just for and against television itself but also when presenting other topics.

In the following two extracts from Libby Purves's Introduction to her book, *How Not To Be A Perfect Mother*, her topic is another kind of transition:

1) A mother's duty is quite clear: it is to be perfect. Mothers, as we all know, are sacred. They are sweet, loving, caring, self-denying madonnas.

They are always there. They have tender bosoms and endless patience. A mother is like the legendary pelican, ripping her own breast to feed her young. Any mother would lay down her life for her child. . . .

Well, yes, true enough. I am a mother, and I would lay down my life for my children, but I see no reason to do it every single day. Under the mantle of every mother lies an ordinary, disgruntled human being: there is no special saint-factory churning out tranquil and self-sacrificing madonnas. Every carefree, adventurous, selfish girl-in-the-street is at risk of being conscripted to wear a mother's halo. And the transition from healthy, adult selfishness to the status of maternal angel can be a painful one: rather like a butterfly trying to climb back into the chrysalis.

2)   Confronted by this tyrant, you drop everything and swim with the tide, serving the baby and forgetting that you ever had preferences of your own. At first, this makes good sense; for a few months after the birth, nobody should expect much beyond survival and the odd quiet drink in front of the television. The problem is that the habit of self-obliteration tends to carry on for too long, reinforced by the sentimental picture we have of mother-hood. Sometimes, the reasonable doctrine of 'demand feeding' continues unreasonably for eighteen years, and widens to embrace demand washing-up of teenage midnight feasts and demand lending of the family car every Saturday night. Even in the early days, we overdo the sacrifice: we leave the house on freezing days with the children wrapped up like Eskimos, but too preoccupied to put on our own coats. . . . We walk miles in blizzards to buy finger-paints (well, I did, once). After a few years of this, we end up dressed like bag ladies and apologising to everybody. For the most extremely unselfish mothers, the ones with no pleasures of their own, are often the ones who feel most guilty and depressed.[7]

To the checklist of features for good persuasive writing, one more option could be added: narrative. Extract 1 describes a transition back from butterfly to chrysalis. In extract 2, time passes: 'At first . . . carry on for too long . . . continues unreasonably for eighteen years. . . . Even in the early days. . . . After a few years of this, we end up . . .' A narrative of graphic frames (like incidents in a comic) persuades by its inevitability. It cites no statistic or authority as evidence. Extracts 1 and 2 are the 'old' picture's narratives. The new one will show these are *not* inevitable and can of course be avoided.

Social change

Opinion writing and demonstrations of opinion flourish in times of major social change. For this reason, when change reaches a point of unstable intensity, opinion can be suppressed, books and pamphlets banned, writers and demonstrators intimidated. Arguments which favour a new picture threaten institutions aiming to protect old standards, or so it seems. But the conflict is hardly ever that simple. Sometimes the social fracture runs straight through the institution itself. The following two contrasting opinions carry the sense of breakdown and change that Sue Townsend's republican article reflects, even though the topic here is collective worship in schools:

1   In asking for a review of compulsory school prayers, [Dr. John Habgood, Archbishop of York] was doing no more than stating realities which every teacher and most parents know. Prayers forced on fidgety children and given by unbelieving teachers are not only hollow; they are counter-productive. Better to have non-sectarian assemblies and periods of study of all religions than the fruitless prayers of one.[8]

2   Speaking to a conference of evangelical Anglican clergymen, [Dr. George Carey, Archbishop of Canterbury] was applauded when he said that, despite the current debate on worship in schools, 'I should like to emphasise the value I continue to attach to a collective spiritual act at the start of each school day.' He said young people required spiritual foundations on which to build their lives. 'We should redouble our efforts to reach out to the children and young people of our land. Many of them are seeking for spiritual realities.'[9]

[Passage 2 continues]: Dr Carey's speech was dramatically interrupted and he was forced to leave the lectern when a group of demonstrators from Outrage!, the militant gay rights group, broke into the chapel, chanting 'Church of hatred'. The 1,500 delegates broke into hearty hymn-singing while police ejected the demonstrators.

Which Archbishop do you support? In the last few years we may have become less tolerant of hypocrisy, and so might expect certain institutions to change or even disappear. Or are these abolitionist views too extreme?

A new picture?

Many people are seeking to improve the material realities of their lives, and in circumstances of deprivation and unfair treatment it may not be easy to imagine a new picture where social problems are solved and communities restored.

You may choose a topic that involves you personally because of your own circumstances. You may not be able to achieve the idealistic overview which many of the extracts above have done. If that is the case, you can hardly be blamed for it. Your writing might, as an alternative, reveal no new picture but simply describe the real one you are experiencing. As I explained in Chapter 5, no individual or family exists as a sealed unit uninfluenced by the changes going on around them. You could decide to write from your own experience and with an issue also in mind.

SURVEY ARTICLES

The aim of the survey article is to draw attention to a topic of public interest and general social relevance. It does not necessarily state an opinion but may recommend a course of action, a change of attitude, or make practical suggestions. A survey can investigate an issue which affects people of a certain age or social group. It produces evidence to show that this issue exists, and that it should influence our thinking. A survey might focus on changes in public behaviour or attitudes, or on the need for a change. It might investigate a case history, advocate something or forewarn us about something. The writer might report an event and then show us the background, the context. But the main body of the survey will be its evidence. The evidence must be presented so that we feel it deserves our attention: the writer is in control; the writer knows something we need to know and will benefit from knowing.

To illustrate, I have divided up the following survey article into sections. As you will see, the organisation looks much clearer this way than it does when read as a series of paragraphs in a newspaper. Here is the piece in full:

Title: 'Flatmates from Hell' by Roger Tredre

Introductory. Topic as Narrative
It starts with the little things: the unscrubbed bath, the unwashed dishes, the socks on the living-room floor. Then the little things become bigger; the unpaid share of the gas bill, the 'borrowed' clothes, the continuous late-night thump of the stereo system. Gradually you come to realise that you are living with the flatmate from hell.

Media review
The new British thriller *Shallow Grave*, which is striking a powerful chord with twenty-something audiences, is set in flat-share land – that world most of us briefly inhabit during our student years and as we make our first stumbling steps on the career ladder.

Sitcom writers have long perceived the tensions of flat, or house, sharing as a rich source of comic potential, as in *Man About the House* with Richard O'Sullivan in the Seventies and *The Young Ones*, the cult series of the early eighties that made stars of Rick Mayall and Nigel Planer.

But the flat-share that goes wrong is very far from being a joke, as Bridget Fonda's character discovered in the film *Single White Female*. In *Shallow Grave*, the three flatmates are clearly ill-suited from the beginning and, after an unexpected death turns them into partners in crime, they end up, literally, at each other's throats. It shows in extremis the devastating effects of personality clashes in an enclosed environment.

Return to topic
Those who have shared flats (or still do) never forget the downside of the experience: the sleepless nights, the arguments over the television, the enforced intimacies.

Theme 1: Example of conflicts. Personal narrative
Carol, 30, still shivers when she remembers how the tensions that developed between her and a man with whom she and two other women
shared a flat during her student days in Manchester finally exploded into
violence. 'He was a disaster from the beginning. Everything got out of hand
during my finals. I had an exam in the afternoon, and so I didn't bother to
do the washing up after my lunch. He just flipped and attacked me. I ran
from room to room and he kept coming after me, throwing me against the
wall. Finally I locked myself in the bathroom.'

Conclusion drawn
Carol was shaken by the experience. 'I moved in with my sister. I wouldn't
share with anyone again unless I knew – and trusted – them inside out.'

Theme 2: Being the flatmate from hell. Personal narrative
Ruth, 29, found herself in the uncomfortable position of being perceived
as the flatmate from hell. 'I moved in with four men when I started work
in London. They were convinced that now all their meals would appear by
magic and all the cleaning would be done. Boy, how wrong they were. But
the final straw for them was when I started bringing women lovers home.
At three in the morning, one of them pushed me against the wall, put his
hand against my throat and said, 'One of us has got to go.' I left the next
morning.

Conclusion drawn
Ruth, like many flat-sharers who have run into trouble, will not make the
same mistake again. 'You should never think you can get on with anyone.
Beware of gender differences, and make sure your sexual proclivities won't
upset anyone.'

Theme 3: Sexual jealousy. Personal narrative
Intra-flat sexual jealousy is a classic cause of catastrophe. Karen, 25,
recalls sharing a home with three women at university, one of whom
developed an obsession which finally came into the open at a fraught
dinner-party. 'She rushed out into the street screaming out, "You're
stealing all my men." She later left without paying her rent money for the
previous term on the grounds of "mental cruelty".'

Theme 4: Money. Personal narrative
Money is another common cause of splits. The division of phone bills can
be the subject of heated debate. David, 24, was always low on cash when
he shared a flat after university. 'I hardly ever used the telephone but the
other two insisted on splitting the bill three ways. When they started
leaving Post-it notes for me detailing how much I owed, I knew I had to
get out.'

Theme 5: From home to partner. Author's comment
Not all flat-sharing experiences are doomed to fail. For many it represents a reassuring step on the path from living at home to living with a partner. Jeremy, 26, says: 'Ideally, you and your flat-mates should create a mutual support system. You become like an extended family with everyone taking on family-type roles. Some members of the flat always naturally assume parental responsibilities.'

The expert
Dr Dorothy Rowe, the psychologist and writer, says, 'In an ideal world, everyone would play at being adults, and flatmates would work together as a co-operative. But it rarely works out like that. Young people don't have any experience of living in groups other than their experience of family life. So they tend to slip into allotted roles of parent and child.'

Theme 6: 'Those who regress.' Personal narratives
The flatmates who regress into the role of children cause the problems. Sarah, 28, found herself unwillingly playing the parent to a woman called Eleanor. 'She was messy and grubby and desperate to find a boyfriend. One night I was woken in the early hours by the people who lived below hammering on the door saying that water was pouring in from the bathroom. I ran in and found Eleanor in the bath with the tap running. She was completely drunk, stark naked, and had a bluish tinge to her face. I thought she was dead. She recovered, but I decided I'd had enough.'

Carol, 32, who was the mother-figure in a flat-share with another woman and two men, also had her work cut out. 'They were all mad about unusual pets. The house was full of animals, including two snakes, an iguana, a cat and a tarantula. Then the man in the room next to me put straw down on his carpet and came home with a Vietnamese pot-bellied pig. It ran riot 24 hours a day. That was when the house self-destructed.'

What can you do? Personal narrative
Getting rid of the flatmate from hell is a tricky business. The legal grounds for a flat 'divorce' are fraught with danger, particularly if there are unpaid bills in dispute. Graham, 27, had problems getting rid of a flatmate who was regularly drunk and sick on the living-room carpet. He did finally find an opportunity to apply pressure. 'He had this shifty friend who came home. I realised he was a drug-dealer, and he had a sawn-off shotgun in a bag. It gave me all the leverage I needed.'

Overall conclusion drawn
What are the characteristics of a perfect flatmate? Let's imagine someone who has no sexual partners, discreetly goes away at weekends, cleans everything all the time, and joins in with enthusiasm whenever we decide to have a late-night party. Dream on. Such a flatmate – the flatmate from heaven – simply does not exist.[10]

Notes and comments

This article is aimed at a specific audience: the twenty-somethings with flat-sharing experience, but also at the wider audience of *Observer* readers. The media review ensures contact with the wider readership by naming a relevant film on current release, as well as popular television series which attracted attention in the recent past. Even if you haven't shared a flat for twenty years, you might have seen *Shallow Grave* or watched *The Young Ones*. Even if your experience of flat-sharing turned out well, you will still be easily persuaded that things go wrong, and will be eager to discover what can and does happen in flat-share land. This writer has a very clear sense of it. Look at the introductory narrative. He likes illustrative detail.

Since this is a survey he foregrounds the experience of other speakers rather than his own. Each theme is stated in one or two short sentences, and is immediately followed by a personal narrative from *one* identified speaker whose actual words (supposedly) are quoted. The name may be a pseudonym, but each story aims to suggest that the writer is face to face with his evidence.

Carol and Ruth (themes 1 and 2) draw conclusions and offer advice, but to have this happen with every speaker would probably interrupt the pace of the reading, and might even turn the whole piece into a series of do's and don'ts. While Carol and Ruth's advice is serious, the tone of the final paragraph is light, not patronising or condemnatory.

Theme 6, only, includes two speakers, but this is the last one before the concluding paragraphs. Instead of a violent scene (as in theme 1), the group of themes ends with a comic shock: the Vietnamese pig.

The expert is not an essential feature, but here it has helped to draw themes 5 and 6 together. Had that not happened, the series would have seemed a randomly arranged list – violence, exploitation, sexual jealousy, money – with no obvious order.

The title is referred to at regular intervals (three times, and again finally as 'the flatmate from heaven').

Examining the structure of this survey we can see the degree of resemblance between its parts. Together they form a tightly constructed series of units, arranged so that its readers sense a development of the themes, rather than just a list. We can also recognise a regular pattern within each unit: brief statement; narrative illustration; conclusion. No statement is allowed to stand on its own, and this principle – that argument must be illustrated – holds for opinion as well as survey writing.

An invented character

Instead of researching the topic with actual speakers, the writer below has invented one deliberately. Because she explains clearly what she is doing and why, this device enables her to focus her comments on the topic she is investigating and to do this again through narrative:

He is well-spoken, well mannered, and well dressed; loyal, honest and conscientious. He is in his twenties, healthy and with a clean record, apart from an episode of speeding one night after someone's 21st birthday bash, for which his licence was endorsed. He is Nice But Dim, and he and his like have no place in today's hi-tech, cut-throat world. Let us call him Humphrey.

Humphrey and his parents are bewildered by his failure to find the sort of job that his father and grandfather effortlessly held. They took it for granted – associates of his father, some family contact – would find a niche for Hum in the city. He wasn't asking for much, or so he thought: a panelled office and a decent house in London, a small country place until he inherited Daddy's, and public school education for the sprogs – though family trusts would help out with that. This was how he and his forefathers had always lived: it was the upper middle's birthright. Nobody doubted that.

Over the past ten years, Humphrey and his parents have moved from shocked disbelief to reluctant acceptance of the fact that those days are over and he is unlikely to get a job of that sort, or indeed of any sort.[11]

'Birthday bash . . . the sprogs . . . Daddy . . .' She has begun to invent his words for him, or to supply him with those of his own class. This article also makes use of its readers' media knowledge by including a photograph of Harry Enfield posing as the character Nice But Dim from his recent series. It follows inevitably that characters invented as evidence must be stereotypes: that is their function. But the writer will need to know in some depth the thinking process, behaviour and attitudes of the originals if these are to be the topic of a survey.

SURVEY-WRITING EXERCISES

1. Choose a survey article from a newspaper. Invent a method of dividing it into units. Write notes on the structure of each unit and how these are arranged in a series. You may not find the same degree of regularity as in 'Flatmates from Hell'. The aim is to find a variety of types of structure. Choose articles which, in your judgement, work well for their readers. Choosing pieces from different types of newspapers or magazines will help you to gauge their different target audiences. Can you match structures with audiences?
2. When writing a survey, it is important to draw in your audience and establish a connection between audience and topic. One obvious way of doing this is to think about the cultural images – *the shared reference* – they will recognise as a group. For newspaper readers, as we have seen, the shared

reference often turns out to be images from the media. But if you are writing for a smaller group – a local community, school or university campus, for example – the shared reference will include images specific to that community, as well as wider ones known to everybody.

Write the beginning of a survey article. Think about the audience, the topic, the means of contact and the shared reference. If you have written for a specific group, try rewriting the piece for a wider one. What adjustments would you have to make to the content and style of your writing?

3.   The following statements have been taken from a survey article and scrambled. They are printed below but in the wrong order. Rearrange them to find the original order. One clue is narrative and tenses of verbs. Afterwards, check the correct sequence (p.211).

From 'A Gallery Opens – After 18,000 Years' by David Keys
250 images so far . . . several hundred more await discovery.
In 1996, a survey and research work will start in earnest . . . and could last
    for at least 30 years.
Chauvet returned to the site with Jean Clottes, a French cave art expert.
There is also an engraving of an owl . . .
All of this however is some way in the future . . .
On the walls of the French caverns are paintings and engravings of 13
    different species of animals . . .
Chauvet and his colleagues slowly removed the rubble . . .
For the time being, the function of Europe's cave paintings remains a
    mystery.
In the centre of the main chamber what appears to be a kind of altar still
    has a bear's skull placed on it.
As fresh as the day they were made some 18,000 years ago.
Microscopic examination of flint implements will reveal . . .
When Clottes entered the cave he found himself face to face with a wall
    covered with magnificent painted horses' heads, wild oxen . . .
Stone Age art is extraordinary not only for its naturalistic beauty but also
    because of the time in which it flourished and the mysterious fact that it
    died out utterly . . . at the end of the last Ice Age.
The peak of the style coincides with the peak of the glaciation.
'I felt I was standing in front of some of the great artistic masterpieces of
    mankind.'
An investigation of the soft cave floor will probably yield the information
    of most value . . .
Huge stalactites and stalagmites, some formed into the most bizarre shapes,
    loom large.
Early naturalistic art . . . therefore seems to have been inspired quite
    specifically by the Ice Age and its challenging climate.
They were the first human beings to enter the cave since the Ice Age.

They may represent gods or ancestral spirits . . .

Scenes of complicated ritual and initiation . . .

It was a tiny draught of warm air emanating from the pile of loose rocks that led to the greatest prehistoric art find for half a century.

And on the soft cave floor are a myriad of footprints of the Stone Age people themselves . . .

Whatever its symbolism the art would have played some role in welding together society at a time when the climate was worsening.[12]

4.   Write a survey article using the following points as a checklist:

* Have you included quotations from people with firsthand experience of the topic?
* Have you made use of quotations from an 'expert'?
* Have you made use of narratives in the structure?
* Does your approach generate contact between topic and audience?
* Have you supported your statements with illustrations?
* Do the narratives lead somewhere or draw conclusions?
* Is the evidence for your conclusion clear?
* Imagine yourself as the reader. Is your interest being led forward, so that you want to go on to the end of the article?

Survey writing can have other outcomes, as I shall explain below, but one quality it teaches above all is the importance of the reader, and even though they may not be aware of it all the time, readers need encouragement. To structure the content of writing enables readers to trust and so accept what they are reading. In itself, structure is a form of persuasion.

WRITING ACROSS THE GENRES

Each form of writing, including those I have covered in this chapter, can stimulate experiments in the other forms.

Given the opening paragraph of the piece about Nice But Dim (see p. 207), how might we describe the difference between the writer's treatment of this character and his counterpart in fiction? If you were investigating this character through a story, would you be happy with the passage as it stands, or would you want to write it in some other way?

Many characters in fiction start out life as a sketch, and the initial treatment may have stereotype qualities that crudely reflect a background or occupation. The next step will be to individualise them, to move them into close-up, to find them a style that is not so obviously conditioned. Characters researched through fiction and drama are localised and specific.

Opinion writing can have its counterparts in fiction or as a scene in a short play. Having explored your opinion by writing an article, you could reinvestigate it in another form. Opinions mean conflicts (there is always

someone who disagrees or obstructs) but they can also mean powerful
sensations: imagination, anger, a sense of injustice or belief, an image of
something desirable or detestable, which either way establishes personal
identity.

The form ready-made to deal with this is poetry. But the need to persuade
is not the only drive in poetry of course. Close to it is the desire to evoke,
realise, excite, to arrange words into rhythms, to see the world as worth all
our attention. A poem can also be a survey. While selecting words and ideas
from the article on prehistoric cave art, I could sense them trying to change
themselves into poems.

'Flatmates from Hell' describes scenes between people in small groups. In
its own words, flat-sharing 'shows . . . the devastating effects of personality
clashes in an enclosed environment', and such scenes are a gift for theatre
writing. If any of them suggest dialogue to you, experiment, write it down
and see if the scene will produce other developments from those in the stories:
it might have a stronger ending, or a less conclusive one. You may read other
articles which will immediately suggest a scene, a conflict or a world you
know and recognise even if the incidents are different.

Minimal knowledge, maximum imagination

All through this book I have spoken about the importance of searching for
details, about close-up focus, about making an extra effort of attention with
topics and ideas, about not being fully satisfied with the obvious and tired
view of things – in other words, about going one step further into experience.
We want to go further, but the trigger for this impulse can be the fact that we
start off by knowing so very little. Learning just one fact, as in Peter
Redgrove's poem about spiders (p.98) can ignite a range of images in the
writer's imagination. Knowing too much could have the opposite effect.
Catching a glimpse of a couple on a beach could spark off a story like V. S.
Pritchett's about the Corams. A glimpse is sometimes enough. Writing a
scene with characters from a soap opera in fiction would be difficult because
we know too much about them. We are likely to know rather less about the
people in our own families.

One of the gifts that writers possess is knowing when a glimpse has become
a trigger. Something is fired, is alive with ideas because so little is known.
The world is generally so full of things that are unfamiliar to us that the idea
of 'making strange' might be misnamed: they are strange already, and in a
sense we are trying to make the really strange things more present and more
familiar to ourselves. Success is in the effort, not the achievement, since what
fascinates most are those things we know about the least. Imagination takes
over when the more obvious ways of knowing are not available.

How else can we explain the writer who researches one topic exhaustively
through writing? It is because they can quite literally never know enough;

the strangeness persists. Peter Shaffer records the impulse that eventually turned itself into his play *Equus*:

> One weekend over two years ago, I was driving with a friend through bleak countryside. We passed a stable. Suddenly he was reminded by it of an alarming crime which he had heard about recently at a dinner party in London. He knew only one horrible detail, and his complete mention of it could barely have lasted a minute – but was enough to arouse in me an intense fascination. . . . A few months later my friend died. I could not verify what he had said or ask him to expand it.[13]

If by writing across the genres I mean dutifully transposing an anecdote (such as the above) into a play or short story in order to explore differences of technique, that would be worth doing, but not as worthwhile or as valuable in the end as responding to a scrap of story with imagination. Certain facts, anecdotes, images, settings, will flow with energy. The writer feels a freedom to explore them, and when that happens the invitation must be taken up. In my view, writers (whatever their age) who are beginning to write and explore writing are just as susceptible to that sense of freed energy as those with experience, and may even be more so.

APPENDIX: 'A GALLERY OPENS – AFTER 18,000 YEARS'

1 It was a tiny draught of warm air emanating from the pile of loose rocks that led to the greatest prehistoric art find for half a century.
2 Chauvet and his colleagues slowly removed the rubble. . . .
3 They were the first human beings to enter the cave since the Ice Age.
4 Chauvet returned to the site with Jean Clottes, a French cave art expert.
5 When Clottes entered the cave he found himself face to face with a wall covered with magnificent painted horses' heads, wild oxen. . . .
6 'I felt I was standing in front of some of the great artistic masterpieces of mankind.'
7 Huge stalactites and stalagmites, some formed into the most bizarre shapes, loom large.
8 In the centre of the main chamber what appears to be a kind of altar still has a bear's skull placed on it.
9 And on the soft cave floor are a myriad of footprints of the Stone Age people themselves . . . as fresh as the day they were made some 18,000 years ago.
10 On the walls of the French caverns are paintings and engravings of 13 different species of animals. . . .
11 250 images so far . . . several hundred more await discovery.
12 There is also an engraving of an owl. . . .
13 An investigation of the soft cave floor will probably yield the information of most value. . . .

14 Microscopic examination of flint implements will reveal. . . .
15 All of this however is some way in the future. . . .
16 Stone Age art is extraordinary not only for its naturalistic beauty but also because of the time in which it flourished and the mysterious fact that it died out utterly . . . at the end of the last Ice Age.
17 Early naturalistic art . . . therefore seems to have been inspired quite specifically by the Ice Age and its challenging climate.
18 The peak of the style coincides with the peak of the glaciation.
19 In 1996, a survey and research work will start in earnest . . . and could last for at least 30 years.
20 For the time being, the function of Europe's cave paintings remains a mystery.
21 They may represent gods or ancestral spirits. . . .
22 Scenes of complicated ritual and initiation. . . .
23 Whatever its symbolism the art would have played some role in welding together society at a time when the climate was worsening.

Notes

1 STRUCTURE AND STYLE

1 George Orwell, 'Politics and the English Language', *Inside The Whale and Other Essays*, London, Penguin, 1957, p. 146.
2 Paul Nash, Letter to his wife, February 1917, see *Modern Painters*, Autumn 1994, Vol 7, No 3, pp. 57–8.
3 Bertholt Brecht, *Poems 1913–56*, London, Methuen, 1976, p. 448.
4 Andrew Rawnsley, *Observer*, 26 February 1995.
5 Angela Carter, 'The Werewolf', *The Bloody Chamber*, London, Penguin, 1981, p. 108.
6 Angela Carter,'The Company of Wolves', ibid., p. 110.
7 John Fowles, 'The Enigma', *The Ebony Tower*, London, Jonathan Cape, 1974, p. 187.
8 Woody Allen, 'Selections from The Allen Notebooks', *The Norton Reader*, 6th Edition, New York, London, Norton, 1984, pp. 77–8.
9 J. G. Ballard, *Empire of the Sun*, London, Grafton, 1985, p. 87.
10 See George Orwell, his quotation from an essay on psychology, op. cit., p. 144.
11 Toni Morrison, *Beloved*, London, Pan Books, 1981, pp. 210–11.
12 Alan Bennett, 'Soldiering On', *Talking Heads*, London, BBC Books, 1988, p. 70.

2 AUTOBIOGRAPHICAL WRITING

1 Isadora Duncan, *My Life*, London, Sphere Books, 1968, p. 7.
2 John Berger, *Keeping A Rendezvous*, London, Granta Books, 1992, pp 43–53.
3 Marianne Faithfull and David Dalton, *Faithfull*, London, Michael Joseph, 1994, p. 1.
4 Michaela Denis, *Leopard In My Lap*, London, W. H. Allen, 1955, p. 11.
5 *You Can't Kill The Spirit, Yorkshire Women go to Greenham. People's History of Yorkshire – Four*. Bretton Women's Book Fund, 1983, pp. 14–17.
6 Tony Parker (ed.), *Soldier Soldier*, London, Heinemann, 1987, p. 237.
7 Sylvia Plath, from *Johnny Panic and the Bible of Dreams*, London, Faber, 1977, pp. 123–30. Also published in *The Art of Sylvia Plath* (ed.) Charles Newman, London, Faber, 1970, pp. 266–8.

3 WRITING POEMS

1 Tony Harrison, 'Them and [Uz]', from *Selected Poems*, London, Penguin, 1984, p. 122.

2 William Shakespeare, *Macbeth*, Act II, scene i.
3 John Milton, *Paradise Lost*, Book IV.
4 William Carlos Williams, *Selected Poems*, New York, New Directions Books, 1968, p. 63.
5 Robin Bell, *Scanning the Forth Bridge*, Calstock, Cornwall, Peterloo Poets, 1994.
6 W. H. Auden, *Collected Shorter Poems*, London, Faber, 1966, p. 92.
7 Miroslav Holub, *Poems Before & After*, Newcastle, Bloodaxe Books, 1990, p. 52.
8 Ted Hughes, *Wodwo*, London, Faber, 1967, p. 177.
9 Elizabeth Bishop, *The Norton Anthology of American Literature*, 4th edition, London, New York, Norton, 1994, p. 2455.
10 Norman MacCaig, *Voice Over*, London, Chatto, 1988, p. 47.
11 Ibid., p. 38.
12 W. S. Graham, *Collected Poems 1942–77*, London, Faber, 1977, p. 68.
13 Ted Hughes, op. cit., p. 182.
14 Charles Causley, 'The Death of A Poet', from *Collected Poems 1951–1975*, London, Macmillan, 1975, p. 155.
15 Sujata Bhatt, from 'The Reaper', No. 16, Santa Cruz USA, p. 46.
16 Thom Gunn, *Collected Poems*, London, Faber, 1993, p. 248.
17 Paul Mills, *Half Moon Bay*, Manchester, Carcanet, 1993, p. 70.
18 Adrienne Rich, *The Fact Of A Doorframe, Poems Selected and New. 1950–1984*. New York, London, Norton, 1984, p. 172.
19 Ted Hughes, *Winter Pollen*, London, Faber, 1995, pp. 191–211. See also Sylvia Plath, *Ariel*, London, Faber, 1965, pp. 11, 13 and *Crossing the Water*, London, Faber, 1971, p. 14.
20 Peter Redgrove, *My Father's Trapdoors* (Jonathan Cape, 1994), *The Independent*, 24 February 1995.
21 M. J. Cootes, *England Since 1700*, London, Longman, 1982, pp. 137–8.

4   WRITING SHORT STORIES

1 Margaret Atwood, 'Happy Endings', *The Secret Self*, (ed.) H. Lee, London, Everyman Dent, pp. 370–3.
2 J. D. Salinger, *The Catcher in the Rye*, London, Penguin, 1958, p. 22. First published in Britain, 1951.
3 *Stand Magazine*, Vol 21, No 3, 1980, p. 63.
4 V. S. Pritchett, 'You Make Your Own Life', *The Complete Short Stories*, London, The Hogarth Press, 1993, p. 130.
5 David Lodge, *Nice Work*, London, Penguin, 1988, p. 13.
6 V. S. Pritchett, 'Handsome is as Handsome Does', op. cit., p. 38.
7 David Lodge, op. cit., p. 15.
8 Ibid., p. 17.
9 A. S. Byatt, 'Art Work', *The Matisse Stories*, London, Vintage, 1994, pp. 33–4.
10 D. H. Lawrence, *Sons and Lovers*, London, Penguin, p. 32. First published by Heinemann, 1913.
11 Woody Allen, 'The Kugelmass Episode', *Side Effects*, London, The New English Library, 1981, pp. 45–59.
12 Martin Amis, 'Let Me Count The Times', *The Penguin Book of Modern British Short Stories*, pp. 369–82.
13 Albert Camus, *The Plague*, London, Penguin, 1960, p. 88. First published in Britain, 1947.
14 James Herbert, *Lair*, London, New English Library paperback, 1979, p. 12.
15 Kate Chopin, 'The Story Of An Hour', first published in *Vogue*, 1894.
16 Carson McCullers, *The Ballad of the Sad Cafe*, London, Penguin, p. 7. First published in Britain, 1953.

17 Virginia Woolf, *To the Lighthouse*, London, Penguin, 1964, pp. 5–7. First published by Hogarth, 1927.
18 J. D. Salinger, 'A Perfect Day for Bananafish', *For Esme with Love and Squalor and other Stories*, London, Penguin, 1986, pp. 2–3. First published in USA, 1953.
19 Margaret Atwood, *Bodily Harm*, London, Virago, 1983, pp. 253–54.
20 Angela Carter, *The Passion of New Eve*, London, Bloomsbury Classics, 1993, pp. 22–3. First published 1977, Gollancz.
21 From *Nerve* by Dick Francis, London, Pan Books, 1976, p. 5. First published Michael Joseph, 1964.
22 *The Thurber Carnival*, London, Penguin, 1945, pp. 304–5.
23 From *The Aran Islands* by J. M. Synge, London, OUP, 1962, pp. 171–7. First published 1907.
24 'The Stone Boy' by Gina Berriault, 1957, originally appeared in *Madamoiselle*, USA.

5 THEATRE

1 Harold Pinter, *Family Voices*, *Pinter Plays Four*, London, Methuen, 1981, pp. 283–4.
2 Ibid., p. 283.
3 Ibid., pp. 290–1.
4 Ibid., p. 294.
5 Ibid., p. 295.
6 Ibid., p. 296.
7 *US*, RSC Production, London, Calder and Boyars, 1968, p. 126.
8 Peter Brook, Preface to *US*, ibid., pp. 10–11.
9 Caryl Churchill, *Top Girls*, *Churchill Plays Two*, London, Methuen, 1990, 57–8.
10 Peter Brook, *The Empty Space*, London, Penguin, 1968, pp. 125–6.
11 James Roose-Evans, *Experimental Theatre*, London, Routledge & Kegan Paul, 1970, p. 196.
12 Kate Kellaway, review of *Blasted* by Sarah Kane, *Guardian*, 22 January 1995.
13 Heinrich Ibsen, *Ghosts*, Act Three.
14 Victoria Wood, 'The Reporter', *Up To You, Porky*, London, Methuen, 1985, p. 43.
15 Ibid., p. 44.

6 WRITING TO PERSUADE

1 Steve Conor, *The Independent*, 27 January 1995.
2 *Guardian*, 10 January 1995.
3 Ibid.,
4 Ibid., 27 January 1995.
5 J. Meyrowitz, from *Short Essays*, (ed.) G. Levin, New York, London, Harcourt, Brace, Jovanovitch, 1986, pp. 253–7.
6 Ibid.
7 Libby Purves, *How Not To Be A Perfect Mother*, London, Fontana, 1986, pp. 11–13.
8 'Time for Church and State to Part', Leader comment, *Observer*, 8 January 1995.
9 'Carey Backs Daily Prayers in School', Martin Wroe, *Observer*, 8 January 1995.
10 'Flatmates from Hell', Roger Tredre, *Observer*, 22 January 1995.
11 Angela Lambert, *The Independent*, 7 December 1994.
12 *The Independent*, 3 February 1995.
13 Peter Shaffer, 'A Note on The Play', *Equus*, London, Penguin, 1973, p. 9.

Bibliography

The dates below indicate recent editions.

RECOMMENDED READING

Poetry

Attridge, Derek, 1982, *The Rhythms of English Poetry*, London, Longman.
Baldwin, Michael, 1982, *The Way to Write Poetry*, London, Elm Tree Books.
Brownjohn, Alan, 1969, *First I Say This, A Selection of Poems for Reading Aloud*, London, Hutchinson.
Brownjohn, Sandy, 1986, *Does It Have to Rhyme?*, London, Hodder & Stoughton.
Harding, D. W., 1974, *Experience into Words*, London, Penguin.
Hughes, Ted, 1979, *Poetry in the Making*, London, Faber.
Livingstone, Dinah, 1993, *Poetry Handbook*, London, Macmillan.
Mort, Graham, 1991, *The Experience of Poetry*, Open College of the Arts, with the Open University Press.
Pirrie, Jill, 1987, *On Common Ground*, London, Hodder & Stoughton.
Powell, Brian, 1968, *Words Large as Apples. English through Poetry*, London, Heinemann.
Tamplin, Ronald, 1993, *Rhythm and Rhyme*, Milton Keynes, the Open University Press.
Tunnicliffe, Stephen, 1984, *Poetry Experience*, London, Methuen.

Fiction

Baldwin, Michael, 1986, *The Way to Write Short Stories*, London, Elm Tree Books.
Bradbury, Malcolm (ed.), 1977, *The Novel Today* [Essays by Lodge, Fowles, Lessing, Bellow, etc.], London, Fontana.
Burroway, Janet, 1987, *Writing Fiction* (2nd edition), Boston, Toronto, Little, Brown & Co.
Chambers, Ross, 1984, *Story and Situation: Narrative Seduction and the Power of Fiction*, Manchester, Manchester University Press.
Haffenden, J., 1985, *Novelists in Interview*, London, Methuen.
Lodge, David, 1992, *The Art of Fiction*, London, Penguin.
Mort, Graham, 1992, *Storylines*, Open College of the Arts, with the Open University Press.

Palmer, Jerry, 1991, *Pot Boilers*, London, Routledge.
Toolan, Michael J., 1998, *Narrative: A Critical Linguistic Introduction*, London, Routledge.

Theatre

Ash, William, 1982, *The Way to Write Radio Drama*, London, Elm Tree Books.
Barker, Clive, 1977, *Theatre Games, A New Approach to Drama Training*, Methuen Drama.
Berry, Cicely, 1993, *Voice and the Actor*, London, Virgin.
Brook, Peter, 1980, *The Empty Space*, London, Penguin.
Brook, Peter, 1989, *The Shifting Point: Forty Years of Theatrical Exploration 1946–1987*, London, Methuen.
Esslin, Martin, 1980, *The Theatre of the Absurd* (3rd edition), London, Penguin.
Gallagher, Tom, 1985, *The Way to Write for the Stage*, London, Elm Tree Books.
Gooch, Steve, 1988, *Writing a Play*, London, A & C Black.
Innes, Christopher, 1993, *Avant Garde Theatre*, London, Routledge.
Jellicoe, Anne, 1987, *Community Plays: How To Put Them On*, Methuen Paperback.
Johnstone, Keith, 1980, *Impro: Improvisation and the Theatre*, London, Methuen.
Mason, Bim, 1992, *Street Theatre and Other Outdoor Performances*, London, Routledge.
Read, Alan, 1993, *Theatre and Everyday Life*, London, Routledge.
Roose-Evans, James, 1994, *Experimental Theatre; From Stanislavsky to Peter Brook*, London, Routledge.
A. C. H. Smith, 1972, *Orghast at Persepolis*, London, Eyre Methuen.

Language and Writing Skills

Close, R. A., 1974, *A University Grammar of English Workbook*, London, Longman.
Crystal, David, 1995, *The Cambridge Encyclopaedia of the English Language*, Cambridge, Cambridge University Press.
Hines, John, 1985, *The Way to Write Magazine Articles*, London, Elm Tree Books.
King, Graham, 1993, *Crisp Clear Writing*, London, Mandarin.
Newby, Michael, 1987, *The Structure of English: A Handbook of English Grammar*, Cambridge, Cambridge University Press.
Newby, Michael, 1989, *Writing: A Guide for Students*, Cambridge, Cambridge University Press.
Orwell, George, 1967, 'Politics and the English Language', *Inside the Whale and other Essays*, London, Penguin.
Pirie, David, 1985, *How to Write Critical Essays, a Guide for Students of Literature*, London, Methuen.
Quirk, Randolph, Greenbaum, Sidney, Leech, Geoffrey and Svartvik, Jan (eds), 1985, *A Comprehensive Grammar of the English Language*, London, Longman.

General

Abbs, Peter, 1982, *English Within The Arts*, London, Hodder & Stoughton.
Brande, Dorothea, 1983, *Becoming a Writer*, London, Papermac. First published 1934.
Brindley, Susan (ed.), 1994, *Teaching English*, London, Routledge.

Cixous, Hélène, 1986, *The Newly Born Woman*, Manchester, Manchester University Press.

Elbow, Peter, 1981, *Writing with Power*, Oxford, Oxford University Press.

Fairfax, John, 1989, *Creative Writing*, London, Hamish Hamilton.

Fairfax, John and Moat, John, 1981, *The Way to Write*, London, Elm Tree Books, Hamish Hamilton.

Flower, Tony and Mort, Graham, 1993, *Starting to Write*, Open College of the Arts, with the Open University Press.

Freeman, Mark, 1993, *Rewriting the Self*, London, Routledge.

Monteith, Moira and Miles, Robert (eds), 1992, *Teaching Creative Writing*, Milton Keynes, the Open University Press.

Olsen, Tillie, 1980, *Silences*, London, Virago.

O'Rourke, Rebecca, 1994, *Written on the Margins, Creative Writing in Cleveland*, Department of Adult Continuing Education, The University of Leeds.

Scholes, Robert and Comely, Nancy R., 1985, *The Practice of Writing*, New York, St Martins Press.

Thomas, Sue, 1995, *Creative Writing: A Handbook for Workshop Leaders*, Department of Adult Education, The University of Nottingham.

SOME RECENT ANTHOLOGIES

Poetry

Adcock, Fleur, 1987, *The Faber Book of Twentieth Century Women's Poetry* London, Faber.

Allnutt, Gillian, D'Aguair, Frank, Edwards, Ken and Mottram, Eric (eds), 1988, *The New British Poetry 1968–88*, London, Paladin.

Astley, Neil (ed.), 1988, *Poetry With An Edge*, Newcastle, Bloodaxe.

Berry, James (ed.), 1987, *News from Babylon. The Chatto Book of West Indian Poetry*, London, Chatto.

Enright, D. J. (ed.), 1980, *The Oxford Book of Contemporary Verse*, Oxford, Oxford University Press.

Finnegan, Ruth (ed.), 1978, *The Penguin Book of Oral Poetry*, London, Penguin.

France, Linda (ed.), 1993, *Sixty Women Poets*, Newcastle, Bloodaxe.

Heaney, Seamus and Hughes, Ted (eds), 1982, *The Rattle Bag*, London, Faber.

Hulse, Michael, Kennedy, David and Morley, David (eds), 1993, *The New Poetry*, Newcastle, Boodaxe.

Markham, E.A.(ed.), 1989, *Hinterland: Caribbean Poetry from the West Indies and Britain*, Newcastle, Bloodaxe.

Moore, Geoffrey (ed.), 1983, *The Penguin Book of American Verse*, London, Penguin.

Morrison, Craig and Motion, Andrew (eds), 1982, *The Penguin Book of Contemporary British Poetry*, London, Penguin.

Porter, Peter (ed.), 1982, *The Faber Book of Modern Verse*, London, Faber.

Rumens, Carol (ed.), 1990, *New Women Poets*, Newcastle, Bloodaxe.

Thwaite, Anthony (ed.), 1984, *Six Centuries of Verse*, London, Thames Methuen.

Fiction

Bradbury, Malcolm (ed.), 1988, *The Penguin Book of Modern British Short Stories*, London, Penguin.

Brown, Stewart (ed.), 1990, *Carribean New Wave: Contemporary Short Stories*, London, Heinemann.

Cobham, Rhonda and Collins, Merle (eds), 1987, *Watchers and Seekers, Creative Writing by Black Women in Britain*, London, The Women's Press.

Ford, Richard, 1992, *The Granta Book of American Short Stories*, London, Granta.

Holstrom, L. (ed.), 1990, *Inner Courtyard Stories by Indian Women*, London, Virago.

Kenison, Katrina (ed.), *The Best American Short Stories 1994*, New York, Houghton Mifflin.

Lee, Hermione (ed.), 1987, *The Secret Self, I and II: Short Stories by Women*, London, Dent.

Moffatt, James and McElhery, Kenneth R. (eds), 1956, *Points of View, an Anthology of Short Stories*, New York and London, Mentor and The New English Library.

Oates, Joyce Carol (ed.), 1992, *The Oxford Book of American Short Stories*, Oxford, Oxford University Press.

Pritchett, V. S. (ed.), 1981, *The Oxford Book of Short Stories*, Oxford, Oxford University Press.

Silkin, Jon, Tracy, Lorna and Wardle, John, 1987 *Best Short Stories from Stand Magazine 1956–1987*, London, Methuen.

General index

absurd drama 170
academic essays 2; asking questions in 187–8, 192; main concepts 188–9; organisation of 192; passive verbs in 193; and readers 186–7, 188, 191, 192; topic statements 188–91; use of quotation in 193
anecdote 100, 102–4, 129
Arturo Ui, the Resistable Rise of 165
attitude: in autobiography 63, 65; in fiction 130
audience 151–2, 168–9, 171, 174, 178, 179, 181, 182, 184, 203, 207
autobiographical writing: summary of main points 64; why autobiography? 43

Blasted 172–3
Bond, James 122

Caretaker, The 175, 180
Catcher in the Rye, The 103
centre of experience: in autobiographical writing 49–50, 60, 64; of revelation in fiction 113; in plays 175–6; in poems 87, 88, 96, 97
character-rhythm 100, 105, 109–13, 129–30
characters: in feature articles 206–7, 209; in fiction 101, 104, 106, 109–13, 116–117, 129–30, 209; in plays 173–4, 176, 180, 209
clichés 28–31, 80
creative process 4, 39, 184–5, 210–11
creative writing 2–5
Crucible, The 162

Death of a Salesman 175, 190

defamiliarisation 71, 97–8, 210
dialogue: in fiction 125–6; in theatre 151, 182–3

editing, redrafting and revision 27, 28, 39, 65–6, 191–2
Equus 210–11
expressionism 97

fiction: characters in 116; crisis and closure 115–6; motifs 116; novels and short stories 101, 125–6; plot in 113; point of view 106–114; protagonist 114; as revelation 113; settings 115, 118–19, 128–9; and theatre 151–2; time in 115–16, 132; trigger events 114, 132
film 42, 105, 203
focalisation 107
focus and perspective: close-up and wide angle 42; in fiction 105–9; in poetry 74, 76; in theatre 158

grammar (*see also* sentence awareness) 7
Greenham Common 57–60

Hitler, Adolf 165, 188–9
humour 192, 198–9

imagination 4, 5, 6, 62, 69, 70, 71, 85, 171, 172, 210–11

Just Between Ourselves 175

Kathakali dance tradition 171–2

metaphor 32, 71, 86–7, 88

Author index

Index of main works